Procurement Management

STRATEGY, ORGANIZATION, AND DECISION-MAKING

E. RAYMOND COREY

Professor of Business Administration

Harvard Graduate School of Business Administration

Foreword by James M. Hill, Jr.

CBI PUBLISHING COMPANY, INC.
51 Sleeper Street   Boston, Massachusetts   02210

Library of Congress Cataloging in Publication Data

Corey, E. Raymond
    Procurement management: strategy, organization, and
    decision-making.

    Includes index.
    1. Industrial procurement.   2. Industrial
procurement—United States—Case studies.   I. Title.
HD52.5.C64   658.7'2   78-5826
ISBN 0-8436-0759-9

Printing(last digit): 9 8 7 6 5 4 3

CREDITS

It is to David, Tom, Fred, Margaret, Joy and Mary
and to their mother,
who is the most skillful purchasing manager I know,
that this book is dedicated.

Contents

Foreword

To the businessman in the free enterprise society, the development of a market strategy is an old and familiar exercise in corporate planning. Indeed, the term "strategy" has been applied to a number of facets of business management.

But until recently strategy has been a stranger to most engaged in the acquisition of materials. Purchasing tactics—or techniques—have held the attention of purchasing executives almost exclusively. And this narrower focus was probably justified by the long-standing and nearly universal acceptance of an industrial environment in which basic materials were thought to be—in practical, if not theoretical terms—limitless in supply, and in which the law of supply and demand governed pricing. In such a world success in procurement was determined by short-term tactics that produced the most competitive results in terms of cost and availability.

By the mid-70s it had become abundantly clear that the world in which the professional buyer lived was changing dramatically and permanently. The market control of prices through changes in the relationship between supply and demand could no longer be relied upon, as illustrated by the continuing escalation of labor costs in a period of high and increasing unemployment. The view of limitless supply was abruptly altered by the oil cartel, and reinforced by any number of new restrictions on the mining, fabrication, and distribution of materials. Government regulations to prevent industry abuse of the environment, to protect the employee, to promote socio-economic objectives, and to guard against ultimate depletion caused significant changes in cost relationships between materials, pricing some completely out of traditional markets.

The impact of change has been felt by general management as quickly as it has been understood by purchasing executives. The need to integrate material requirements into the short- and long-term strategy of corporate planning has become apparent, and many companies have been quick to act.

The most obvious material strategy is the assurance of long-range supply. This involves both product planning (to utilize materials with long-term availability at reasonable cost) and source planning (which ranges from long-term supply contracts for basic materials to the outright acquisition of basic material properties). Other material strategies are concerned with logistics management, inventory management, and the nature of material control systems.

Organizing to carry out strategic decisions is both a tactic and a strategy. For example, the organization may be structured to produce tactically the strongest possible position in a price-volume sensitive commodity of cost importance to the product being marketed. At the same time, the organization may be structured as part of the strategy for vertical integration to protect a scarce, but essential, raw material. In other words, the form of the organization can be both the plan and the instrument.

As strategies are developed, it becomes apparent that they are interrelated. Tactics tend to stand alone, but material strategies not only interact with each other, but also with other company strategies such as marketing and asset control. This elevates the task of the procurement executive to the level of general management, and demands an understanding of not only other functions within the organization, but their relationship to each other and to the basic objectives of the enterprise.

Since strategic planning is relatively new to the field of materials, it is not surprising that there is little to be found in the literature to help the purchasing executive. *Procurement Management: Strategy, Organization, and Decision-Making* breaks new ground, and is valuable as a practical guide to the kind of thinking that goes into the setting of strategies. Being based upon the experience of several large firms, it addresses theoretical concepts with real world illustrations. It is a book for thoughtful procurement executives and general managers who wish to shape their procurement organization and plan material strategy with as much care as they plan facilities or attack markets.

James M. Hill, Jr.
Corporate Director,
Procurement
Raytheon Company

Acknowledgments

This study was born out of my strong interest as a teacher and writer in the field of industrial marketing to learn at first hand how industry actually buys. There was little in the literature that was helpful. Researchers and writers have dealt with procurement on either a theoretical plane primarily for academic consumption or on a technical level helpful for buyers. What seemed to be lacking was an understanding of the problems of *procurement managers,* those charged with planning and organizing procurement, with assuring the optimal effectiveness of day-to-day purchasing decisions, and with developing strong and viable sourcing systems. Their responsibilities are great, indeed, as is their potential for making major contributions to the success of the organizations they represent.

My "laboratory" comprised six major American corporations in five industries: General Motors (automotive), International Business Machines (computer), Raytheon (electronic), PPG Industries (industrial materials), General Foods (packaged foods) and Heinz USA (also packaged foods). Interviews were conducted in these six companies with well over a hundred buyers and managers, not only in procurement, but in other functions involved in procurement decision-making, such as engineering, manufacturing, marketing, control, and finance as well as general management. The objective was to understand first how procurement was structured in each company at the headquarters, division, and plant levels. Then specific procurement decisions were selected for intensive study, decisions relating to purchases of raw materials, production parts, supply items, plant and office equipment, and major capital investments. In each instance key personnel described the nature of the purchasing problem, the search for sources of supply, negotiations with potential vendors, the influences both external and internal that came to bear on making buying decisions, and subsequent relations with the selected sources. These data provided some rare insights on procurement management in practice. They became the basis for generalizations that I believe extend in significance well beyond the companies and industries studied. What was observed in these six companies has direct relevance, as well, for other large and small companies, for profit and nonprofit institutions, and for manufacturing and service organizations.

Procurement Management: Strategy, Organization, and Decision-Making has considerable relevance, too, for industrial marketers when it comes to understanding industrial buying behavior. How do buyers perceive sellers' strategies? What factors lead the buyers to select one supplier instead of another? How can industrial marketers most effectively retain their positions with existing customers? How can they break into new accounts? How is selling to corporate-level buyers different from selling at the plant level? Studying the purchase-and-sale transaction from the purchaser's point of view certainly leads one to greater depths of understanding in industrial marketing.

One further word about the source material. The cooperating organizations have willingly allowed me to use their names and to discuss the actual products being purchased. To protect proprietary information, however, I agreed that all names of company personnel, vendor companies, and competitors would be disguised as well as quantitative data not publicly available. With this understanding, managers in these six organizations answered questions put to them in considerable detail, volunteering additional relevant information, and adding insights gained through their years of experience.

For making all this possible I am greatly indebted to: John W. Brislin, Director of Purchasing, International Business Machines Corporation; Ralph L. Cobb, Vice-President, Group Executive, General Foods Corporation; James M. Hill, Jr., Corporate Director, Procurement, Raytheon Company; Edgar T. Mertz, Vice-President, Operations, Heinz USA; Richard Sperring, Vice-President, Supplies, PPG Industries; and Robert B. Stone, Executive-in-Charge, Purchasing Activities, General Motors Corporation.

In studying at first hand the procurement operations they manage, I gained a great respect for the complexity of their work and the high degree of managerial skill it requires. In particular, I came to understand that procurement as a management function is undergoing considerable change, change that has been forced on it by events in the external environment. The Arab oil embargo, the shortages of 1972–73, the increasing government involvement in matters relating to procurement, the rapidly growing use of management information systems—a trend in big companies, generally, away from geographically decentralized structures—all these factors have had, and will continue to have, a profound effect on procurement strategies, organization, and decision-making processes.

The field work for this study and the work on the preparation of the manuscript was funded by the Division of Research of the Harvard Business School with supplemental grants from Proctor and Gamble and the Marketing Science Institute. I hope that the end result will be perceived by these several sources of support as worthy of their expressions of confidence in the initial proposal.

I want to express my thanks to three persons who were of great help to me in this undertaking. Mr. Roger Bennett, now Assistant Professor at McGill University, worked very closely with me in the collection of data from the six companies. Dr. Ron Schill, Associate Professor at Brigham Young University, gathered useful information from one of these companies during a year at the Harvard Business School as a Visiting Scholar. Mr. Morton Galper, Associate Professor at Babson College, performed the literature search on which Appendix A is based.

Professor Richard E. Walton, Director of the Division of Research at Harvard Business School, should also be recognized here for his encouragement and his valuable insights and suggestions in shaping this study initially. At the other end of the process, Associate Professor Benson P. Shapiro of the Harvard Business School Faculty reviewed the manuscript and contributed many useful suggestions toward making this a more readable book. While I gratefully acknowledge these invaluable contributions, I do myself take full responsibility for the statements, concepts, and conclusions in the text.

Ms. Elizabeth Griffin and Mrs. Sharon Yates very skillfully and cheerfully managed the tremendous details of taking rough handwritten drafts of field interviews and chapters through multiple iterations to the final manuscript. Finally, my wife, Charlotte Worrall Corey, was a mainstay of the entire undertaking, and I am most grateful for her encouragement and support over the three years from inception to completion of this work.

Introduction

Procurement Management: Strategy, Organization, and Decision-Making looks at procurement from a top-management viewpoint, relates procurement to other business functions, and integrates it as an element in total corporate strategy. This study is descriptive in nature, seeking to depict from firsthand observation the way procurement works in large corporations, what strategies are used in coping with the supply environment, how it is organized, and the decision-making influences to which it is subjected. What may be observed in large corporations is applicable as well to medium and small companies and to nonprofit organizations. Thus, the basic concepts developed in this study are relevant for the procurement function regardless of the size or nature of the institution.

Chapter 1 identifies the elements of purchasing strategy and develops a three-part typology of strategic approaches that buyers use and the particular circumstances under which each is appropriate. Chapters 2 and 3 discuss the four basic elements of any strategy—procurement scope, supplier selection, price-quantity factors, and buyer-seller negotiations—and suggest the range of considerations that come to bear on the choices the buyer makes along each of these four dimensions. The discussion also develops understanding of strategy syndromes, that is, the interrelatedness and cohesiveness of the several elements in achieving a strategic integrity.

Chapters 4 and 5 deal with procurement organization. Chapter 4 considers the reasons for the current strong trend toward the centralization of procurement activities in large organizations and the countervailing pressures for decentralization. It considers, as well, the dynamic factors in the economic and political environment that are currently working to shape where procurement is positioned. I also attempt to predict future organizational directions. Going beyond this overview, Chapter 5 looks at *what* specific procurement activities are typically carried out *where* in the organizational structure. It looks at the structure of purchasing departments per se and at the specialization of work that is reflected therein.

Chapters 6 and 7 describe purchasing decision-making processes: how sourcing decisions are made and the internal influences that come to bear on the process. These final chapters discuss the involvement of other functional areas in the procurement process—engineering, production, marketing, and general management. Chapter 6 also describes procurement audit and performance-measurement systems as influences on purchasing decision-making processes.

As a guide to the reader, Appendix A serves mainly to position this study among some of the more widely used books in procurement. It describes each of six texts, its major ideas, and its particular contribution. The purpose is to indicate the scope of what has been written in the procurement field and to position this book in the literature.

Appendix B consists of 10 case studies, the purpose of which is to allow the reader to study some specific situations in depth and to serve as a basis for discussion in a classroom setting.

The observations on which this study is based come primarily from six major U.S. companies representing five different industries: General Motors, International Business Machines Corporation, Raytheon Company, PPG Industries, General Foods Corporation, and Heinz USA. Each is a leading company in its field. It is a reasonable presumption, therefore, that the effectiveness of the procurement function in each case has made a major contribution to its growth and profitability. Hence, these particular companies were chosen with the expectation that much could be learned from the approaches their managements have taken to the development and management of sourcing systems. The practices that were observed in these companies were in fact highly professional and may usefully serve as models from which to learn.

The largest of the six companies, General Motors, recorded sales in 1977 of $55 billion, of which $47.5 billion were made in the U.S. Its profits in that year were $3.3 billon. General Motors' major business is the manufacture of cars and trucks, of which it produced and sold 8.9 million worldwide in 1977. Other product lines include buses, locomotives, motor homes, earth-moving equipment, diesel engines, turbine aircraft engines, navigation systems, major household appliances, automotive and truck parts and accessories, and systems and components for military and space agencies. In 1977 General Motors' average worldwide employment was 797,000 people, and it was the largest manufacturing company in the world. Its purchases of goods and services in 1977 were $27.6 billion, or approximately 50 percent of its sales dollars.

International Business Machines had sales in 1977 of $18.1 billion, half of which were in the United States and half abroad. Its earnings after taxes were $2.7 billion. IBM is the world's largest manufacturer of computers. In addition, it is a major supplier of office equipment, including copier-duplicators; electric typewriters; high-speed printers; and educational and testing materials for school, industry, and home use. Its products are both leased and sold. In 1977 its employees numbered 310,000.

Highly diversified, Raytheon Company's major field of business is electronic systems and components, including navigation, weapons, and communications systems for both government and industry. Raytheon divisions and subsidiary companies also make major household and industrial appliances, such as refrigerators, freezers, and microwave ovens; medical equipment; and data-handling systems. Still another division publishes textbooks, and one subsidiary is engaged in the construction of chemical and petrochemical plants. Sales in 1977 were $2.82 billion, on which the company earned $113 million after taxes.

PPG Industries' major lines are glass for building construction and for automotive and aircraft applications; paints and protective coatings for both consumer and industrial markets; industrial chemicals; and fiberglass. PPG sales in 1977 were $2.51 billion; its profits were $91.7 million. The number of employees at year end was 36,600. In 1977, PPG purchased $1.42 billion in materials and services, an amount equal to 56.9 percent of its revenues.

General Foods, the largest processor of coffee in the United States and the sixth largest manufacturer of packaged foods in this country, had net revenues of $4.91 billion in the fiscal year 1977 (Ending April 2, 1977) and after-tax profits of $150 million. Its well-known brand names include Maxwell House (coffee), Post (cereals), Birds Eye (frozen foods), Jell-O (desserts), Kool-Aid (soft drinks), Swans Down (cake mixes), and Gaines (pet foods). It had also diversified into such areas as fast-food service restaurants and seeds and gardening aids. General Foods' purchases of materials, supplies, and services amounted to $3.84 billion in fiscal 1977, or 78.2 percent of sales revenues.

Also a major producer of processed-food products, Heinz had worldwide sales of $1.87 billion and a net income of $84 million for its 1977 fiscal year (Ending April 27, 1977). Sales by Heinz domestic companies (including those in U.S. possessions) were $1.2 billion in fiscal year 1977. Heinz is a leading manufacturer of ketchup, pickles and relishes, canned soups and vegetables, baby food, canned tuna, frozen desserts, and pet foods. Worldwide purchases of food ingredients; packaging; and other materials, goods, and services amounted to 71.6 percent out of every sales dollar, or $1.34 billion in 1977.

Industrial procurement is that function in organizations concerned with the acquisition of goods and services both from outside suppliers and from internal sister divisions. In manufacturing companies, such as General Motors, the procurement function typically accounts for the expenditure of amounts upward of

50 percent of sales. In retailing and wholesale organizations the comparable figure would be in the 65 to 80 percent range. Clearly, the procurement function has a significant impact on corporate profitability or, in the case of nonprofit organizations, on cost efficiency.

By way of definition, *procurement* or *purchasing* includes:

1. The determination of what to buy, that is, the physical and performance specifications of the goods or services to be bought and the quantity to be obtained.
2. The identification and selection of potential sources of supply.
3. The qualification of sources and of the products they will supply.
4. The design of the request for quotations (RFQ) and the solicitation of bids.
5. The negotiation of prices, terms, and conditions with selected vendors and the allocation of purchase amounts among them.
6. The monitoring of supplier performance and the conduct of ongoing supplier relations, including often
   · the management of technical interchange activities
   · delivery schedules and transportation arrangements for incoming shipments
   · audits of vendor costs
   · accounting for equipment and materials owned by the buyer and located on the vendor's premises
   · feedback on vendor performance
   · the resolution of delivery, product quality, and service problems
   · the handling of any claims against the vendor for failure to perform
7. The establishment of procurement policies, control systems, and performance-measurement systems.
8. Sometimes the management of inventories of purchased parts, materials, and supplies.
9. Often the disposal of waste and scrap materials.

The term *sourcing* is broader in definition than procurement in that it includes all that is meant by the latter and in addition embraces certain matters of policy and broad strategy. One of these is the company's posture with regard to make-or-buy options. Another has to do with the use of foreign sources of supply and the firm's willingness to incur the possible supply risks that might entail. Another is the structuring of long-term relations with supply industries, which may involve making multiyear commitments to purchase in return for suppliers' making major financial investments in manufacturing capacity. A *sourcing system* is the complex of outside suppliers and internal manufacturing sources for all the materials, component parts, supplies, machinery and equipment, facilities, and services the organization requires.

The purchase of materials and parts that go into the products a business makes and sells are called *product purchases*. The procurement of supplies, capital equipment, and services that are used in the manufacturing process but do not become part of the end product are called *nonproduct purchases*. This distinction, as will be seen later, has important implications for procurement organization and decision-making processes.

Since purchases are often made by buyers who are not part of the organizations to which those supplies will be delivered for use, the term *user location* is intended to refer to plants, laboratories, and offices that are on the receiving end of procurement decision-making.

The language of procurement includes other terms that might usefully be described at the outset. *Supplier* and *vendor* are used interchangeably to refer to the outside companies and to the sister divisions from which purchases are made. Some of these sources are *manufacturers* that make the products they sell. Some are intermediaries, such as distributors, agents, jobbers, and wholesalers who sell the products made by their sources of supply. To distinguish among these several terms, a *distributor* buys merchandise from a number of sources, carries it in inventory, and sells to a large number of customers. Like a distributor, a *jobber* also takes title to the goods he sells, although he may or may not carry those goods in inventory. When he makes a sale, he may have the goods shipped directly to his customer from his manufacturing source. A jobber typically sells limited lines, buying in bulk and selling in smaller lots for negotiated prices. *Agents* and *brokers* do not take title to the goods they sell but instead typically represent a limited number of sources and are compensated by a percentage commission on sales. Agents tend to have long-term relationships with the principals they represent. Brokers may deal with a constantly changing complex of sources.

Supply industries are sometimes described in this text as *oligopolistic,* meaning that a limited number (two to eight) of large suppliers account for the bulk (60 percent or more) of industry sales and that the product-planning, pricing, and capital investment decisions of each significantly influence the strategies of the others. Similarly, buying industries are termed *oligopsonistic* when a limited number of large buyers account for a high percentage of total purchases of certain product categories.

Finally, among the commonly used acronyms in purchasing, three are especially worthy of note. An *RFQ* is a request for quotations. It describes the particular product specifications, delivery requirements, and contract terms relating to a proposed purchase and requests a supplier to respond with a sales offer. The offer will include the prices and terms under which the seller is willing to meet the buyer's requirements.

A *CPA* is a corporate purchase agreement. Sometimes also referred to as a *CWA* (corporate-wide agreement), it is a contract negotiated at some central point in the organization for a particular class of products at specified prices for a fixed time period and on which user locations may draw to meet their needs as they arise. Among other categories of goods, CPAs are often negotiated for *MRO* items. These are nonproduct maintenance, repair, and operating supplies.

The above terms and acronyms are sufficiently pervasive to warrant early recognition. Others will be defined as they come up in the text.

Overall, *Procurement Management* is intended for members of general management and procurement management. This book should be useful in adding conceptual perspectives in the areas of strategy, organization, and decision-making. Such perspectives might usefully contribute to the design of more effective procurement functions.

For those involved in day-to-day purchasing activities, this book will help them relate their important work to the work in other functional areas and to the ongoing missions of the total enterprise.

For students of business and academicians it is offered for what it might contribute toward the better understanding of a vital organizational function.

Procurement
Management

1 Procurement Strategy Models

A strategy is a plan of action designed to achieve given goals and objectives. Both buyers and sellers have strategies for dealing with the other. The kinds of marketing strategy sellers develop and implement generally are well articulated within firms and in the literature. By contrast, procurement strategies—plans of action for obtaining supplies and for dealing with sellers—often are not clearly understood. Yet well-conceived and skillfully executed procurement strategies are highly critical to the success of any organization. Overall, an organization's growth and profitability will be affected greatly by its ability to secure supplies and to gain the benefits of new technologies from its supply sources.

Procurement strategies vary so greatly from one purchasing situation to another because each situation is unique. Thus, every strategy has to be tailored to the type of product being purchased, the stage of the procurement cycle, the past purchasing history, the nature of the supply environment, and the buying company itself: its resources, its negotiating strength, and its purchasing policies. However, all procurement strategies seem to be variations and modifications of the three basic models that are described in this chapter.

The three models are most clearly distinguished from each other in terms of the basis for determining price, that is, cost-based negotiations, market-price-based negotiations, and competitive bidding. Each strategy model is a synthesis of mutually reinforcing elements that form an integrated whole. When strategies lack internal consistency, the result will almost certainly be a failure to achieve procurement goals.

Each of the three sections that follows begins with an illustrative case example of a strategy model and concludes with an analytical commentary.

The Cost-Based Price Model: Developing and Purchasing New Production Equipment at IBM

In late 1972, engineers at an IBM development center designed a feasibility model of a complex new machine to be used in the manufacture of logic chips.[1] The new machine, of a highly advanced design, would contain a network of pipes made of different materials, both plastic and metal, which would carry chemicals such as hydrofluoric acid, argon, hydrogen, and nitrogen. It was essential that each pipeline be kept apart from every other pipeline and that the machine include elaborate sensing and shut-off mechanisms to guard against leakages. It was also mandatory that the system be completely sealed off from all impurities. The requirement was for more than 150 such machines for production purposes. While IBM engineers had developed a prototype, more technical development work was required. One or more suppliers would be needed to work intensively with IBM engineers for the duration of the design-and-development phase and to supply production units when this phase was completed.

The buyer assigned to develop a source for this equipment began by forming a team to identify and evaluate potential suppliers. The team included quality-control and design and drafting personnel, industrial engineers, and purchasing managers. The team began its work by preparing a list of potential vendors. The list eventually included five possible sources. In visits to each one, the team assessed the company's drafting, fabrication, and engineering capabilities; its management strength; its accounting controls; its purchasing function; and its ability to segregate the project from other jobs and to maintain security and technical confidentiality. A particular concern was the supplier's hourly rate, that is, the price for labor, general and administrative overheads, and profit.

Only one vendor, Special Machine Tool (SMT), seemed well qualified on all counts, and IBM negotiated a time-and-materials (T&M) contract with this supplier for 25 units for delivery in the last quarter of 1973 and the first quarter of 1974. The contract stipulated an hourly rate ($12.59) and provided that IBM would reimburse the vendor at cost for all materials used on the contract. IBM had the right to inspect work in process and to audit project accounts and files. Among other matters, the contract dealt with the control of engineering changes, insurance arrangements, payment terms, the treatment of confidential information and security control procedures, and rights to patents coming out of the development work. An important clause in the contract identified those individuals who would represent each party in the ongoing relationship. Also covered were delivery procedures, product performance standards, and test procedures that would be used in evaluating and accepting finished units.

In a six-month period the work required frequent contacts involving a number of people at IBM and SMT. Engineers from the two companies worked closely

---

1. Logic chips are electronic components utilizing extremely dense microcircuitry and are used in data-processing equipment.

together on design development and engineering changes. No IBM engineer, however, was to have direct contact with SMT representatives until the purpose of his or her visit or communication had been approved by the buyer in charge of vendor relationships. This provision was to avoid confusion in authorizing changes and to assure full consideration of their effect on cost. Although this rule was supposed to be strictly enforced, it was occasionally disregarded, with the result that expensive changes were made by engineering personnel without full consideration of cost effects.

Five months after the first agreement was signed, a second was arranged for an additional 15 units, and this was followed by a final T&M contract for 38 units, due to be completed in March 1975. By mid-1974, SMT had completed and delivered the first 40 units and had completed half of the work on the next 38. At that point, although engineering change orders continued to come through, the decision was made to attempt to negotiate a fixed-price contract for additional units. The buyer explained why a fixed-price contract was preferable to a T&M arrangement at this stage.

> I think SMT is an honest company and our contract terms allow us to audit what they charge us. Even then T&M works out to be an expensive way of doing business. It requires a colossal amount of supervision. There are weekly reports, checks on work-in-progress, auditing work sheets, requesting estimates for the next stage and checking costs against estimates, and other control measures. The buyer is in contact with the vendor many times each day.

SMT and one other, much larger company, were asked to bid on 85 more units. The RFQ requested that the overall bid be broken down to show the hourly rate, the parts and materials component in the price, and any charges for subcontracted services. SMT quoted $1.62 million and supplied the cost breakdown as requested. The second company submitted only one total figure, $5.01 million, with no cost breakdown. The decision was made to negotiate with SMT.

The IBM negotiating team included two purchasing managers and two cost engineers. One cost engineer had developed manufacturing cost estimates for every component, working from engineering drawings and cost-data books that he had built up from previous experience and that contained time factors, both set-up and run times, for a large variety of operations. He estimated materials costs by working both from data supplied by the IBM Corporate Purchasing Staff and from purchasing journals. He visited SMT facilities to see the tooling available so that he would know what processes were being used. He assumed that there would be perfect conditions and trained operators, and he developed cost estimates for the 158th unit (25 + 15 + 38 + 80). He added 5 percent for scrap-and-flow loss; 2 percent to allow for the use of temporary tools, jigs, and fixtures; 5 percent for quality control; and 9 percent for purchasing burden. Then, using an 85 percent learning curve,[2] he backed up his costs to get an estimate for the first unit. He next checked the data on hours and materials for the 25, 15, and 38 units already made and found that his estimate for the first unit was within 4 percent of actual cost. His check, however, had indicated a 90 percent learning-curve effect on hours per unit.

In the negotiations, SMT was represented by one of the two owners of the business, two engineers, and one cost estimator. The sessions opened with a discussion of learning curves. The IBM cost estimator demonstrated that SMT had in fact been operating on a 90% learning curve. But, he argued, it should be possible to move to an 85% curve, given the longer runs, reduced set-up time, and increased continuity of workers on the job that would be possible with an order for 80 units. The owner agreed with this analysis and was willing to reduce his price by 4%.

However, as each operation in the manufacturing process was discussed, it became clear that some IBM cost estimates were too low because certain crating and shipping expenses had been overlooked. These oversights were minor, however, and in the following discussions the two parties arrived at a common understanding of specifications and reached agreements on the costs of each manufacturing operation.

At this point, SMT representatives expressed great concern about the possibility of inflation in materials costs. The IBM negotiators volunteered to include a form of price escalation in the contract, as previously agreed among themselves. IBM representatives suggested that if overall materials costs changed by more than 10 percent, the price could be adjusted accordingly. However, if one party took the initiative to have the price revised, the other could require an analysis of *all* parts and materials invoices in arriving at the new price.

Another concern of the SMT representatives was that a large amount of overtime and subcontracting would be required to meet IBM's specified delivery schedule. IBM negotiators thought that a relaxation in the delivery schedule might be possible if a price concession could be obtained. In response the SMT team offered a 5 percent discount, and this was accepted. As a result of these negotiations the SMT price was reduced almost 20 percent below its original bid price.

In a subsequent meeting called to negotiate the prices of certain pipes to be used in the system, it became apparent to an IBM cost estimator that SMT representatives had seriously underestimated their costs. He pointed out this apparent error because he could not understand why SMT had quoted such a low figure. He wanted to be sure that SMT was using the correct manufacturing

2. The use of an 85 percent learning curve applied to labor-related costs is based on the assumption that with each doubling of production quantities the number of hours used to make each unit will decrease by 15 percent. The choice of an 85 percent learning curve was based on the cost engineer's experience.

process. In any case, if SMT estimators had made a mistake it should be noted. It was IBM's policy to seek a fair price both for itself and for its suppliers. IBM procurement managers believed that if a vendor was losing money on a job there would be a tendency to cut corners. In addition, the IBM negotiator felt that by pointing out the error he generated some goodwill that would help in future sessions.

The IBM team also sought to negotiate a contract with the second supplier that had submitted a bid, but to no avail. This supplier's prices were much higher than SMT's, and its representatives were unwilling to discuss cost-price breakdowns. After two meetings and several months of correspondence, IBM broke off negotiations. The general business turndown had slowed the program, so that there was no longer a desperate need to find a second supplier merely to satisfy delivery schedule requirements. An IBM buyer commented on the need for another vendor:

> We would like to have had another vendor working for us but present demand doesn't justify it. Based on our change of requirements, it was no longer necessary to develop another supplier. Given our cost estimates and SMT's experience, this was the best business decision. To second source would cost us a premium.
>
> There are worries, though. SMT is a $4 million company and we have too much of its business. One fire and it could be wiped out, and we would be in a mess. That doesn't stop me from sleeping at night, but it does worry me. We're concerned that the vendor keep work-in-progress to a minimum and that warehoused product be kept at a location away from the plant. We insist on reports on both matters.
>
> The fact that we have a large proportion of SMT's business is a concern. We've met with SMT management to keep them appraised of our long-term requirements so they can assess the impact on themselves. As our requirements have decreased, we have arranged to stretch out the fixed-price order.
>
> If we need more units, we'll go back to SMT—but they'll have to lower their prices because of the learning curve. It would take a lot of effort to bring more suppliers on stream. Another source would have to have:
>
> Good engineering/drafting capability.
> The ability to do most of the work in house.
> Good prices.
> A good record of past performance.
> A financially sound position.
> The ability to comply with confidential agreement terms.

But even so, there would be all sorts of problems in bringing him on stream and delivery is critically important. I'm in contact with SMT three or four times a day and that contract is going smoothly. You can imagine the problems involved with a new supplier. All the same, though, IBM likes a competitive environment and that's the way I like to live, too.

The *cost-based price model* is the basis for a close working relationship, typically symbiotic in nature, between vendor and customer. The salient features of the strategy initially are: (1) a single supplier; (2) a single item being developed and purchased; (3) a time-and-materials pricing arrangement; and (4) contracts initially negotiated for short durations and limited quantities. Then the price arrangement may evolve into a firm fixed price; other suppliers may be solicited, but negotiations may continue to be vendor-cost-based.

Because of the stringent requirements having to do with technical competence, manufacturing capabilities, and cost and security controls, the initial screening of potential suppliers had to be quite rigorous. It was important, too, that engineers be involved in the evaluations, both because the appraisals were largely of a technical nature and because the IBM supplier relationship would be conducted largely on a technical level throughout the contract. IBM engineers and supplier technical personnel would be working closely for almost two years. Thus, it was critical to determine in the beginning whether the individuals involved could work well together and communicate easily in resolving complex technical problems.

Given the nature of the work, it might have been clumsy and inefficient to involve more than one supplier. That being the case, it was important that IBM's development work on the new machine was well along before a supplier was selected. By the prototype stage the general directions and technical requirements were well known, and the requirements of an outside supplier could be spelled out with some degree of certainty.

Ideally, the objective in qualification procedures is to eliminate all the variables that tend to differentiate suppliers by setting up standards that each must meet to be considered. Then price differences remain the sole determinant. Thus, it would have been desirable if more than one supplier had survived IBM's qualification screening, because then the choice could have been based on price alone, in this case the hourly rate. It may be, as in this instance, however, that the standards are necessarily so stringent that vendor selection never reaches the point of price competition. Broadly speaking, in such a case the final choice is the result of engineering evaluations together with assessments of vendor management capabilities.

In this case, the pricing is of particular interest. It was carried out with the implicit objective of arriving at an arrangement that would be fair for both buyer and seller. SMT's profit was included in its hourly rate, and IBM negotiators never asked for a breakdown of that figure into its components of labor, overheads, and profit. In total, the hourly rate was accepted as reasonable in the absence of having two or three qualified bidders as a check.

Given the nature of the work, a time-and-materials pricing arrangement was the only practical possibility. The design and machine specifications were far from frozen. Engineering changes that would affect costs were being made with great frequency. Bidding on a fixed-price basis under these circumstances would not have been feasible.

Although resorting to a time-and-materials price basis imposed tremendous auditing burdens on IBM personnel, it also had a great advantage. It gave IBM representatives an opportunity to monitor the work and track cost behavior and thereby gain detailed knowledge of the work that would be useful in subsequent negotiations.

The second-stage price negotiations that did arrive at a fixed-price arrangement focused on all of the different elements of cost, a key one being learning-curve effects. Several aspects of those negotiations are well worth noting:

1. The IBM cost estimators prepared for these discussions by developing a detailed buildup of cost factors to arrive at a target price. In doing so they relied on publicly available cost information, on their knowledge of SMT's facilities and processes, on SMT's cost performance during the development phases of the work, and on their own expertise in cost estimating.

2. In cost-based price negotiations it is essential that buyer and seller be working from common assumptions and understanding regarding product specifications and the processes to be employed. This consideration underscores the importance of structuring the buyer-supplier relationship in the development stages so that the buyer's engineers go through, and do not bypass, the purchasing managers in dealing with supplier personnel. If purchasing managers go into negotiations with an inaccurate understanding of the work, their negotiating effectiveness may be seriously weakened.

3. As for agenda, it is useful to note that it was planned so that detailed cost discussions were cleared away first. That resulted in developing a common understanding of, and agreement on, cost factors. Then IBM made two moves that reduced the final price significantly. It assumed the risks of inflation in materials costs by agreeing to provide for escalation in the contract. These risks are much less formidable to a large buyer than to a small supplier, and the escalation provisions could protect the vendor's profits by guarding against the devastating effects of materials price increases. In fact, in 1974 price inflation was a major concern. The second move was to stretch out the delivery schedule. This concession would enable SMT to improve cost performance and to pass on the cost savings in the form of a price reduction.

It is not surprising that at this point in the negotiations it would have been difficult for IBM to introduce a second source. SMT had the strong advantage of having gone through a learning-curve experience. No competitor would be likely to have lower costs for the work, nor could another competitor quote with as much confidence: another bidder would be likely to build safety margins into the quotation to offset possible errors in estimating and to take into account the inherent inefficiencies in breaking in plant administrative and engineering personnel on new and unfamiliar work.

Adding a second source would also have been likely to reduce the unit-cost efficiency of the first source by reducing its manufacturing quantities. In a case like this one, having two sources would almost certainly have increased the cost of the procurement.

Finally, it is important that buyer and seller representatives had developed close working relationships and that the seller was performing satisfactorily. Those considerations would tend to reduce the desire of IBM personnel to add another supplier, with all the complexities such a move would incur.

An inherent disadvantage of single sourcing is, of course, the risk of a work stoppage or a catastrophe at the supplier's plant that could hold up the buyer's schedules at some considerable cost. That risk was not easily offset in this case, even though work in progress was kept at minimum levels and it was required that the warehouse locations used would not be close to the plant.

The second disadvantage is that the buyer forgoes the benefits of having multiple suppliers willing to compete on a price basis for a given volume of business. In this case, the loss in bargaining power is probably offset by the buyer's having negotiating strength in other ways. Primarily, the work is a significant part of the vendor's total load, and losing it might seriously affect his business. In addition, the buyer may, and probably will, be the source of future business. Finally, the buyer has an important psychological advantage in negotiating: he or she knows the vendor's costs. For all these reasons it is likely that, for the near term at least, negotiations will result in fair and reasonable prices.

It is useful to note an inherent internal consistency in IBM's strategy. The developmental nature of the work in the early stages would lead to: (1) planning a narrow (one item) procurement; and (2) working as a practical matter with one supplier rather than with several. But such a relationship forgoes the benefits of competition. In these circumstances, cost-based price negotiations become appropriate as a way of assuring that the price is fair for the seller and optimal for the buyer.

The Market-Price-Based Model: Sourcing for Steel Requirements at General Motors

> We talked to the suppliers about what percentages of our requirements we would like to buy from them. . . . We didn't talk price. You can't bargain individually with the steel companies on base prices.

So commented one member of a four-man steel-buying team at General Motors in discussing negotiations with GM's ten steel suppliers for the 1976 model year.

At General Motors, steel purchasing was primarily the responsibility of Warren MacNair and a team of three. They were Dick Lamphere, who worked with MacNair at the GM central office; Allen Lyman, a member of the Chevrolet central office procurement organization; and Ralph Reisman of the Fisher Body purchasing group. MacNair was also responsible for the purchase of tires, nonferrous metals, and plastic materials. He reported to Jim Cowan, executive in charge of purchasing activities.

Steel is the largest purchase that GM makes. As of 1975, the average car contained 3,400 pounds of steel, of which 2,500 pounds was bought by GM in the form of sheet and bar stock and 900 pounds came from GM suppliers as frames, mufflers, springs, and other steel parts. GM's direct purchases from U.S. steel companies amounted to roughly $3 billion in 1974, an amount that represented 12 to 13 percent of total U.S. steel production. Overall, the U.S. automobile industry accounted for 18 to 22 percent of total domestic steel output.

In 1974, steel, among many other materials and manufactured products, was in short supply in the United States. GM had difficulty getting all the steel it needed. Moreover, in the face of shortages, steel producers' pricing practices took some new turns. Prior to 1974, all had typically quoted the same base prices, but these began to vary, often depending on cost factors. Mills that used higher percentages of scrap, for example, increased base prices to account for sharply rising scrap costs. Other mills raised base prices to secure the resources for capital expansion. Generally, the industry abandoned freight equalization[3] and began quoting FOB mill. Mills also quoted varying prices for width-and-gauge extras,[4] whereas previously these extras, too, had been typically the same from one producer to another. Finally, in the face of shortages, secondary sources such as brokers and warehouses charged significantly more for steel than the primary producers did. In the last half of 1974, the base price at the mill for hot-rolled steel was 12.5 cents a pound, while spot prices from warehouses and secondary processors were in the 18 to 26 cent range. In the fourth quarter of 1974, GM purchasing managers estimated that the company paid premiums to secondary sources. The majority of premiums were paid by GM parts suppliers and passed on to their customers. A small portion was due to having to fill GM plant emergency needs from the stocks of local steel warehouses.

It was against this background that MacNair, Lamphere, Lyman, and Reisman went into negotiations with GM's domestic steel suppliers in April 1975.

Early in 1975, as in past years, each GM plant purchasing manager was

---

3. In some industries, including steel, it was common practice to set the freight component of the price to the buyer at a level that equated to the cost of freight to the point of delivery from the nearest mill of any steel supplier.

4. One of the extras in steel pricing is the width-and-gauge charge. For every combination of thickness (gauge) and width a certain charge is specified in cents per pound and added to the base price. Other extras may include charges based on quantity ordered, type of packaging specified, and cutting-to-size requirements.

requested to prepare a plan for meeting his plant's steel requirements for the 1976 model year, beginning July 1, 1975. These plans, due February 28, were to be based on corporate planning-volume figures issued by the Central Office, which reflected sales forecasts for the 1976 model year by product line.

At the Chevrolet Division's Warren Plant, which made axle and brake assemblies and wheels, the Central Office memorandum on planning steel requirements came to assistant purchasing agent Pat Clements. His work in preparing a "pattern" for the Warren Plant is illustrative of what went on in many GM plants.

The steel-sourcing cycle at the Warren Plant started with the receipt of an estimate, issued by Lyman's office, which established guidelines for developing the pattern for the coming model year. This letter included data that gave some indication of model-year planning volumes by car line. This information was submitted as "units of cars," not as "tons of steel." The local plant Production Material Control Department interpolated these planning volumes, breaking them down by part number and calculating the annual tonnage required by part number. Parts were grouped by categories of steel (i.e., hot-rolled sheet, strip, hot-rolled carbon bar, etc.). On a continuing basis, Clements received detailed specifications, by part number, showing grade of steel and all size information. During the year, the buyer was kept informed of the level of steel quality received from the various mills. He was also informed of mill-delivery performance through normal dealings with the Production Material Control Department. All this information was considered prior to allocating business for the coming model year. Clements said: "On the basis of current model year performance, I know who should be rewarded with increased business, whom to penalize, and where to maintain a status quo." According to Clements:

Significant changes in the new pattern from the current pattern must be carefully documented with cogent reasons. Eventually, the entire pattern must be approved by Central Office. On small-tonnage items (forty tons or less per month), you'll normally have one source. When the tonnage per month, per part is great enough, you will establish multiple sources. Pattern variations from model year to model year will normally be affected on these parts. In normal times, steel prices vary little between mills. However, during the end of the 1974 model and first half of the 1975 model year, there were frequent and varied price adjustments with little similarity between mills. Some abandoned freight equalization, others had higher base-prices, mill prices for extras such as mill bond (plastic coating) varied, etc.

Clements tried to favor the mills closest to the Warren Plant in sourcing for the 1976 model year. Although most of the mills had reinstituted freight equalization during the 1975 model year, he was concerned that this pricing convention might be changed again if shortages recurred.

In the case of two major suppliers, he felt constrained to alter significantly the 1976 pattern percentages because of corporate agreements. Without the corporate agreements, Clements would have reduced his allocation with one mill for reasons of poor delivery and lack of responsiveness to requests for technical help. The percentage with the other major mill would not have been altered because of its overall good performance at the Warren Plant.

As for other suppliers, Clements gave one a 3.5 percent increase because of good delivery performance and useful technical contributions. Another was reduced by 4 percent, once again for reasons relevant for GM's overall steel-sourcing strategy. This company had done nothing to plan for the expansion of its steel-producing facilities and had not evidenced strong interest in supplying the automotive industry. This 4 percent could be allocated to another supplier that had helped GM considerably to get steel when it was in short supply. In addition, the latter supplier was planning a facilities expansion and gave every evidence of having made a long-term commitment to the automobile industry. Except for such considerations as these, there was little basis for choice among suppliers on the volume of hot-rolled and cold-rolled steel for production parts. According to Clements:

> All the major steel mills make pretty much equivalent products. There is little to choose quality-wise. From time to time, you'll receive some dirty steel and you hear about it from the production people, especially on something like a wheel rim which is the most difficult part we make. Working with the Inspection Department, the buyer must do whatever he can to minimize the frequency of such problems.

After Clements drafted his steel-sourcing plan, he submitted it to Lyman at Chevrolet Central Office. When he received approval for it, he issued contracts to suppliers stipulating for each steel specification the percentage of the Warren Plant's requirements each supplier would receive for the 1976 model year. He asserted: "Then I make sure the steel company representatives that call on us know what the new allocations will be and the reasons for any change." Each month, Clements sent a report of actual orders against contract and steel inventory levels to Lyman with appropriate explanations for any variances from plan.

At the Central Office, Dick Lamphere received all the proposed steel-sourcing patterns from the divisions. It was his task to consolidate these data and to develop an overall pattern for GM, taking into account both division preferences and the strategic considerations emanating from the headquarters steel-buying team under MacNair. Since steel had been in very short supply in 1974 and GM had experienced difficulty in meeting its requirements, a key factor in developing the pattern for 1975–76 was the actual pattern for 1974–75. By taking 1974–75 purchases as a basing point for 1975–76 when it was anticipated there would not be steel shortages, GM would be giving business to its suppliers in proportion to what they had made available to it out of their scarce supplies in the prior year.

The new plan, of course, did not exactly replicate the prior year's sourcing pattern in percentage allocations of steel purchases from different suppliers. It did reflect some rewards for suppliers that had been particularly responsive to GM's needs.

The sum of the proposed divisional patterns and the preferred sourcing plan developed by the corporate buying team varied by 400,000 tons out of a total requirement of 8.5 million tons. Lamphere then aligned the divisional proposals by working with Reisman and Lyman to make shifts, mainly in the plant plans in the Fisher Body and Chevrolet Divisions, which were the two largest steel-using divisions.

In early April, meetings were held with each of the GM's ten steel suppliers to discuss the percentage of GM's requirements for the 1976 model year each would supply. At these meetings, GM was represented by the buying team of Lamphere, Lyman, and Reisman; supplier representation generally included a sales vice-president, the Detroit district manager, and product managers for the large-volume items. Some suppliers might argue in such meetings for increased allocations based on factors such as past performance, their historical shares of GM's business, and future expansion plans. However, no changes in this sourcing program were made in the course of the April meetings.

In late April and early May there were a series of discussions with steel suppliers on prices. The GM steel-buying team's objective in these meetings was to achieve a reinstatement of freight equalization and a reduction of width-and-gauge price extras for those suppliers that had raised them above prevailing levels in 1974. The theme that GM negotiators stressed was, "We don't want to pay one dollar more a ton for the same steel to any one supplier over another."

Initial conversations were held with one of GM's larger suppliers, and this company agreed to return to freight equalization. With this concession and taking account of width-and-gauge extras, at this point its prices were lower than those of six other suppliers. GM then negotiated with the latter group to roll back on the extras.[5] At the end of this series of meetings (all held at the General Motors Building in Detroit), all GM steel suppliers had reinstituted freight equalization and had like prices on extras. These prices, it should be noted, applied to all their customers, not only to GM. Because of the Robinson-Patman Act, the GM negotiating team would never negotiate for a price lower than that at which the supplier was selling to another of its accounts which might be competing with GM; nor would GM negotiators knowingly accept a discriminatory price.

As the spring of 1975 went on, the three-man team was joined by Lindsay (Vice-president of Procurement and Production Control in the Central Office), Cowan, and MacNair in calls on the top officers of the steel companies, the board chairmen, and the presidents. The steel supplier's Detroit district manager was almost always present at each of these meetings.

5. In general, extras in steel pricing might amount to roughly 20 percent of the total price.

The discussion agenda generally ranged across the supplier's plans for capacity expansion, research on new products, and energy problems and the steps being taken to cope with them. The GM team members also took the opportunity to do some "jawboning" with individual companies on list-price-level increases. They argued that in coming out of a slump in car sales it was important for the automotive industry to get the 1976 model year off to a good start without the handicap of higher steel prices that would have to be passed on to consumers in increased car prices. They pointed out, too, that the steel industry in 1974 had been relatively profitable, while the automobile industry had suffered badly, with sharp earnings declines and even losses in some cases.

With the price picture and the sourcing pattern having been worked out for the 1976 model year, the GM steel-buying team settled back to monitor actual performance against plan. At the Warren Plant, Clements sent monthly reports to Lyman in the Chevrolet Division with explanations for any deviations from plan. In the meantime, Lamphere continued to hold monthly meetings with groups of plant buyers to learn of any steel-supply problems and to keep them current on developments of general interest in GM's steel-sourcing program. He also made adjustments in the sourcing plan as problems of late delivery or quality were experienced with individual suppliers.

From time to time he received calls from plant buyers where there were difficulties with certain suppliers. Normally, after learning the facts, he got in touch with the supplier's Detroit district representative.

At the Central Office, MacNair was thinking about the longer-run sourcing pattern for GM:

> The 1973–1975 period has given us a good opportunity to evaluate suppliers—their ability to control costs, willingness to invest in new capacity and management attitudes toward serving the automotive industry. That gives us the basis for evolving a long-run sourcing program that can be implemented gradually. In fact, we're already negotiating today for new steel capacity for the 1980s.

What has just been described is an example of the *market-price-based negotiating strategy*. In sourcing such a critical material as steel, GM objectives are: (1) to assure long-run availability of steel; (2) to assure that the steel will be of suitable quality; and (3) to obtain the lowest prices—in that order. Assuring availability is a matter of long-term commitment to a group of suppliers, in this case domestic, and of encouraging their investment in new plant capacity as demand grows. Getting steel of suitable quality is primarily a matter of day-to-day monitoring of vendor product quality as it arrives at GM plants and of taking corrective action when necessary. Obtaining low prices seems more a matter of bargaining between the steel and automotive industries, both because of the oligopolistic nature of the supply industry and because of GM's unique position as the industry's largest customer. The Robinson-Patman Act precludes the steel companies' giving GM a lower price than any of its competitors. In addition, the price of steel to GM significantly influences steel-price levels generally. Thus, for a large buyer like General Motors, its objectives in steel-price discussions must be to assure that its competitors do not, in some way, get the benefit of lower steel prices. Of equal importance, General Motors' negotiators must assure that its steel suppliers treat the automotive industry as favorably as possible, and at the same time have financial incentives to continue reinvesting in facilities. And that, indeed, is a delicate balance! Bargaining for long-run supply availability and low current prices would seem to require considerable diplomacy on both sides.

Nor is steel sourcing at GM a unique situation. The model is relevant for negotiations between large buyers and large sellers of materials and other commodities in oligopolistic or oligopsonistic industry structures. General Foods negotiating with the large chemical producers for supplies of food-grade chemicals is another example of market-price-based negotiations.

It is interesting to note in the General Motors case that the execution of its strategy progressed in three stages. First was the allocation of purchases—not really negotiated with suppliers—but unilaterally decided and announced. Clearly, allocations are made to individual suppliers based on quality of service at the plant level, willingness to supply GM during shortages, restraint in exploiting the shortage condition to raise prices excessively, willingness to expand capacity to meet long-term needs, and interest in serving the automotive industry. Allocations are determined, then, through a system of rewards. As the steel buyer at the Chevrolet Warren Plant commented: "On the basis of current model-year performance, I know who should be rewarded with increased business, whom to penalize, and where to maintain a status quo."

The longer-term considerations are factored in at the GM Central Office level, and allocations proposed at the plant level are modified accordingly.

The second stage of negotiations was price discussions. It is significant that these discussions came later than the meetings in which suppliers were informed what percent of GM's steel purchases each would be given. As noted, General Motors cannot bargain to get lower prices than other steel users. It can, however, significantly influence general price levels. On the theme that "We don't want to pay one dollar more a ton for the same steel to any one supplier over another," GM negotiators in 1975 successfully pressed for a reinstatement of freight equalization and reduced pricing extras. In effect, it rolled back pricing elements that made for price differences among suppliers to the lowest *total* price levels.

In the third stage of discussions—this time with top corporate officers of the steel-producing companies—GM negotiators "jawboned" to hold down the inevitable price increases in the period ahead. They argued the commonality of interest of both the steel and the automotive industries in the level of new car sales. If steel prices could be held down, car prices would be lower and sales higher. Then, in an implicit appeal to a sense of fairness in the split of profits between steel suppliers and automotive producers, GM negotiators noted the relatively greater profitability of the steel industry in 1974 versus the sharp earnings declines in the automobile industry. In this third stage, too, the discussions probed steel producers' plans for capacity expansion, new-product research, and coping with the mounting cost of energy. They demonstrated GM's natural interest in the long-term health of the domestic steel industry. This was the pattern of negotiations in the spring of 1975.

Another dimension of GM's steel-sourcing strategy was based on what happened in 1971–72 when General Motors moved to buy steel from foreign producers. To quote the head of the buying team: "We really felt that the domestic industry needed an injection of more competition." In 1970, following two substantial price increases within ten months on the part of domestic suppliers, GM managers decided to buy from foreign mills. The increases were supported by the contention that then existing price levels did not yield sufficient profits to support long-run expansion of steel capacity. The lack of planning for steel capacity had been a matter of concern at GM, too, and added some impetus to its decision to seek buying positions with mills abroad.

By 1972, GM was purchasing 15 percent of its cold-rolled steel requirements (7 percent of its total requirements) from mills in Germany, France, Luxembourg, the Netherlands, and Japan. Foreign steel prices were 5 to 12 percent below those charged by domestic suppliers and averaged $25 a ton less on a landed-cost basis to GM.

The sourcing of a percentage of their steel requirements abroad by GM and other large steel users, however, not only had an impact on the domestic steel industry, it also hurt GM in ways that had not been anticipated, according to MacNair. With the decline in demand on the U.S. producers, the majority of mills attempted to move steel through distribution channels by giving steel brokers and warehouses lower prices than were made available to large user-customers. In addition, some steel mills began to quote below-list prices to individual accounts to meet the equally low offers of competitors. Such offers were not made to General Motors, possibly because a low price to such a large buyer would soon become the general market price.

In the meantime, the largest producers, GM's largest suppliers, had suffered substantial reductions in tonnage, as much as 30 to 40 percent in cold-rolled sheet. As their profits eroded, they increased prices. As domestic prices went up, the prices of foreign steel also rose.

In July 1972, GM executives made a study of the company's policies on steel buying and of the future outlook. (MacNair had just assumed top responsibility for steel buying at GM, having worked with his predecessor since November 1971.) The study articulated some growing concerns about going further down the road on which GM had started a year earlier. A major one was the dependability of foreign sources for GM. In the long run, it seemed evident that worldwide demand for steel was growing at a much more rapid rate than U.S.

demand and that foreign output would be drawn toward the more rapidly developing countries. In the short run, there was the matter of the great distances from foreign mills and the need to carry large inventories to guard against any interruptions in supply. According to MacNair:

> We had a chance to study our cost experience with using foreign steel and estimated that $10 of the $25-a-ton saving was used up in the added costs of handling—we needed extra people to uncrate foreign steel and put it in condition for us to use—and of working capital for inventories.

In addition, GM financial officers anticipated currency revaluations that would effectively increase the cost of foreign steel to U.S. customers. They couldn't predict "when" or "how much" but felt that revaluations were quite probably imminent. In the face of these concerns, GM executives noted with some alarm that U.S. producers were closing marginal mills and not replacing their capacity. Finally, after they surveyed industry economics, they concluded that potentially the United States could be the world's lowest-cost steel-producing country because of its ore and energy supplies. As a result of the study, MacNair went to Europe and Japan in October 1972 to explain to GM's steel sources abroad that GM would concentrate its steel purchases for domestic production with U.S. producers but would continue to buy abroad for its plants in foreign countries. In the fall of 1972, GM cut its foreign purchases in half and phased them out completely in 1973.

Thus, the effort to introduce more competition by buying from foreign mills was short-lived. But the point is that it was a dimension of GM's sourcing strategy. It also suggests the limitations of price bargaining. Pressed too vigorously by buyers, it may easily jeopardize long-run supply availability.

In many respects, steel buyers and suppliers behave as though they recognized their long-run mutual dependency. The year-to-year bargaining, however, has the characteristics of an adversary relationship, each party maneuvering to achieve some advantage in what ultimately comes down to how the profits that come from the production and sale of automobiles will be shared between the automotive industry and its key supply industries. Additionally, the steel companies are understandably concerned about the effect of price negotiations with the automotive industry on steel-price levels in their other markets.

In the market-price-based model, it is absolutely essential to have a multi-supplier sourcing system. While prices are essentially determined in strict conformance with published market prices and are the same for all customers in a using industry, the large buyer has some ability to influence overall price levels by introducing new competitive elements. Also, by working on price differences among suppliers at the lowest levels, he can bring pressure to achieve price uniformity among them. Hence, procurement planning calls for massing total requirements across the corporation and for buying a wide range of items from each supplier. Negotiations focus on longer-range considerations, such as adding new steel capacity and new-product development. Too, significant bargaining strength derives from the ability of the large buyer to shift purchase volumes among suppliers.

Few organizations, of course, have the bargaining power of a General Motors in dealing with an oligopsonistic supply industry. But in other industries where buyers and sellers are relatively large and limited in number, it would be natural for one buying organization, usually the largest, to exercise leadership in negotiating prices and terms on critical materials. The smaller buyers and sellers, then, may be greatly dependent on the outcome of the yearly negotiations between the leaders and may have relatively little ability to affect prices.

The Competitive-Bidding Model: Negotiating with Electronics Parts Distributors at Raytheon

Five years ago we were concentrating firmly on achieving the largest possible rebates. Since then we've thought much more about what we want from our distributors. Rebates are still important but what we need more are service, competitive pricing and quality.

This comment by Bob Odegaard, a senior purchasing specialist at Raytheon's corporate office, referred to supplier selection criteria in preparing the 1976–77 Approved Electronics Distributors List (AEDL). Plant buyers utilized this list to purchase a wide range of electronics parts. While Raytheon buyers negotiated with manufacturing sources for the great bulk of these items, local distributors were also used, particularly for small quantities ordered either routinely or for "rush" delivery. Purchases from distributors in 1975–76 had exceeded $8 million, and on this volume Raytheon had received rebates of approximately $400,000. Plant buyers were required to use the AEDL. In 1975, 90 percent of the dollar value of all electronic components purchased from distributors were supplied by vendors on the AEDL with whom the Raytheon specialist had negotiated corporate purchase agreements (CPAs).

In January 1976, Odegaard sent all Raytheon buyers who used the AEDL a short questionnaire for ranking distributor performance on both service and product quality. In February, he mailed RFQs to all distributors who had been on the list for the year commencing April 1, 1975, as well as to three new suppliers recommended by plant buyers. The information requested in the RFQ is shown below.

PROPOSAL INSTRUCTIONS

    I. *Performance Plan for Raytheon*
        A. *Account Penetration and Service*
            a) List by location your planned sales to Raytheon. Describe the

operation of the outside sales and operating staff. Include the frequency of visits to each location.

B. *Delivery Performance*
   a) With lead times lengthening in 1976, tell us how your organization will keep the Raytheon plants appraised of open order status and how often you will update the information.

C. *Special Product Service Features*
   a) Do you have any special service programs or relationships with manufacturers such as "on-line" stock availability checks, or "Hot Line" communication arrangements that you would offer to Raytheon?

D. *Inventory Stocking*
   a) What lines are stocked in depth locally that are used by Raytheon?

E. *Actual vs. Planned Performance*
   a) How will you report actual sales performance with the locations during the year?

F. *Special Capabilities*
   a) List special local in-house service capabilities such as marking, testing, programming, engraving, connector assembly, etc., which you have available.

G. *Quality Control*
   a) Name the individual specifically responsible for quality control and inspection of material for Raytheon.

II. *Line Coverage*
Supply a matrix which describes your major lines. The vertical axis should list the manufacturers. The horizontal axis should include the following:
   a) Commodity
   b) Authorized franchised distributor for New England (Yes-No)
   c) Approximate combined value of inventory at all locations at cost

You should list commodities in the following order:

1. Diodes
2. Transistors
3. Integrated circuits
4. Capacitors
5. Connectors
6. Filters
7. Potentiometers
8. Wire and cable
9. Lamps
10. Relays
11. Switches
12. Transformers, coils and chokes
13. Resistors

III. *Financial and Management Data*
Supply the following information as part of your proposal.

1. Financial results for the calendar year 1975.
2. Include ownership details and number of employees, cash terms of sale and F.O.B. point.

IV. *Price Proposal*
A minimum level of business cannot be guaranteed because a multiple number of sources will exist. You may elect to propose any arrangement or combinations of discount, cost, earned credit, or plateau agreements. No earned credit exclusions will be permitted except for those subsidiary agreements specifically negotiated beforehand with Corporate Procurement. If you are quoting a plateau agreement, choose plateau points in even $100,000 increments. This is not to imply that you should provide a break at each $100,000 level.

V. *New Ideas*
Please surface three or four specific ideas on how we can improve our business relationship. Consider such things as:
· Simplified paperwork approaches
· Computer terminal applications
· Special stocking plans you would implement
· Ways to make sales calls more effective
· Better coordination with your inside sales organization

The price submissions requested gave distributors latitude to structure their own pricing schedules. In conformance with prior bidding conventions, they were invited to submit plateau schedules if they desired to do so. This was a schedule of rebates, expressed as percentages of varying annual dollar-volume order levels that the distributor would refund to Raytheon. Thus, for example, a rebate schedule might be submitted in this form:

Annual Sales to Raytheon	Percentage Rebate
($000)	
$ 0–100	1%
100–300	4
300–600	7
600–	10

In the past, Odegaard's predecessor had negotiated with distributors to gain as much as possible in year-end rebates. Odegaard, however, placed somewhat different emphasis on this element of the procurement.

I'm sure I'm still measured on the rebates. But that's not the most important item. We don't want to "pay for our rebates" by having a distributor quote higher prices to us so he can cover his costs. We use our buying power to obtain rebates but, even more important, is the service these small firms can give us.

In commenting further, Odegaard indicated that he would be quite selective in whom he qualified for the AEDL:

We want to keep the list reasonably small. There's no point in having distributors on it who offer nothing that the others already have. We have a finite amount of business, and the more the shares of the business are divided, the less important a place on the list becomes. Removing those who do not perform enables us to keep management control.

Specifically, Warshaw and Cox, two Raytheon suppliers on the West Coast, would be reappointed. Of the remaining fourteen that had bid, Odegaard was concerned about the position of five vendors. One of them, Barth, had offered nothing new and seemed to have no greater interest in providing good service than it showed in 1973. Odegaard could see no reason to add this supplier to the list, especially since it had not performed well in the past.

Abbot was a small area firm that specialized in wire. It had received low performance and quality rankings from the plant buyers, but Odegaard thought that it had done a good job as a wire supplier during the past few years. He was anxious to encourage small businesses.

Murfree was a local minority supplier that had not been in business long. Odegaard believed its performance was likely to improve.

Robertson and Knowlton were the third and fourth largest electrical distributors in the country, with sales of $70 million and $65 million in 1975, respectively. Both companies had stocking locations in each major area of the United States, and both had a district stocking location in New England. Odegaard said that their relatively poor performance and, in particular, their decline from 1974 to 1975, were due to local management changes. He suspected that their district managers had built up too much inventory at the beginning of 1974. They were dismissed when the economic recession struck, and their replacements were not as good either as salesmen or as supply managers as their predecessors. Knowlton had nothing unique to offer Raytheon. At one time it had been the best supplier of RCA components, but Boardman now performed better. Robertson supplied Texas Instruments components, but these could also be purchased from Watson. Odegaard commented:

The most important point I always bear in mind is that my negotiations with the distributors accurately reflect the judgment of the sixty buyers who use the distributors' services. Full weight of the buyers' judgment as indicated on the rating sheets must be reflected in the suppliers selected. We've reached a situation where 90 percent of the dollars paid to distributors go to firms on the AEDL and I think that's a great success. But we have to continue providing good service to the buyers by making the right distributor selections.

A very significant volume of purchases is placed using *competitive-bidding* procedures. Either suppliers are unwilling to base negotiations on cost factors, or it is simply not feasible to do so given the nature of the purchase. On the other hand, market prices are not so rigidly established as to leave little room for price bargaining. In the present case, the suppliers are distributors who are free to set their own prices and typically compete vigorously with each other on a price basis. In other situations, when the suppliers are manufacturers, the products might be differentiated by performance characteristics and specifications, or might be designed to meet the buyer's requirements. Under such circumstances market prices either do not apply or do not rigidly constrain the seller in competing for business as it might in, say, the steel industry.

In addition, factors besides price became important in the vendor-selection process. Thus, in sourcing electronics parts *from distributors* at Raytheon, where service and delivery are especially critical, the plant buyers' ratings of distributor performance would be a prime consideration.

The most important aspect of competitive-bidding strategy is the selection of a sufficient number of qualified vendors. The buyer's primary objective is to have enough vendors to provide effective competition for his business but not more than would allow a meaningful sales potential to each vendor. There has to be a certain "critical mass" of sales volume available to the vendor to induce low price quotations and to evoke high levels of service if awarded a contract. On the other hand, a buyer that has too few suppliers could in time find he is dealing with a live-and-let-live attitude on the part of each, with the result that price competition is dulled and service levels deteriorate. The right number would be a function of the particular set of circumstances, that is, the amount of business available, the size of vendor companies and their abilities to handle given volumes of business, the suppliers' manufacturing-cost functions for the items being purchased, the types of services required by the customer, the availability of qualified suppliers, and the modes of competitive behavior that are characteristic of the supply industry.

The vendor-selection process also has a qualification dimension. In the Raytheon case, it was relatively simple and consisted primarily of: (1) examining the lines each distributor carried to assure that user locations would have available the items and brands they needed; and, as previously mentioned, (2) having line buyers at user locations rate vendors on past service performance. In other situations, supplier qualification may be an immensely complex and drawn-out process. It may involve engineering evaluations of the vendor's product quality, technical resources, and manufacturing facilities; and it may include evaluations of financial strength, management control systems, and managerial resources.

The qualification stage is an essential means of narrowing the list of potential bidders. It is also a necessary part of preparing for subsequent negotiations with those vendors who pass the initial screening. What becomes apparent from the evaluations is that all potential suppliers are not, in fact, equal and that the ultimate selection is not simply a matter of price. Some vendors carry lines that are particularly well regarded in the plants and laboratories. Some have especially wide lines and can satisfy a range of user requirements on one order form. Some have a reputation for providing excellent delivery and technical service. Some qualify for consideration as small and/or minority-owned businesses. Ultimately, then, the bidding-and-negotiating process has to result in the development of a vendor complex able to satisfy user-location needs for products and services at favorable, but not necessarily at the lowest, price levels.

In this case, one feature of the RFQ that tends to be characteristic of the competitive-bidding model is the use of purchase volume as a variable to induce competitive pricing. Each bidder has an incentive to offer attractive volume rebates at levels of business above his current volumes with Raytheon. In theory, suppliers may be tempted to price incrementally. They will reason that if variable costs and overheads can be covered at existing volume levels then additional business will add to profits at any price above variable cost, provided that no additional overheads are created by the sales increment. It is, of course, to the buyer's advantage to induce this pricing behavior. In a sense, the buyer is seeking to benefit from the seller's economies of scale. It will be to his advantage to award larger purchase volumes to fewer suppliers as long as: (1) the seller's unit costs are reduced; (2) the seller is willing to share the cost benefits with the buyer in the form of lower prices; and (3) the buyer's purpose is not defeated because the vendor complex narrows down to so few firms that they no longer compete vigorously for the business the buyer has to offer.

These are the essential features of the competitive-bidding model as illustrated in Raytheon's negotiations with electronic parts distributors: (1) a supply environment in which pricing behavior is not rigidly constrained through price leadership and in which individual suppliers have considerable pricing freedom; (2) the use of bidding on price-volume combinations to get the lowest prices from all vendors as a group; and (3) the shaping of a vendor complex that will service the customer's total requirements and meet broad procurement-policy objectives, even though some members might be paid more than others. Some other competitive-bidding situations include a fourth element in the model, the use of price quotations for individual elements of the procurement package, such as for different items and different shipment quantities. Such breakdowns serve two purposes. The first is to enable buyers to purchase different items in varying amounts from different suppliers in a way that optimizes the total procurement. The second is to provide a bargaining tool to negotiate low total prices with vendors through a focus on apparent price discrepancies within and across the sets of quotations submitted by individual bidders, thus inducing bidders to rethink their costs.

The Elements of Strategy

The foregoing discussion draws on three widely different examples: purchasing a new piece of production machinery at IBM, sourcing steel at General Motors, and procuring electronics parts from distributors at Raytheon. Each is illustrative of one of the basic procurement strategies. They are distinguished from each other primarily in terms of pricing modes: (1) cost-plus pricing; (2) market-price-based negotiations; and (3) competitive-bidding. But each strategy is composed of four basic elements: the product scope of the procurement; the number and type of suppliers selected; the pricing mode; and the negotiating strategy.

Procurement Scope. The beginning point in procurement strategy is the determination of what will be purchased and the nature of the buying-selling commitment on both sides. Will the contract scope be broad or narrow with respect to the number of items? Will it be specific or open-ended as to quantity? What performance standards and quality criteria will be specified? Will there be penalty clauses for failure to perform? What time period will the purchasing commitment cover?

Procurement scope is critical in that it significantly influences the number and type of suppliers who will be willing and able to quote. It is a key factor in determining the degree of competition that will be generated among potential suppliers for the buyer's business.

As may be seen from the three examples described above, the product scope of a procurement tends to be quite narrow in a cost-plus procurement and somewhat less so in a market-price-based situation, which tends to cover various specifications of one product type, such as steel. Product scope may be relatively narrow or very broad in a competitively bid procurement.

Supplier Selection. The second key element in procurement strategy relates to the numbers and kinds of suppliers with whom the buyer will contract. Normally, buyers tend to purchase from enough vendors to assure that there is effective competition for their business. On the other hand, buyers typically refrain from acquiring so many sources that none is motivated to compete vigorously on price and to provide good service; in addition, they want to prevent relationships, particularly of a technical sort, from becoming unmanageable. There tends to be a very limited number of suppliers, often only one, in a cost-plus-procurement situation, whereas in a market-price-based strategy it is essential to have multiple sources. In the competitive-bidding model, the buyer may elect to purchase from one vendor at any point in time, but it is essential to have multiple sources available for purposes of assuring competition.

Supplier selection goes beyond type and number of vendor. It involves fashioning a sourcing system in which individual suppliers of the same item may play different roles. One may make important technical contributions; another may be the industry price leader; another may serve to introduce greater price competition. Hence, vendor-selection strategies must often be concerned with designing the total supplier system so as to obtain some form of optimal combination of service, low price, and long-run supply availability.

Finally, an element of supplier selection relates to the nature of the selection process itself. The whole system of identifying and qualifying suppliers, a system in which engineers as well as procurement managers may be involved, obviously affects the outcome in terms of numbers and types of suppliers. Hence the selection process must be regarded as a strategic component in procurement strategy.

Price-Quantity Determination. This factor seems clearly to be the most complex dimension of procurement strategy. There are three basic approaches to determining price: (1) pay the recognized market price; (2) use competitive bidding; (3) calculate the supplier's cost and add a margin for overheads and/or for profit. Which one may be appropriate in any given case may be determined by: (1) the type of product being purchased—whether it is, for example, of standard design or custom-manufactured, and whether manufacturing costs can be calculated with relatively high certainty; (2) the nature of the supply industry—whether it is oligopolistic or relatively less concentrated; and (3) market conditions—whether supplies are readily available or shortage conditions prevail.

Going beyond these basic considerations, price-quantity strategy also involves the matter of risk-sharing. For example, how will the risks of cost-factor inflation or deflation be assigned to either party? This question introduces the whole matter of providing contractually for cost escalation; when it is appropriate, how it should be written into contracts, and how changes in cost factors should be determined for pricing purposes.

Another area of risk relates to fluctuations in the buyer's requirements. In some instances, stated contractual amounts are firm commitments on the part of the buyer. Very often, however, they are approximations, and failure to take the agreed-upon quantities may not result in having to pay penalties commensurate with the shortfall.

Another element of price-quantity strategy is the form in which price quotations are to be submitted. The RFQ may ask for a single price, or it may specify price breakdowns for different items, for supplier tooling, for different delivery quantities, or for different delivery points. The RFQ may specify that different prices be quoted for different volumes. It may ask that quotations be given in dollar amounts or as a percentage of the supplier's published list prices. The choice of a price structure establishes the framework for subsequent negotiations and will, in itself, be a factor influencing the negotiating strength of buyers and sellers, respectively. It is the data base from which bargaining proceeds.

Negotiating Strategy. This is a powerful, final determinant of the prices and terms of a procurement. Bargaining is preconditioned and is bounded by what the buyer is ultimately willing to pay and what the seller is ultimately willing to accept. These conditions in turn are determined by general supply-and-demand conditions; by the unique benefits the seller may be able to offer the buyer (such as product advantages and superior technical service); and by what the buyer may be able to offer the seller (i.e., large volume, technology, and a strengthened position for getting future business from this customer and others). While these factors set the stage, the bargaining range and the possible outcomes are typically quite great.

Negotiating strategies will vary considerably among the three models. In cost-plus situations the focus of discussion becomes cost factors, and the buyer's strength rests on his knowledge of the seller's costs and on his engineering competence. Market-price-based negotiations put stress on the buyer's ability to allocate purchase volumes among suppliers to reward and penalize based on supplier performance in areas such as delivery, service, and technical contributions. Buyers may shift purchase volumes, as well, in recognition of one supplier's move to increase prices or another's move to lower general market-price levels.

In competitive-bidding modes, negotiating strategy will often focus on the detailed examination of various combinations of price-and-quantity and delivery-and-product specifications submitted by individual bidders to seek the most favorable offer from any one supplier as well as the optimal overall sourcing arrangement.

Negotiating strategy takes into account the location for bargaining, usually either the supplier's premises or the buyer's. Another critical element is the composition of the negotiating team and the role each member will play if the buying company is represented by more than the individual buyer. Another is the sequencing of items on the agenda. Going further, there is the matter of making trade-offs, that is, the concessions the buyer is willing to make in return for reduced prices or accelerated delivery or even to assure availability of supply.

Negotiating tactics are a particularly critical dimension of procurement strategy, involving the use of power as well as ethics in intercorporate relationships. Tactics have important psychological overtones in that negotiators are individuals with certain personality traits. As in any bargaining situation, the outcome of procurement negotiations is significantly affected by the willingness to take risks of a corporate nature. Additionally, the assessment of the personal risks and rewards that may accrue to the negotiators themselves is always an element in any bargaining confrontation. That clearly affects willingness to concede, to hold out, or to compromise.

The two chapters that follow examine more closely each of the four elements of procurement strategy.

2 Procurement Scope and Supplier Selection

The basis for procurement planning is the design of the Request for Quotations (RFQ). The basic parameters in RFQ design are what items will be covered, what quality levels will apply, what the buyer's commitment will be as to quantity, what the duration of the contract will be, and how prices will be quoted by suppliers. These dimensions of RFQ design will determine to a large extent who is qualified to bid and their interest in competing actively for the business. In addition, the RFQ sets the backdrop for subsequent negotiations, contract terms and conditions, and longer-term buyer-seller relationships.

A good example of creative RFQ design is to be found in the procurement of computer-room furniture at IBM, where this equipment was purchased under corporate contracts. Procurement responsibility for computer-room furniture rested with Bob Pitt, manager of the corporate-contract group in the corporate-purchasing staff.

Before 1970 office-furniture purchases had been largely decentralized. There were pricing agreements with four major manufacturers, under which any IBM location could buy any item at discounts off list price ranging from 10 to 30 percent. The pricing agreements were arranged primarily for the convenience of supplying the smaller computer rooms and for individual replacements at the plants. Whenever large quantities were required, buyers would arrange for the manufacturers to bid on each order.

In 1969, the manager of corporate contracts at IBM headquarters formed a small task force of buyers who were responsible for computer-room equipment purchases at vaious IBM locations to investigate possible ways that IBM could buy furniture more efficiently and at a lower cost. It was concluded that a single corporate contract under which IBM plants and offices could place orders at contract prices would lead to the greatest overall savings.

The corporate-contract group then gathered what data were available on the purchasing history for computer-room furniture at IBM and asked buyers at ten large IBM locations to evaluate the four existing suppliers. It was learned that the bulk of total expenditures was accounted for by seven items: tape-reel cabinets, consoles, operators' chairs, side chairs, tables, A-disc files, and B-disc files.

At the end of 1969, each of the four suppliers was asked to bid on all of IBM's computer-room furniture purchases. The contract would be for one year only so that IBM could gain experience for subsequent procurements. It was suggested that the bids be submitted separately by companies for the seven major pieces and that other items be quoted in terms of a percentage discount off list price. Quotations were solicited on total annual volumes of $750,000 and $1.5 million. One company, Record Protection, submitted bids substantially below those of the other three companies on every major item and was awarded a contract for 1970 at the $1.5 million level. Buyers at IBM user locations were so notified and were informed that it was mandatory to use the contract for all the items it covered.

In 1970, however, furniture purchases were sharply curtailed because of declining economic conditions, and IBM failed to meet its $1.5 million commitment. Although Record Protection legally might have required IBM to pay the difference between the prices Record Protection quoted at the $750,000 and $1.5 million levels, it did not do so. The contract was renewed on the same terms for 1971, and it was renewed again for 1972, this time at prices for the $750,000 commitment level.

In late 1972, the procurement was once again put out for bids, and suppliers were asked to quote on a two-year agreement. It was reasoned that it would take a new supplier six months to become used to IBM's requirements, and a supplier would have a better chance of performing satisfactorily if given a longer period. In addition, a two-year contract could result in lower prices. Once again, suppliers were asked to bid separately on the seven key items at varying commitment levels and to indicate penalties for failure to meet commitment.

Record Protection again emerged as the low bidder and was awarded a two-year contract. Prices would be fixed for 1973. For 1974 the prices of the seven major items could be raised by a maximum of 5 percent corresponding to any increase in Record Protection's costs, while list prices and discounts on other items would remain firm for IBM. To support claims for price increases in 1974, Record Protection would permit IBM to audit its manufacturing costs for the console and the tape-reel cabinet.

In 1974, demand for this equipment increased dramatically. At the same time, many materials came into short supply, resulting in an extension of Record

Protection's lead times. To avoid delivery delays, the supplier volunteered to warehouse a one-month supply of major items and to bill IBM on shipment. In 1973 IBM spent $2.6 million on computer-room furniture and about $4.5 million in 1974.

Owing to the experience gained from the 1973–74 contract, the RFQs that were sent out to the four manufacturers in October 1974 were far more complex than the 1972 version. First, vendors were invited to quote different prices for different parts of the country. (It was estimated that IBM purchased 79 percent of its computer-room equipment in the East, 2 percent in the Midwest, and 19 percent in the West.) Second, bidders were asked to quote on both one- and two-year contracts. Third, they were asked what sort of stocking program they would propose. Fourth, it was suggested that they quote separate prices for individual orders against contracts over $10,000 and under $10,000. (The $10,000 amount was approximately a full truckload.) Finally, bidders were requested to suggest ideas for lowering IBM's overall computer-room furniture costs.

As an initial observation, it is interesting to note the way in which RFQ design evolved as IBM corporate-contract specialists gained experience in buying office furniture. In addition, in this case one can see the influence of a changing supply environment, since shortages and inflation became major factors in 1973–74.

Looking now at the several dimensions of the procurement design, the most basic one was the *product scope,* that is, the specific items that would be purchased under the contract. It covered all computer-room furniture for all of IBM's U.S. locations. The scope paralleled the vendor's product lines, and the purchase volumes incurred by massing requirements tended to generate strong price and service competition. At the same time, placing large orders for a full range of requirements in this product category simplified order routines at the user locations. Such a product scope depends, of course, on the ability to establish commonality of requirements. Doing so is a prerequisite to negotiating a corporate contract.

A possible risk, however, in massing requirements for procurement purposes is that the number of suppliers who are able and willing to bid may be significantly reduced. At Raytheon, for example, corporate contracts were negotiated for the company's complete needs for hand tools in the New England area. The corporate-contract specialist was able to conclude what were regarded as very favorable agreements in successive periods with one particular supplier. He was having difficulty, however, in getting others to bid. Few vendors had the resources or wide enough lines to service Raytheon through the company's computerized ordering system.

Thus, the product scope in any contract may be determined, in part, by such considerations as: (1) the scope of potential vendors' product lines; (2) the extent to which the scope of the procurement may have the effect of preselecting and limiting the number of qualified suppliers; (3) the convenience of negotiating with a limited number of suppliers to cover a wide range of requirements; and (4) the simplification of ordering routines on the part of user locations.

Procurement scope is also a function of pricing mode. In cost-based pricing, contracts seem typically to cover either one item or one family of products with a limited number of items. In cost-based-pricing strategies, the degree of cost detail that needs to be negotiated is such that contracts must generally focus sharply on one job for the supplier.

In market-price-based negotiations in which the buyer's essential objective may be to bargain for supply availability and simultaneously to try to hold general price levels down, contracts tend to cover all of the products the buying company purchases from a supplier. Examples here are the purchase of food chemicals at General Foods, glass bottles at Heinz USA, and steel at General Motors. Similarly, in competitive-bidding situations, contract scope is shaped such that it generates competition. This means massing identifiable requirements common to multiple user locations to focus bidding attention on large-volume items, as in the case of procuring computer-room furniture at IBM.

Contract duration is a second aspect of RFQ design. Note the range of considerations in this case. Initially IBM corporate-contract specialists selected a one-year period to gain experience with a new procurement program; it was a pilot run. They would have an opportunity to make strategic adjustments relatively soon in the duration of the program.

Later they elected to negotiate two-year contracts. By doubling the commitment, IBM specialists encouraged vendors to quote lower prices. They also made it more attractive for a new supplier to compete against Record Protection. A two-year contract might provide significant learning-curve opportunities, if not in manufacturing, then in servicing the IBM account.

Other factors that influence contract length are:

1. Predictability of needs. If requirements are difficult to forecast within a range necessary for the vendor to plan his production schedules, contracts are typically made for short periods. In fact, contract length on production items seems to be directly related to the buying plants' production-planning cycle.
2. Market-price volatility. In circumstances where prices are primarily market-determined and where these prices are extremely volatile, as, for example, in the case of electronic components, both buyer and seller are normally unwilling to make contractual commitments beyond a year.
3. Stage of product development. In situations where the product being purchased is in the development stage and where the supplier and customer are going through a mutual learning experience, contracts may be short to provide frequent checkpoints. Each successive negotiation may be carried

out with the benefit of additional data on product design, production process, and costs.

Perhaps the most fascinating aspect of the procurement design for computer-room furniture is the way vendor responses on price had to be structured. IBM buyers asked for:

1. Individual prices for the seven key items accounting for a large percentage of dollar volume.
2. Percentage discounts off list for the remainder.
3. Prices for one- and two-year volumes.
4. Prices for three different shipping zones.
5. Prices for shipments in truckloads and less than truckload quantities.
6. Suggestions for price reductions.

The advantages in structuring price quotations in this way lies primarily in the opportunity it provides for developing different sets of sourcing options and for selecting the lowest price combination consistent with service and convenience of ordering. Another advantage is that it facilitates comparisons among bidders by focusing on key elements in pricing. But perhaps the most important consideration is that price breakdowns of this sort provide a useful basis for discussion in subsequent negotiations with individual suppliers. Much more will be said on this point in Chapter 3 on determining prices through competitive bidding.

Vendor Selection

Under normal supply-and-demand conditions, vendor selection is a matter of choosing from among a number of qualified sources. In periods of shortage, however, buyers have to put considerable effort into identifying potential sources and persuading them to make supply commitments. It would be useful, therefore, first to look at the vendor-selection process under the more prevalent circumstances of sellers actively competing for business. Then attention can be given to techniques of persuasion when customers are aggressively competing for limited supply sources.

The process by which a buyer ultimately arrives at a contract agreement with a seller may be conceived of as a series of cuts, each one narrowing the list of candidates. The initial stage is identification; the second is qualification; the third may be bidding; the fourth, negotiation. Finally, a deal is made with one or more vendors.

The Identification Process. In making up the list of potential suppliers (identification), buyers naturally tend to list first the companies with which they are currently doing business. The tendency of the buyer to stay with suppliers he knows and with whom user locations are satisfied is so strong that, as an offset, buyer performance is often measured in part by the number of new suppliers introduced into the sourcing system. New suppliers may broaden the base of sources, bring in new ideas, and add an element of price competition. But bringing in new suppliers involves both uncertainties and administrative costs. These factors, combined with satisfactory performance on the part of existing suppliers, considerably reduces incentives to seek new sources.

When the need does arise, however, the buyer's sources of information for identification purposes are varied. They include such practical reference points as other buyers, trade publications, vendor catalogues, and *Thomas' Register of American Manufacturers* (Thomas Publishing Company, New York). In addition, some buyers routinely maintain notebooks with relevant information on potential vendors. In some companies there are regional vendor conferences to which all potential suppliers of certain products are invited. There they have an opportunity to be briefed on the buying company's requirements and to discuss their product qualifications with the buyers present.

A frequent concern is that minority-owned businesses be included on bidders' lists as a matter of policy. Often such concerns seem to be identified, not by buyers, but by those in procurement organizations who have specific responsibilities for building up the volume of corporate business with minority vendors.

The Purposes of Qualification. A list of potential sources delineates the pool of potential suppliers to be covered in the evaluation and qualification process. The initial objective of this process is to weed out those who are obviously not qualified regardless of price. Beyond that, the purpose may be to gather all the information, *in addition to price,* about each source that should be considered in the final selection. Alternatively, the qualification stage may be designed to pass only those who are qualified on the basis of exacting criteria so that the final award may be made on *price alone.* As a purchasing manager at an IBM development center explained: "It [is] an IBM policy that once a supplier [has] been approved it should be treated on an equal basis with all other potential vendors. Thus the lowest bid would be accepted automatically. . . ."

This difference in the concept of qualification requires some discussion. The difficulty inherent in evaluating all factors by which vendors may be compared when making a final selection is that comparison factors must be weighted, and weightings are necessarily arbitrary. For example, at one stage in selecting sources for catalysts for the catalytic converter,[1] General Motors purchasing managers ranked seven candidates on thirteen different counts, including price. Among the other factors evaluated were engineering capability, production-control procedures, quality-control procedures, management depth, financial

---

1. An automotive component used to filter engine-exhaust emissions.

stability, and "housekeeping." Each factor was weighted on a scale of 1 to 6, 1 indicating greatest importance. Each potential supplier was then ranked on a 1 to 7 scale for each factor. Individual rankings were multiplied by factor weights for each supplier and then summed to provide a total score for each. Under this system the one with the lowest score would be considered the best candidate and the high scorer would be least acceptable.

The difficulty of such a mechanical approach to vendor evaluation is that factor identification, weighting, and scoring yield a numerical yardstick of averages that may not truly distinguish the important from the unimportant. Mechanically applied, the system might turn up as a strong candidate a vendor who is totally unacceptable on one count but overcomes the scoring deficiency with high rankings on other counts.

In contrast, using these evaluations only to assure that all vendors to be considered clear certain hurdle requirements, and then to base selection on price, avoids this problem. If, however, standards are set at too high a level (as they may be under strong engineering influence), the hurdle-requirements approach may arbitrarily screen out all or most of the possible sources at an early stage. Then few, if any, bidders are left.

It would seem that vendor screening might well proceed initially in terms of applying hurdle tests only to eliminate sources which clearly are not qualified in essential ways. Then, by weighing differences in price against a limited number of other factors that differentiate suppliers, the final selection could be based on assessments of trade-offs. To complete the quotation from the buyer at the IBM development center: "With time-and-materials contracts very occasionally we decide not to give the contract to the lowest bidder if, for example, another supplier has superior facilities and is likely to give better service."

Areas for Evaluation. There are four basic areas to be evaluated in qualifying suppliers of production parts and manufacturing equipment. The first is a *technical assessment* of the product to be purchased (if it exists at this stage), particularly of the supplier's manufacturing and engineering resources. In most cases, this type of evaluation is carried out by technical personnel in departments outside purchasing, such as industrial engineering, product assurance, and process engineering. The more quality-sensitive the end product, the more exacting and exhaustive the evaluation procedures should be. At Raytheon, government contracting officers require rigid vendor-certification procedures and may provide extra funding to cover the cost. At IBM, where the requirement is self-imposed, qualification for a single component from an outside supplier may cost many thousands of dollars and take a year or more to complete. Separating the technical-qualification function from procurement assures that vendor selection will not be influenced prematurely by price factors. Furthermore, it gives engineering control over, and responsibility for, the quality of materials and components that go into the end product.

A second area is *business evaluation,* which covers a range of factors including managerial competence, accounting and control procedures, financial condition, and security controls. Normally this assessment is made by purchasing managers.

Another part of the screening is the application of *purchasing-policy criteria* laid down by top procurement management. Such policies may, for example, impose a limit on the amount of purchases from any one supplier to avoid having a supplier become overly dependent on the buying company. Other policies may require that minority-owned suppliers be given special consideration.

Finally, a part of the evaluation may sometimes be *user-location ratings* of vendors currently or formerly supplying the company. The factors included in such ratings usually relate to delivery service, technical assistance, and product quality. For example, such ratings were used by Raytheon in selecting electronics-parts distributors. User-location ratings are particularly useful as "red flags"; that is, for alerting the purchasing manager to poor performance by suppliers at particular locations. They signal the need to get more information to determine either to discontinue using the supplier or to take such corrective action as may be needed.

User-location ratings serve another purpose: they are clues to the purchasing manager that he may have to do some "internal selling" to gain user-location acceptance of a vendor he believes to be fully qualified. Such a supplier may be well regarded by all but one or two user locations and may have performed well. But for some reason—and it seems to happen often—he has irritated one or two of his clients, perhaps through deficient service or personality clashes.

The Sourcing System

A critical dimension of sourcing strategy is the *composition* of the vendor complex: What type, how many, and what roles will each vendor complex play in serving the buying company's needs? As for type, as a practical matter, the choices relate primarily to manufacturers versus distributors and, in some instances, domestic versus foreign firms. One can compare, for example, General Motors' decision to buy steel directly from manufacturers with Raytheon's decision to buy electronics parts from distributors as well as from manufacturers. What are the strategic considerations that make for these different choices? A basic one is the level and type of service required. Raytheon needed immediate local availability for large numbers of parts in small quantities. Local distributors were best suited to meet this requirement. With large quantities and with predictable usage patterns, it is practical to buy direct from the manufacturer and to avoid having a distributor's margin included in the price.

Another factor is long-run supply availability. General Motors wanted a buying position with steel manufacturers both to protect its sources in the event of shortages and, as a large buyer, to encourage the development of steel capacity to meet demand in the 1980s.

An additional consideration involved in this kind of choice is the characteristic pricing behavior of manufacturers and distributors. In General Motors' experience, steel manufacturers pursued relatively stable pricing policies. Steel warehouses, by contrast, tended to exploit shortage situations by pricing much higher than manufacturers and by undercutting steel-mill prices to users in periods of excess supply. They were able to price below their supplier by "giving away" the margins they received as resellers in the form of reduced prices to users.

Finally, the type of product service required is a consideration in the choice between buying from distributors or from manufacturers. Typically, though not always, manufacturers have superior technical-service resources and are equipped to provide field services related to the use of the products they sell. Primarily, distributors perform resale functions: warehousing, delivery, and credit. They also typically carry wide product lines and are accustomed to handling small orders.

The choice between domestic and foreign sources is also illustrated in the sourcing for steel requirements at General Motors. The advantage in sourcing abroad seems essentially to be one of price. However, risks involving continuity of supply must be set against any price benefit, since shipping disruption due to strikes, armed conflict, or nationalistic intervention on the part of supply-country governments is ever present. Added packaging and inventory costs also must be weighed against any price benefits from foreign sources. Another consideration is the difficulty of relating to a distant supplier on technical product-service levels.

The Strategy of Numbers. In connection with the earlier description of the competitive-bidding model the number of suppliers in a vendor complex was discussed. Key considerations were: (1) there should not be so many that the buying company is no longer perceived by each supplier as an important customer; (2) there should not be so few that price-and-service competition among suppliers diminishes. There are other considerations. An important one, also mentioned earlier, is the nature of the supplier-customer interface. Considerable technical development work and engineering interchange would argue for one or two suppliers at the most. Such relationships require enormous amounts of time and energy, security control, and individuals on both sides who relate well to each other. Plainly, it is usually impractical, uneconomic, and inefficient to work simultaneously with a number of suppliers on developmental efforts. By comparison, the simpler and the more routine the relationship, the more vendors one may want and need.

Three other considerations work as effective limits to multiple sources. One is that the cost of qualifying suppliers may be very high, and, particularly in the case of defense work, government funding may not be available for that purpose. Another is that splitting the available volume of purchases among several suppliers may make it impossible for any one purchaser to achieve economies of scale in production and servicing. Then the customer must suffer a penalty in the prices paid for maintaining multiple sources. Finally, there is the matter of simplifying ordering routines. This is a consideration particularly in connection with purchase agreements that are centrally negotiated but decentrally used. In negotiating for supply items, for example, there may be a price advantage in buying some items from one vendor and some from others. A significant deterrent, however, is the confusion that this might cause in ordering routines at the plant level.

As this discussion suggests, there is a natural tendency toward single-sourcing when the buying company is not forced by the magnitude of its requirements to use multiple sources. A further explanation for this tendency is the opportunity one vendor may have in a development situation to gain a learning-curve advantage over potential competitors: if he lowers his price accordingly, other suppliers may find it difficult to overtake his cost advantage. In particular, if the entrenched supplier is willing to share his cost data with his customer and to negotiate on that basis, he can make it very unattractive for his customer to second-source.

Single-sourcing also may develop when a vendor has proprietary technology or is contributing on a continuing basis to product development. In such situations a symbiotic relationship evolves out of close working relationships, and there is no apparent reason or incentive to change so long as users are satisfied.

Stability of Vendor Relations

If the economy is right we inquiry all parts to ensure lowest possible purchase costs. In a strong inflationary period or period of acute material shortages, we attempt to extend contracts at existing prices to stabilize costs. If the supplier doesn't want to extend, we'll attempt to negotiate a mutually acceptable agreement. If negotiation efforts fail, we will go to general inquiry (i.e., competitive bidding) but the vendor will usually try to work an agreement rather than risk losing the business to a competitor. On our part we don't want to risk interrupting continuity of production.

We try to maintain stability in our relationship with vendors for other reasons as well: (1) some tooling is incompatible with other suppliers' equipment or too complex to move, and the cost and lead time for new tools is too great to consider changing sources—on frames alone we probably have $20 million in tooling with three suppliers, (2) suppliers' engineering contributions must be rewarded and manufacturing expertise must be recognized—some suppliers have special know-how that others do not. It's important to preserve those sources and encourage further progressive efforts.

These are comments of the general purchasing agent at Chevrolet who shortly thereafter became the Chevrolet director of purchases. He gives three reasons why stability of vendor relationships is important in building a strong sourcing system. First, stability encourages the supplier to make technical contributions to both product design and manufacturing processes. Second is a very practical consideration: by investing in tooling to be used in suppliers' plants, GM, of necessity, commits both itself and the supplier to a longer-term relationship than if GM-owned tooling was not involved. Third and somewhat less obvious, inflation may encourage longer-term relationships. The assumption is that in periods of inflation the prices in existing contracts are likely to be as good as, or lower than, a new set of prices determined through putting all purchased parts out for a new round of competitive bidding. By contrast, when "the economy is right" there will presumably be opportunities to lower prices by getting bids from new suppliers and by encouraging existing ones to be more competitive in their pricing or risk losing the business.

Auditors at General Motors disagree, however. Quoting from a speech made by the GM general auditor at the Central Office to GM purchasing offices in July 1972:

> There are a few other miscellaneous purchasing comments which often repeat themselves in our audit reports. For example:
> 1. Carryover parts are not requoted on an annual basis or for several years. There is often a feeling that vendors might request price increases because labor and material prices are increasing; however, we seldom find documented evidence that requoting would generally result in increased prices. After all, if a vendor is hurting he will ask for a price increase anyway. If he has been content to carry the old price forward for four or five years, he must have a comfortable price. Why not look for price decreases where volumes have increased or where vendors have reduced their costs due to better methods or increased efficiency.

One would have to agree with the general auditor's viewpoint. In defense of the general purchasing agent, however, it should be recognized that a general inquiry for competitive bids on 17,000 parts is a tremendously costly and time-consuming effort. The rewards in terms of reduced prices on purchased parts are doubtful at a time when there are strong inflationary factors at work in the economy, particularly if there are shortages at the same time.

There are other factors that foster long-term relationships. Foremost among them is the need for vendors to amortize any investments they may have made in taking on a contract. Commitments of three to four years or longer are not uncommon to allow vendors to amortize capital investments through the price of the product they have contracted to supply.

Stable buyer-seller relationships are also characteristic of situations where the system through which the supplier serves the customer is detailed, complex, time-consuming to put in place, and not quickly changed. Such a system was the one Raytheon developed with its supplier of small hand tools. The computer program for listing, ordering, pricing out, billing, and keeping track of orders outstanding for 20,000 items took months to develop and "debug." To redesign the computer program, which would be necessary if suppliers were changed, would be a formidable undertaking.

Similarly, there is a built-in deterrent to shifting vendors when the supplier maintains consigned stocks in the customer's plant or has special-purpose storage facilities, as is often the case whether purchases are made from distributors or direct from manufacturers.

However, factors that encourage stable, long-term vendor relationships and single-sourcing tend also to encourage, in the long run, payment of higher prices for lack of effective competition. The disciplines that are enforced through procurement-practice codes, purchasing-performance reviews, and internal audits are critical as offsets. The stress these disciplines place on getting competitive bids and bringing new suppliers on-stream is essential to a strong procurement function. More will be said about this in Chapter 6 in the discussion of procurement decision-making processes.

Vendor Roles in a Sourcing System

In multiple-source supply systems individual vendors play different roles. In a well-planned vendor complex, suppliers complement each other in their contributions to the buying company.

A useful example of vendor roles in a supply system comes out of the sourcing of glass bottles at Heinz USA. This large packaged-food manufacturer purchased in excess of $35 million of glass containers in 1974, of which ketchup bottles amounted to more than $15 million. For ketchup bottles, Heinz relied extensively on the three largest glass-producers (which together accounted for 45 percent of total glass-container industry capacity) and on one smaller company. Allegheny Glass met 38 percent of Heinz USA's ketchup bottle requirements; Green River Glass, 30 percent; Shearson Container, 28 percent; Medford Corporation (the smaller company) 2 percent; and other small manufacturers, 2 percent.

According to Ken Robards, the Heinz glass buyer, different suppliers played different roles in his sourcing pattern. Major shares went to Allegheny and Green River because Heinz's heavy seasonal needs required suppliers who could meet these peaks. Profit margins on ketchup bottles were lower than on other glass containers, and the small companies did not want to invest in molds to make glass only for short periods. A company like Green River, Robards indicated, gave Heinz superior service, good quality, and technical assistance. A company like Medford (the smaller company), however, was "in the picture" to insure competitive pricing by the larger suppliers and to "keep them honest." Medford was qualified to serve as a larger supplier at two Heinz plants, but in that respect Robards saw no particular advantage for Heinz in terms of price, quality, or service. Green River was Heinz's largest supplier of bottles of all types and had been increasing its share of business simply because it had outperformed the others. Now Heinz was its largest customer. According to Robards, Green River was willing to work on new designs and was most responsive to requests for prototypes for testing. As one example, the 32-ounce ketchup bottle was very hard to make, and Heinz had had significant breakage problems with it. Green River redesigned the bottle and reduced breakage in one plant by 70 percent.

In this vendor complex, Green River apparently had the most at stake with Heinz—its largest customer—and could be counted on for excellent technical service. Allegheny Glass determined price, for all practical purposes, while Medford was maintained in the complex as the small supplier willing to quote competitive prices to increase sales, thereby giving Heinz bargaining strength in negotiations with the larger glass manufacturers. Shearson, for lack of specific mention, is cast in the role of another supplier, filling a portion of Heinz USA's rather large requirements.

Developing Sources of Supply

The shortages of late 1973 and 1974 placed many buyers in the reverse position of persuading suppliers to take their business. It was not unusual for purchasing managers to visit potential vendors and to make presentations to supplier managements on the advantages of being suppliers to the companies the purchasing managers represented. It was in this era, in fact, that some marketing department members were moved temporarily (or permanently) into procurement assignments. It was an unusual situation and buying companies had to resort to a variety of techniques to get enough supplies to keep production lines running.

A particularly interesting effort to procure an urgently needed component under shortage conditions was the sourcing of automotive leaf springs at GM's Chevrolet Division for the 1974 model year. The requirement arose in early 1972 when the federal government issued automotive specifications requiring that bumper heights on most cars and light trucks be regulated to specific dimensions from the ground, plus-or-minus a quarter of an inch. The new regulation meant that the automotive manufacturers would have to redesign the coil spring and leaf spring systems that cushioned the body of the car. The redesign of coil springs, which were made from round steel bars ½ to ¾ inches thick, created neither engineering nor sourcing difficulties for the Chevrolet Division. But leaf springs did both. Approximately 44 different types were needed to accommodate the different vehicle weights.

As for sourcing, there was a shortage of the steelplate stock from which spring plates were made. Steel mill managers did not like to make this item because it was a less profitable use of their limited capacities. The few qualified leaf spring manufacturers were already committed to General Motors and other automotive manufacturers. And, in fact, demand for this product was declining. Prior to government bumper-height regulations, the trend in vehicle design had been away from leaf springs toward coil springs. So leaf spring manufacturers closed down or diversified into other product lines.

Other factors reduced the effective capacity. Running as they were at a pace of three shifts a day, seven days a week, leaf spring manufacturers had no time for routine maintenance, and production was constantly being interrupted by breakdowns of mechanical equipment and heat-treating furnaces. There were labor stoppages due to strikes as well.

Prior to 1973 the Chevrolet Division had sourced leaf springs from Consolidated Manufacturing, Inc. with four plant locations for making springs, from Spencer Steel Products with two plant locations, and from its own Livonia plant. Consolidated had accounted for approximately 25 percent of requirements, Spencer for 25 percent, and the Chevrolet Livonia plant for 50 percent in 1972. Flat-plate steel for leaf springs was purchased by these manufacturers from Pittsburgh General, Construction Steel, Ferrous Metals, and Bradley Automotive Corporation.

When it became evident that considerably more leaf-spring steel (AISI 5160) had to be obtained, A. F. Lyman (purchasing agent, raw materials, Chevrolet Division Central Office) called on these four suppliers to arrange for sourcing an additional 2500 tons of leaf-spring steel stock. He quickly learned that none of these suppliers regarded either leaf- or coil-spring steel business as profitable and none wanted to take on more of it. Lyman argued that if the Chevrolet Division could not get enough spring steel, it could not meet its automobile production schedule, and would then have to reduce steel purchases overall. Price was not the major issue; the primary concern was quantities required to maintain production of vehicles.

Lyman called first on Pittsburgh General's sales vice-president who told him that he would be unwilling to increase shipments of AISI 5160 steel to Chevrolet. It was an unprofitable item because AISI 5160 had to be made on a 13-inch mill, which represented an uneconomic use of this equipment. In addition, Pittsburgh General was at a freight disadvantage.[2] The discussion was concluded with Lyman saying that if he could not meet his steel needs after talking with other existing and potential suppliers, he would like to be able to reopen negotiations. He was assured that "the door would always be open."

2. The steel companies freight-equalized at the customer's plant location with the supplier whose mill was closest to this point. In this case the Bradley Automotive steel mill in Midland, Michigan was closest to the Livonia plant and freight between these two points was $2.10 per ton. By comparison, the freight to Livonia from the Pittsburgh General steel mill in Erie, Pennsylvania, was $16 per ton.

At Construction Steel, Lyman was successful in increasing this supplier's commitment on AISI 5160 steel. The tradeoff, however, was that Chevrolet release Construction Steel from its commitment to supply Chevrolet with 550 tons per month of steel rod for coil springs. (In retrospect, Lyman regretted having made this deal because subsequently, the Chevrolet Division had increased requirements for coil spring steel, by which time it had effectively lost Construction Steel as a supplier of this item.)

Ferrous Metals' manager of sales in the Detroit office told Lyman that his company would increase its shipments of leaf spring stock to Chevrolet. At that time, Ferrous Metals was supplying .9 million tons a year of steel to Chevrolet and the Detroit manager was concerned that about .17 million tons of body steel would have to be eliminated from this program, if Chevrolet could not get enough leaf springs.

At Bradley Automotive, a competing automobile manufacturer, Lyman learned that not only could Bradley not increase shipments of AISI 5160 steel to Chevrolet but would have to reduce the regular shipment from 22,000 tons to 14,000 tons a year. At that time Bradley, too, was trying to build up its outside sources for leaf springs and had to promise steel to potential suppliers.

Lyman was successful in bringing in two new sources for leaf-spring material. Toledo Steel, which had never supplied Chevrolet with AISI 5160 steel but did sell other grades to this division, was anxious to build its position as a GM supplier. It had an eight-inch mill and a continuous casting process both of which contributed to a relatively low production cost on AISI 5160 steel.

Atlantic Metals, a relatively small supplier, also was willing to make a commitment to supply leaf-spring steel to Chevrolet. Lyman believed that Atlantic managers wanted to develop a plant base load[3] with Chevrolet because General Motors had a reputation for giving long lead times on orders, for paying its bills promptly, and for supporting suppliers in times of trouble. Atlantic Steel, however, needed coke for its steel furnaces. Lyman was able to arrange to buy coke from another steel company and agreed to supply Atlantic with one ton of coke for every ton of AISI 5160 steel the latter made for Chevrolet.

In the meantime, in September-October 1973, Eric Engel, a divisional buyer in the Chevrolet central purchasing organization had compiled a list of over fifty potential sources for springs. To develop the list he used such references as *Thomas' Register,* trade association directories, and word of mouth. His basic objective was to locate Gogan-machine capacity[4] and negotiate for leaf-spring plate production. He found that most of the manufacturers on his list were making springs wider than 2½ inches, usually for trucks, and that the process

---

3. Baseloading means committing a significant part of plant capacity to serving a relatively stable and continuing requirement as a way of covering large portions of fixed overheads.

4. In manufacturing leaf springs, flat steel stock is heat-treated and then clamped on a steel drum in a Gogan machine to give the leaf spring its curved shape. The Gogan machine represented the capacity bottleneck in this process. It was loaded by hand labor and the drum had to rotate slowly. New "Gogans" had a lead time from the machine manufacturer of 15 to 18 months.

was incompatible for widths 2½ inches and under. The wider, thicker plates needed slower manufacturing cycles that could not be practically changed to accommodate lighter materials.

In negotiating in October-November 1973 with the remaining domestic manufacturers on his list, Engel was prepared to offer each a percentage of Chevrolet's leaf-spring requirements for a year. He was at a disadvantage in negotiating, however, because buyers for one of GM's competitors were offering multiyear commitments, in some cases for a specific number of springs. Engel explained to potential suppliers that future design specifications and quantities were not available to permit the writing of contracts for longer than one year. Market demand might change suddenly; Chevrolet engineers might go back to coil springs. According to Engel:

> My biggest selling point was the reputation of GM Purchasing. GM is known to stand by its commitments. Also if a supplier gets a one-year contract and keeps his commitments, he can be reasonably sure of continuing as a supplier to GM. In fact I sometimes quoted a recent magazine article that rated GM Purchasing quite highly.

As a result of his search, Engel completed contract negotiations in December 1973 with two new sources, Hewitt Products and A. F. Rudden. The contracts, each for one year, specified a percentage of Chevrolet's needs at a fixed price. Speaking of negotiations with Hewitt, Engel said:

> Hewitt was quite knowledgeable of current market conditions. He knew what he could produce and he had his materials and energy sources all lined up. And he bargained hard on how much he would commit and how much lead time we had to give him on requirements. He wanted a multiyear contract on a specific quantity per month, building from 8,000 to 35,000 springs a month from April to August 1974 for the 1975 model. I wouldn't agree to 35,000 but would give him a percentage of our requirements that equaled to that amount based on current volumes. Also he was proposing two new plants and wanted some sort of a guarantee from GM to support his applications for a bank loan. But I said he would have to prove out as a GM supplier with his existing plant before we would make a further commitment. He wasn't a proven supplier, however, and our quality engineers would have to inspect his facilities and qualify him before we would sign a contract. By reviewing his plant facilities it was noted that quality control procedure would have to be improved. That put him on the defensive and made negotiating a little easier for me. For example, he didn't have a quality control manual. He came up with one real fast and then I knew he was really interested in Chevrolet business.

Recalling these discussions, Engel commented further: "In the time I've been with GM, I've been in all aspects of production: supervision, quality control, industrial engineering, and plant layout. That's been my big suit in purchasing, the thing that's helped me in jobs like this one, to work with vendors as well as our own engineers and QC [quality control] people."

The other new supplier was A. F. Rudden, a recently acquired subsidiary of Myerson Company. From the outset, Rudden did not want to take on any Chevrolet leaf-spring business. It was primarily a manufacturer of large, heavy-duty truck springs. Because GM was an important customer of the parent corporation, however, the Rudden management was persuaded to take a portion of the requirements on a high-volume, multiple-sourced spring. Nevertheless, Rudden was unable to meet the quality standards and could not meet agreed-upon production schedules. Eventually this supplier agreement was terminated.

Even with the addition of Hewitt and of more output at Consolidated, the buyer was still under pressure to obtain leaf springs in the quantities needed. He negotiated with all his sources to operate through holidays and to stagger vacations in order to avoid the traditional two-week plant shutdown. In return he agreed to pay price premiums. To minimize the risk of work stoppage, every high-volume leaf spring was dual-sourced, that is, for every high-volume spring there were two or more plants that could produce it.

The buyer also set up very tight production schedules on his suppliers' operations. He monitored output in terms of the number of plates by specifications, that were produced. He received schedules, as well, from the GM Assembly Division to which the springs would be shipped. His office then became the control point for meshing supplier output with needs at the several car-assembly locations. Finally, he proposed to Chevrolet Division engineers that, based on sales data for October and November 1973, the number of different types of springs needed could be reduced by eliminating specifications intended for the extreme ends of the vehicle-weight range, which engineering had provided for. Having worked strenuously to develop additional leaf-spring capacity, the buyer then had difficulty in getting the Chevrolet Scheduling Department to place orders based on vendor capacity rather than on sold-order inflow from Chevrolet dealers. The buyer explained: "If they didn't order ahead there would be no way we would catch up when our sales increased as we expected. On G-vans we actually sold 7,000 more than we had forecast and we couldn't have met this demand if we hadn't persuaded Scheduling to order ahead on leaf springs."

Consider the different techniques Chevrolet Division purchasing managers used, first to get steel and then springs to meet the new leaf-spring requirement in the face of a capacity shortage. At his first stop, Pittsburgh General, Lyman did not press this supplier to take on the leaf-spring steel order, but he was able to "leave the door open." That is, if Lyman was not successful in subsequent calls, he could always resume his negotiations at Pittsburgh General. Presumably this large steel producer did a significant volume of business with GM and would be willing to help out in an emergency.

At Construction Steel, Lyman made a trade. This supplier agreed to make AISI 5160 steel in return for a release from his commitment to supply Chevrolet with 550 tons per month of steel rods for coil springs, presumably a less profitable product for Construction Steel. At Ferrous Metals the willingness to supply

AISI 5160 was based on a concern that if Chevrolet could not get enough steel to meet its leaf-spring requirements, it might have to cut back on purchases of steel for car bodies, which Ferrous Metals was supplying.

In each case the negotiations were carried on against a background of GM's long-term relationships with the steel producer and involved other steel products currently being purchased from that company by GM.

Another supplier, Toledo Steel, was motivated to make leaf-spring steel for Chevrolet as a way of building its position with this important customer. A small company, Atlantic Metals, made a commitment, according to Lyman, as a way of baseloading its plant with business from a desirable customer. As part of the deal, Lyman arranged to help Atlantic Metals to buy coke from another steel company in amounts proportional to the volume of AISI 5160 it made for Chevrolet.

In the cases of Toledo and Atlantic, Lyman was successful because of their long-term interests in becoming important Chevrolet suppliers.

Engel, the leaf-spring buyer, did not bargain from a position of strength comparable to Lyman's. Moreover, he was competing for capacity against another automotive company able to offer multiyear contracts while he was authorized only to make one-year commitments. His main selling tools were GM's reputation as a buyer and his ability to relate on a technical level with potential suppliers. The one time he used GM's position with a vendor (Myerson) to exert pressure on its subsidiary (Rudden), he was not successful in bringing this supplier satisfactorily on-stream. Rudden's management did not want to make Chevrolet leaf springs. Not surprisingly, when Rudden was persuaded through the GM/Myerson relationship to undertake leaf-spring production, Rudden failed to meet quality standards and delivery schedules.

Finally, it is important to note, having developed a vendor complex for leaf springs, Engel did all he could to insure that Chevrolet production schedules were kept. He paid premium prices for operating over holidays and staggering vacations. He dual-sourced to minimize the risk of work stoppages. In particular, he was able to get an adjustment in the Chevrolet order pattern and to reduce the number of specifications in order to stabilize the demand on leaf spring suppliers to allow them to get longer production runs.

In conclusion, the experience suggests that a company's ability to obtain sources of supply under shortage conditions depends fundamentally on two rather obvious factors. The first is its reputation for fairness as a customer in all aspects of its relations with suppliers. Such reputations take a long time to build, but their value is great. The second is the importance of the buying company to its vendors. If it is important, then its suppliers are prone to meet its needs in emergencies in the interest of preserving long-term relationships.

3 Pricing and Negotiations

The three strategy models described in Chapter 1 are differentiated initially in terms of pricing behavior. In this chapter, we examine more closely cost-based, market-price-based, and competitive-bid-based pricing conventions. Each is appropriate under different conditions. Each has different objectives, and each calls for widely different negotiating tactics.

Cost-Based Pricing

In cost-based price negotiations bargaining focuses on elements of the vendor's cost structure such as labor, materials, overhead and profit for the item he will supply. Negotiations may result in a time-and-materials contract such as the one the IBM development center had with Special Machine Tool or in a fixed-price contract. In a time-and-materials contract the buyer pays for material costs incurred by the vendor and compensates him for labor, overheads, and profits at an agreed-upon rate per hour of direct labor. In a fixed-price contract the buyer agrees to pay the supplier a specified amount for each unit produced. Often such contracts include escalation clauses so that the price may be adjusted proportionally to increases (or decreases) in the vendor's costs for key materials and labor.

Generally, in cost-based price negotiations the seller's objectives are to get a fair return (on sales or investment or both) and to minimize cost-factor risks while the buyer's objectives are to negotiate a fair price and to get the benefit of vendor-cost reductions that accrue through experience. This implies that the buyer is often willing to assume the risks associated with cost inflation to protect the seller's profits. Usually cost-based price negotiations are appropriate to conditions of cost uncertainty. In addition, they seem typically, but not always, to take place between large buyers and small sellers. There are two reasons. First, the large buyer may be able to assume the risks associated with cost uncertainty more easily than the small seller. Second, large sellers are characteristically unwilling to share cost information with customers. They feel that to do so weakens their bargaining strength. More important, they do not willingly forgo the opportunity for large profits.

An example of cost-based price negotiations under conditions of cost uncertainty is to be found in General Motors enormous effort to develop sources for the catalytic converter. It began with the formulation in 1969 of proposals to control automotive exhaust emissions, by the U.S. Department of Health, Education and Welfare acting under the authority given to it by the Clean Air Act. In September 1970 amendments to the act were introduced in the Congress which considerably shortened the time period in which the automotive industry would have to meet very stringent emissions levels standards. The AC Spark Plug Division (AC) of GM was given the task of developing and manufacturing a converter through which engine exhaust gases would pass to remove carbon monoxide (CO), hydrocarbons (HC), and oxides of nitrogen (NO_x). As ultimately designed, the converter consisted of an outer cover and an inner shell of aluminized stainless steel with a layer of ceramic-fiber insulation in between. The catalyst material was in the form of small ceramic beads coated with a formulation of platinum and palladium. The catalyst was carried in a stainless-steel, louvred retainer inside the inner shell. There were input and output tubes through which the exhaust gases passed, and a removable plug for replacing the catalyst before the 50,000-mile mark. The catalytic converter would go in all 1975 GM cars and light trucks (up to 6,001 pounds gross vehicle weight). It would be positioned on the underside of the car below the front passenger seat. (See illustrations on pages 176–77.)

AC Spark Plug managers had to find sources for platinum and palladium, catalyst beads, and a special grade of stainless steel, and for such fabricated components as the outer cover, inner shell, and louvred retainer as well as tubes, plugs, and insulation. Of particular relevance to a discussion of cost-based pricing are the sourcing arrangements with a South African mining company for platinum and palladium and with the four U.S. suppliers of catalyst material.

Palladium and platinum are found mainly in Russia and South Africa. After careful study and lengthy negotiations, GM managers selected Van Horne, a mining company in South Africa, and negotiated a 10-year contract. To meet GM's anticipated requirements, Van Horne would invest approximately $75 million for new mine shafts and added refining capacity. A large part of this amount would go into building a town to house and care for 10,000 additional workers. GM's annual requirements by 1975 were estimated to be 300,000 troy ounces of platinum and 120,000 troy ounces of palladium. (One troy ounce = 1.097 ounces.)

The prices were set initially at $110 a troy ounce for platinum and $60 a troy ounce for palladium. Thereafter prices would be adjusted annually based on mutually agreed-upon economic indices. Criteria for determining a basis for price adjustments were (1) that auditing of Van Horne's internal accounts would not be involved, (2) that the vendor's incentives for cost reduction would not be diminished, and (3) that prices to General Motors would be reasonably stable. The indices selected were the platinum and palladium producers' prices as reported weekly in *Metalworking News*.

Penalty payments were required for each ounce under the commitment level that GM did not take in any year. In addition, GM would have to pay cancellation charges if it wanted to reduce or withdraw entirely from its contractual commitment. Liabilities under the latter contract clause built up rapidly as Van Horne invested in new capacity in 1973 and before any deliveries were made. After that the prices of the two metals would include amounts for investment amortization, and GM's cancellation liabilities would then decline gradually as it purchased platinum and palladium from Van Horne. The contract would be for ten years in consideration of the need to amortize the Van Horne investment without heavy amortization charges in the early years.

Having arranged sourcing for the metals, managers then searched for domestic catalyst manufacturers who could make or buy ceramic beads (the substrate) and coat them with a palladium and platinum solution. There were tremendous technical uncertainties: the nature of the substrate, the formulation of the solution, and the method of applying the solution to the beads.

In August 1972 two companies were given letter agreements authorizing each one to design plants for making catalysts in two forms. They would be compensated on a monthly basis for engineering work and equipment. In November, a third company was also commissioned to work on plant design. In August 1973 contracts were negotiated with four firms selected by GM managers so that deliveries could begin in April 1974. The contracts were for three years. Price was stipulated in each contract and would be adjusted on May 1, 1974 for the 1975 model year. Price escalation was based on any increases in the prices of ceramic substrate sourced from outside suppliers, cost of fuel, wage increases provided for under the vendor's labor contracts, and increases in the cost of other materials based on the Industrial Chemical Commodity Price Index in the *Survey of Current Business* (U.S. Department of Commerce). A provision in the contracts stated: "In the negotiation of a fair and reasonable catalyst price, the parties agree that such catalyst price shall not be measured solely by cost, with profit being a percent thereof, but that the parties shall also consider in their pricing philosophy the aspect of a fair return on investment."

The contracts included penalties for not taking certain minimum amounts of product from each supplier. They also provided for cancellation charges based on each vendor's investment build-up. In addition, GM assumed a liability to pay for ending inventories of catalysts up to a certain limit in the event of final cancellation.

An important contract provision was one which gave GM the right to require any one supplier to take technology from another at no cost. However, the technology recipient would not be liable for failure to perform to GM specifications if it could not make the technology work. For purposes of price redetermination and possible cancellation settlements, GM had the right to audit its four suppliers' accounting records.

It may be observed that General Motors was, initially, in a very weak bargaining position. GM was being required, not unwillingly though, to develop new technology and mass-produce catalytic converters under rather great time pressures. Its suppliers would all have to build new capacity and the four catalyst sources would need to invest heavily in technical development. It was a situation in which the buyer was destined to assume all the risks if it was to meet its deadlines. What is of particular interest, though, is the structure of penalties, price revision provisions, and audit rights by which price was determined. Unit prices were calculated with the expressed objective of providing sellers with a fair return on investment. In the same spirit, penalty clauses for failure to take the minimum commitment and for cancellation were related in amount to supplier-investment amortization. If suppliers had not been required to invest in new facilities no such penalty provisions on GM's part would have been required. In all likelihood, too, the buyer would not have had to agree to minimum purchase levels.

As for price revisions there is an interesting comparison to be made between those applying to Van Horne, the South African source for metals, and those for the four domestic catalyst suppliers. Because the former sells platinum and palladium in world markets, and because it was not involved in developing new technology, its pricing objective was to get as much per ounce from GM as from its other customers. Accordingly, price revisions were based on the producers' price index.

By contrast provisions for price revisions for the four catalyst suppliers reflected their basic objective: a fair return-on-investment. Price formulas then protected against cost-factor increases.

In the case of Van Horne, price terms did not require that GM audit the supplier's accounts, a burden that GM managers didn't want to take on. Audit privileges did have to be obtained from the four catalyst suppliers. Although auditing would be an onerous chore at best, it would give GM valuable knowledge that would certainly be useful in future negotiations.

The skill in conducting cost-based price negotiations lies initially in understanding the supplier's circumstances and his objectives. Then it is important to develop a price structure, using escalation factors, indices, penalty clauses and audit provisions, which is tailored to the purpose. It is especially important for the buyer to be knowledgeable about factor costs and to set targets for negotiating purposes.

In the case of the catalytic converter, General Motors would have little protection against vendor-cost inefficiencies under the terms of the contract in the early stages. It could hope, however, to get the benefits of improved supplier efficiencies at later stages by moving toward a competitive-bidding pricing mode.

Market-Based Pricing

In a broad range of supply industries price is market-determined in the respect that price levels are the result of market forces, prices are published, and all customers pay the same. There is little room for individual buyers to bargain on price, although large buyers are often able to influence general price levels and the timing of price increases or decreases. Such industries may be oligopolistic in nature (such as metals, chemicals, plastics, heavy electrical equipment) where there is a recognized price leader whom other firms are inclined to follow. Or in industries with a large number of relatively small sellers producing undifferentiated commodities such as wheat, soy beans, and other agricultural products where supply/demand interaction is the main determinant of price. Under these conditions, the buyer's pricing objective is primarily to assure that no competitor is able to buy at a price lower than the one he gets and thereby gain a cost advantage. In fact, buyers will often attempt to negotiate a "most-favored-nations" clause in the contract, under which the supplier agrees to sell to no other customer at a lower price. In addition, the buyer will often avoid, if possible, making fixed quantity commitments, preferring to order to cover production needs. Accordingly, he or she may allocate business to vendors in terms of a percentage of requirements or may indicate a volume range in which anticipated needs will fall.

On their parts, sellers in oligopolistic supply-industries are concerned in individual price negotiations about the effect of the outcome on general market-price levels just as in labor negotiations the bargaining parties are concerned about the precedent any one wage settlement will have on subsequent negotiations. Sellers are also concerned about maintaining their positions with individual accounts and market shares vis-a-vis their competitors.

Both buyer and seller must be particularly cautious about inducing or granting a discriminatory price and thereby violating the Robinson-Patman Act (15 U.S. Code Section 13). This act makes it illegal for a seller to give a lower price to one customer than to other customers who compete with the first, unless the lower price is granted to meet the equally-low price offered to that account by a competitor of the seller or reflects differences in the supplier's costs of manufacture and delivery. By the same token, it is illegal for the buyer knowingly to induce a discriminatory price by misleading the supplier into thinking that in granting such a price he is meeting the equally-low price of a competitor. Accordingly, efforts by buyers in large companies to obtain low prices are likely to focus on seeking to influence market-price levels rather than on obtaining special lower-than-market prices. There is a range of strategic approaches aimed at influencing the general level of market prices, as illustrated in sourcing for glass bottles at Heinz USA.

In the glass food-container industry general price levels tended to be influenced by the published list-prices and terms of Allegheny Glass. Nevertheless, given Heinz's position as a large buyer and the fact that it used unique designs, Robards, the Heinz glass buyer, spent a lot of his time in negotiating on price with his suppliers. Described below are four different strategies he used and some others he considered.

Trade-offs on delivery scheduling. At one time, Allegheny had proposed a 40 cent-a-gross price decrease on a price of $8-a-gross if Heinz would take its production on a steady year-round basis. (This is known as the "dedicated line" concept.) But problems had arisen and Heinz had been unable to take the agreed amounts on schedule. However, to retain its share of Heinz business, Shearson, another glass supplier, had met the Allegheny reduced price but on the usual seasonal delivery basis and thus Allegheny was unable to raise the price to its former level when the "dedicated line" idea was abandoned.

Quantity discounts. Two years before Robards had tried to get lower prices by asking suppliers to bid on a different basis than before. He encouraged individual suppliers to attempt to achieve a large proportion of Heinz's ketchup bottle business by quoting lower prices in return for larger orders on which the supplier might realize the benefits of lower manufacturing and/or distribution costs. They were asked to submit bids on three bases:

(1) To provide all of the glass used for ketchup at any one plant.
(2) To provide all of Heinz's requirements for any one size bottle at any or all of Heinz's plants.
(3) To provide 60 percent of total bottle requirements for Heinz ketchup.

The suppliers, in general, did not respond. Green River representatives said they couldn't handle the volume. Shearson managers indicated that they thought it unwise to be so heavily dependent on one customer. Allegheny gave no reply. It was Robards' guess that such responses came out of a consideration for heavy mold investments required, the relatively low level of profit in ketchup bottles, and a concern that they would have to deprive other customers especially during seasonal peaks.

Shearson, though, did negotiate lower prices for ketchup glass for one Heinz plant on the condition that it would be guaranteed 75 percent of the plant's ketchup business. Shearson had a glass manufacturing plant across the street from this Heinz facility. The other supplier to the same plant, Allegheny, had immediately met the new low price despite the fact that it would have to deliver from 43 miles away.

New Competition. Heinz's strategy with respect to new suppliers changed during 1974 because of a decline in overall demand for glass containers. Plant capacity was available because several traditional users of glass bottles were decreasing, or at least, not increasing their usage. In particular, the packaging of beer was changing with an increasingly large proportion being sold in cans. As for soft drinks, a rapid increase in the price of sugar had led to increased soft drink prices and lower sales. Several manufacturers with spare plant capacity had approached Heinz suggesting that they would like to become suppliers of ketchup bottles. Before 1974 Robards would have been unlikely to have accepted any of these proposals. He would have been concerned that if business picked up in their traditional markets, they would go back to them. Under 1974 conditions, however, he thought he should seriously consider taking on new suppliers. Nevertheless, he was concerned that any new supplier might be subject to counterattack from one of the larger glass suppliers in its traditional market and would, thus, be of use to Heinz for only a short period. He explained that Heinz had to understand the smaller company's total market position with regard to both its customers and its competitors. According to Robards: "If a company gets hurt in its major traditional market while it's supplying us, they may not be able to remain a reliable high-quality supplier to Heinz."

On receiving approaches from other companies Robards attempted to obtain quotes and then used them when negotiating with the three major vendors after he satisfied himself that a new potential supplier had the capability for producing a quality container at the quoted price. In 1973, he accepted one bid from a smaller company to make 14-ounce bottles at a lower price than he had been paying before. This lower price was eventually met by the traditional suppliers. The new company had not developed into a major supplier because it had been unable to maintain quality. Nevertheless, it had since submitted bids on other bottle sizes and Robards expected to accept one of its bids in the near future.

Thus new market conditions had led to a change in Robards' strategy. The small glass companies were looking for new customers and were prepared to reduce their commitments to their existing, declining market segments.

Shifting purchases. In early 1975, Robards reallocated some preliminary orders in an effort to make Allegheny change its payment terms. In late 1974 Allegheny had announced a change in the dates when payment would be required for ketchup bottles. Rather than accepting one-third of the annual amount in each of September, October, and November, it announced a schedule that was financially much less favorable to buyers. The new schedule was also adopted by other manufacturers and represented a considerable change from prior practice.

Because of the high interest rates that had prevailed in the second half of 1974, the change had not come as a surprise to Robards and he came back with a counterproposal. Eventually Robards negotiated compromises with Green River and Shearson on payment terms but not with Allegheny. He believed, however, that Allegheny might eventually reconsider after it had seen some of its orders go to other vendors.

Other possible strategies. Although Robards felt that his strategies to date had kept prices down, he believed that more could be done in the future. Two ideas in particular were: (1) Manufacture glass bottles (2) Change the design of the bottles: remove the panels so that the bottles were round rather than octagonal and lower the height and weight.

What strategic approaches to pricing can be identified? One is the offer, made in good faith, to change the buying company's ordering pattern in a way that saves money for the supplier by allowing him to smooth his production schedule and reduce his inventories. This was the dedicated line proposal. The idea was that the supplier might legally pass on some of the cost savings in the form of lower prices. Even though Heinz was unable to adjust its own production schedules to receive shipments at a constant level, the move accrued to its benefit. Another glass supplier, unwilling to lose its share of Heinz USA's business met the reduced price without the condition that Heinz take shipments on a steady year-round basis. That became the new low price. The strategem relies on the inherent importance to suppliers in oligopolistic industries of maintaining account position and market share.

Similarly, the large buyer may exert pressure on price levels by bringing in new sources willing to grant lower prices to break into a new market segment. This is one way prices move to lower levels in periods of excess supply. Smaller companies, hungry for business, search outside their traditional market segments and take on new competitors. Robards reflected the normal concerns of doing business with small, new suppliers: (1) Can their facilities be adapted to serve the needs of a new market segment? (2) Can they be counted on for the long run? (3) Will the new supplier be hurt in its traditional markets in a way that impairs its strength as a supplier?

A third strategy is to take action against a market leader who raises prices or changes terms in a way that seems unreasonable, given the supplier's cost-profit structure. In this case Robards reallocated some orders to other suppliers in an effort to make Allegheny Glass change its new, and much less favorable, payment terms. The move was effective in persuading some other Heinz USA suppliers to back away from Allegheny's lead and to strike something of a compromise on payment terms.

But note that the attempt to obtain more favorable prices by offering increased volumes to low bidders met with a cool reception on the part of suppliers. Each undoubtedly reasoned that if he quoted a low price, his competitors would meet it and all would be selling the same quantities as before with lower profits. That's exactly what happened when Shearson bid for 75 percent of one Heinz plant's requirements and Allegheny immediately met the low price although its freight costs would be greater than Shearson's.

As for the threat on the part of large users to make glass bottles rather than buy, that is a constant pressure on price levels. Certainly it has been a factor in the case of metal containers where, increasingly, large users in the packaged foods, soft-drink, and brewing industries have set up their own can-making lines.

The threat to make rather than buy would seem less effective in influencing price levels for ketchup bottles, however. Glass container plants, unlike can lines, take relatively larger capital investments and are not easy to operate. At one time Heinz USA did make its own glass containers but sold the facility to one of its suppliers in the late 1940s. According to one member of the purchasing management: "As I remember, the reason for selling it was because we weren't maintaining the plant adequately and the quality of the glass coming out of it was atrocious. We sold the plant to Shearson Glass so they could supply us from this facility. Then, the first five carloads of glass they shipped to us from there we rejected because of poor quality!"

In the purchase of commodities such as wheat, sugar, and soy beans buyers will have little, if any, opportunity to influence market price levels. In products for which there are established commodity exchanges, buyers may have some options as to the timing of their purchases, and they may use hedging as a way of protecting themselves from sharp price increases or price declines.

For a division manager attempting to make sales and profits targets on an annual basis, the essential consideration is that he or she pay no more than competitors for a key commodity, and hopefully less. If the costs are higher, then the manager is faced with the risk of having to raise prices and lose sales volume or accept lower margins.

Because of the importance of the commodity-cost component in packaged foods and beverages, buying companies may retain skilled commodity specialists on their purchasing staffs. But there is nothing the specialists can do to negotiate favorable prices. All they can do is to attempt skillfully to forecast supply-and-demand conditions and recommend strategies that essentially have to do with the timing of purchases.

Price Determination by Competitive Bidding

When suppliers do not willingly arrive at prices through discussions of their costs with customers and when, on the other hand, prices are not purely market-determined, competitive bidding is likely to be the mechanism by which prices are set. The seller's freedom to set his own prices may be the result of his making a differentiated product, such as a component or a piece of capital equipment. Or it may possibly be because the product—or the product package—on which he is quoting is planned to meet the unique specifications of the customer. Third, if the seller is a distributor he cannot legally be bound to resell at prices his sources dictate and may, for all practical purposes, charge what he wants.

The seller's objective in competitive bidding is usually to get as high a price as possible commensurate with the value of the product to his customer.

The use of competitive bidding is strongly encouraged and even required of buyers according to company purchasing rules and regulations. It may, for example, be a rule that for all procurements exceeding a given dollar amount that three bids will be required unless valid reasons for not doing so are explicitly documented and filed for later audit. The competitive-bidding rule is a way of insuring that buyers probe for lowest available price rather than place the business automatically with suppliers they know best.

Competitive bidding may be either "sealed" or "negotiated." Under sealed-bidding procedures, bids are due at a certain time and the award made to the low bidder if his specifications conform to the RFQ. Many federal, state and municipal government organizations are required to use sealed bidding. Late bids are disqualified as a way of assuring that some vendors do not get the information on competitive-bid prices before submitting their own offers. In negotiated bidding, the procedure usually calls for submitting bids by some specified date, to be opened at some appointed hour, with rules against accepting late bids. Then further negotiations may be conducted with the lowest one or two bidders in an effort to get price reductions below the bid amounts. Negotiated-bidding procedures are more characteristic of buying behavior in private corporations than in government agencies.

In negotiated bidding, the buyer's objective is simply to arrive at the lowest price possible, all else being equal, down to the point where vendor performance will not be jeopardized. Sometimes, however, even the latter consideration may not impose any restraints on zealous buyers in bargaining sessions.

The seller's objective is to maximize his profits. Usually that is a long-run objective and applies to his business as a whole. Thus the seller may accept an order from a particular customer, below his full costs, to bring work into his plant that will contribute to overhead. Or he may wish to "buy in," that is, to get an opportunity to serve a particular customer or to gain experience in making some product. His expectation, then, is that this opportunity will lead to further ones for more profitable work.

Given the respective objectives of buyers and sellers, we can now consider the pricing strategies buyers find useful in competitive-bidding situations. Clues are to be found in the way they structure RFQs to obtain from bidders not one but a whole set of prices for varying combinations of volume, delivery schedules, product specifications, and commitment levels. Going back to the procurement of computer-room furniture at IBM, for example, it will be recalled that the corporate contract specialist asked bidders to quote separate prices for the seven major items. He also requested different prices for one and two year's requirements, for each of three different shipping zones, and for truckload and less than truckload shipments to user-locations. In another instance, an IBM purchasing manager buying electronic components requested bidders to submit prices for percentages of the total procurement ranging from 20 to 80 percent at 10 percent intervals for each of thirty items.

In the absence of having detailed knowledge of vendor costs, buyers gain important strategic advantages in asking for such price breakdowns. It forces the supplier to analyze his costs carefully in preparing a bid that quotes on various award possibilities. It serves as a framework for gauging the sensitivity of price to such major cost variables as production volume, production-schedule requirements, freight charges, and service. It provides the buyer, in addition, with opportunities to engage the supplier's negotiators in justifying the pricing pattern reflected across the several price-quantity-service combinations. Comparisons among item quotations may also open up possibilities for exploiting apparent inconsistencies to get lower prices. It gives the buyer the possibility of exploring the effect on price of his allowing for certain changes in requirements that would affect the vendor's costs. For example, he might relax delivery schedules to allow the vendor to stretch out the work in his plant and to benefit from the economies of a more stable work flow. He might discuss possibilities for reducing prices by including materials- and labor-escalation clauses in the contract thereby assuming these risks and taking them out of the supplier's calculations as contingencies. In particular, the buyer has the opportunity, if he chooses to take it, of putting together some combination of awards to two or more suppliers that will result in the lowest overall cost, consistent with the required levels of service.

Asking in the RFQ for different unit prices for different volume levels is widely used in competitive bidding. It may tempt the vendor who stands to increase his business to price the increment of volume at something less than full cost just to contribute to overhead. On the other hand, the supplier threatened with the loss of business in an important account may shade his price to keep a competitor from gaining ground. In the extreme, a negotiating focus on different volume-price combinations in very competitive markets would move suppliers toward pricing on the basis of out-of-pocket costs. It would also gain for the customer, in the form of reduced prices, the benefits of supplier cost reductions.

The essential element for successful competitive-bidding is having two, and preferably more, qualified bidders. In some instances the field narrows down to a single source quoting on a bidding basis. Such circumstances put the buyer at a disadvantage because he needs the vendor to perceive the possibility of losing the business as a sufficiently serious risk so that there is some balance left in the bargaining strength. The supplier may have committed certain plant facilities that would otherwise go idle. He may need the cash flow. He may want a continued relation with the buying company. Then price determination is a matter of finding some compromise that satisfies, as best as possible, the needs and objectives of both buyer and seller.

In conclusion, the buyer has strength in competitive-bidding situations to the extent that (1) he has several qualified bidders and that (2) he has opportunities for contrasts and comparisons among bid-price data within and across bids. It helps considerably, too, if he has developed his own estimates of vendor's costs so he has some practical sense of price objectives as he goes into negotiations.

Negotiating Tactics

A considerable amount, both theoretical[1] and practical,[2] has been written on negotiating. The literature is applicable to bargaining between buyers and sellers but goes beyond that relationship to consider as well labor negotiations, diplomatic relationships, mergers and acquisitions, and interpersonal relations. No effort can be made in the context of this study to treat the subject exhaustively; rather, the details of one bargaining situation will be provided and some of the tactical elements that make for a successful outcome for the purchaser will be described. This case example describes the negotiations of an IBM purchasing team with one of two suppliers of a family of electronic components known as

1. Bartos, Otomar J., *Process and Outcome of Negotiations*, (Columbia University Press, New York, 1974)

Rubin, Jeffrey Z. and Brown, Bert R., *The Social Psychology of Bargaining and Negotiation*, (Academic Press, New York, 1975)

Walton, Richard E. and McKersie, Robert B., *A Behavioral Theory of Labor Negotiations*, (McGraw-Hill, New York 1965)

2. Nierenberg, Gerard I., *Creative Business Negotiating*, (Hawthorn Books, Inc., New York, 1971)

Karass, Chester L., *Give & Take: The Complete Guide to Negotiating Strategies and Tactics*, (Thomas Y. Crowell Company, New York, 1974)

Karass, Chester L., *The Negotiating Game*, (The World Publishing Company, New York, 1970)

TTLs (transitor-transitor logic chips). This team met in September 1974 to plan the negotiations on contracts for first half 1975 requirements. The team consisted of the Systems Products Division (SPD) Component Procurement Group manager of cost engineering and business analysis, a cost estimator, a purchasing manager, and two buyers. Two main goals were set: (1) two major sources should be maintained; and (2) IBM should attempt to achieve a 15 percent overall price reduction. According to the cost estimator, lead times were shortening, suppliers had announced price reductions in their catalogues, and a group vice-president of one of the suppliers, NCC, had publicly stated that the company was on an 80 percent learning curve in the manufacture of integrated circuits.

Cost estimators were often able to estimate the cost of manufactured parts bought by IBM so that time and material costs could be assigned to each operation. In this case it was known that there were 93 operations involved. Labor rates could be obtained from U.S. government publications and materials prices and yield rates could be estimated. An approximate cost breakdown could then be made and, adding estimated overhead and profit figures, IBM purchasing managers could arrive at what they believed to be a reasonable price for the two suppliers, in this case average prices of 61 cents and 59 cents for NCC and IMS, the other supplier, respectively.

In many cases this breakdown was used in negotiating with suppliers. Although in the field of semiconductors, suppliers often refused to discuss costs, the IBM team could use the estimates as a basis for establishing prices below which it would be unwise to negotiate. The team was very concerned that it should not lower prices to such an extent that the contracts became uneconomic for the suppliers. If that occurred, quality and delivery would probably suffer. John Royce, the senior buyer involved, explained: ''When a man's in trouble, he starts taking shortcuts. Then you don't get the product you want. The cost estimates are useful in establishing a negotiation objective, but we don't want to push beyond that.''

In preparing for negotiations, the IBM estimators knew that NCC and IMS had both extended capacity and reduced their workforce. The general semiconductor market was believed to be very soft. NCC had merged two operations into one plant at a low labor-rate location. It was thought that, in this situation, both vendors would try to improve productivity, cut their overheads, and, be willing to accept lower margins.

As a beginning, each company was asked to bid on the most likely percentages of total requirements (20 million units) that would be given to it (60 percent for NCC and 40 percent for IMS) and on volumes 10 percent and 20 percent on each side of that figure. Thus, NCC was requested to submit bids on 40-50-*60*-70-80% of the total volume and IMS on 20-30-*40*-50-60% of the business. The bids and the expected volumes are shown in Figure 3.1 and are compared with prices paid in the second half of 1974.

Figure 3.1. *Quotes Received in 1974* for 1st Half 1975 Requirement*

1st Half 1975 Quantities	Quotations for 2nd Half 1974 Average Unit Prices* NCC	Quotations for 1st Half 1975 Average Unit Prices
(000)		
16,000		63.28¢
14,000	69.53¢	64.33¢
12,000	70.76¢	65.48¢
10,000	72.50¢	67.04¢
8,000	74.76¢	69.02¢
	IMS	
12,000		61.74¢
10,000	66.28¢	62.92¢
8,000	67.70¢	64.30¢
6,000	69.75¢	66.12¢
4,000	72.35¢	68.34¢

*Average unit price is the weighted average unit price of the five major parts that make up about 70 percent of the requirements from each supplier.

NOTE: Contracted quantities for 1974 were 11,250K for NCC and 7,200K for IMS.

From an item-by-item comparison, Alan Chester, a buyer, was surprised that NCC had bid so aggressively and took it as a sign that the market was softer than had been thought. Given the large drop in quoted prices, therefore, the team decided to negotiate with the suppliers in an effort to achieve previously stated objectives of 61 cents and 59 cents for NCC and IMS, respectively. Chester explained: "When bidders suddenly become aggressive in reducing their prices, you owe it to yourself to probe to see how soft the market really is."

The team met several times in preparing its negotiating strategy. It was agreed first that negotiations with NCC should precede those with IMS because there was still a price difference between the two companies that might be probed. Second, it was agreed that the talks would be held at SPD Component Procurement Group offices.

After these decisions had been made, roles were assigned. The team leader was Royce, the purchasing manager. The IBM cost analysis would be presented by the cost estimator, while Chester and the other buyer would be providing general support.

NCC was represented by a program manager who led the team, a product sales manager, a salesman, the district sales manager, and two others. Royce began by asking the vendor's team to review its quote and to suggest where manufacturing-process improvements and price reductions might be possible. He proposed that they talk about any process or product alterations that were being considered or possible changes in manufacturing locations.

The NCC team leader admitted that the prices were negotiable, although he denied the market was soft. A member of the IBM team pointed out that in an article in *Electronic News* an NCC vice-president was quoted as saying that the market was worsening. The supplier's program manager countered by saying that certain technical changes would enable NCC to offer IBM a slight price decrease. Component Procurement Group engineers were called in to discuss these changes. One proposal was to eliminate a quality control test that NCC performed. The test was, in fact, carried out twice: once at the manufacturing line, and a second time after it was assembled.

This proposal was accepted in part by requiring only a sample testing after the assembly operation. Another suggestion, that NCC manufacture the TTLs on an automated rather than manual line, was postponed until the new line could be approved by IBM engineers. In anticipation of this approval, the NCC team leader offered an additional price reduction of 2 percent, bringing the average price for 12 million units down to 64.17 cents and for 10 million units to 65.70 cents. NCC team members said that they would take the risk that the new line would be approved and then asked if IBM would consider a contract for fixed one-year quantities instead of just six months. IBM representatives told them that this was not possible, although the supplier would be given assurance that it would be one of the two IBM suppliers for the entire year.

At this stage the teams separated and caucused. As soon as they returned to the negotiating table, IBM negotiators informed the NCC representatives that their present offer was still above target, and IBM was now requesting a review of NCC's price for 8 million units. When asked why only 8 million was being discussed, Royce said NCC's offer made a larger amount uneconomical. At this stage, the meeting adjourned for lunch.

At the beginning of the afternoon, the supplier made an offer of 63.85 cents for 12 million units, 64.9 cents for 10 million, but 66.8 cents for 8 million. The IBM team restated the fact that these prices were still above target and requested a review of operations to determine what could be changed to develop better prices. The supplier's team argued that because its mix of units was complex, it was difficult to identify cost reduction candidates. After further short discussion, the meeting broke up with the IBM team saying it hoped for a final firm offer the next day.

When they met again the next day, the NCC program manager asked questions about possible variations in both the mix and absolute quantities that would be required after the order had been placed. The IBM team was able to tell the vendor that the mix would, if anything, be richer than expected. Because more profit was made on the more expensive items the NCC team leader said he would be able to lower his price to 62.09 cents for 12 million units.

In addition, the NCC team asked if the proposed mix was firm. They were told that is was firm for 90 days and 80 percent firm for the next 90 days. They then asked if IBM would agree to the first quarter's orders not being rescheduled or cancelled. IBM agreed. Finally, they offered a price of 61.85 cents for 12.3 million units on the condition that NCC was supplied the first quarter's part numbers and quantities within two days. This would allow NCC to plan its production and shipping schedules immediately. Royce accepted these conditions and after settling some minor contractual clauses, the NCC team left for the airport.

Probably the most important phase of this negotiation for the IBM team was what happened beforehand. A considerable amount of time was spent in *determining negotiating objectives*. They were developed with reference, first, to the vendor's estimated manufacturing costs as calculated by IBM industrial engineers using their knowledge of the manufacturing process and publicly available information on materials costs and labor rates. A second area for analysis was the market environment. In this case, lead times were shortening and some price reductions had been announced, suggesting a concern on the part of suppliers about weakening demand. A third area was recent events in supplier organizations that would be likely to shape their bargaining objectives. Here there were (1) the merger of two NCC plants into one operation at a low labor-rate location and (2) the NCC president's public statement that NCC was on an 80 percent learning curve in making integrated circuits. It could be postulated that NCC had the potential for significant price reductions and, given the market environment, its negotiators might be willing to accept lower margins for the 1975 first-half contract. A fourth clue was NCC's bid. It conveyed a degree of anxiety that supported the IBM team's surmise that there was, indeed, an opportunity to obtain lower prices. But it was really in the early stages of the actual negotiations that the team set an ultimate bargaining objective in the 59 to 61 cents range when the behavior of the NCC negotiators implicitly confirmed the strength of IBM's position.

Choice of location for bargaining sessions is another tactical element. Based on the premise that home court always gives you an advantage, the IBM team chose in this case to conduct negotiations in their offices. Vendor representatives would have planes to catch and other business to tend and, hopefully, might make concessions simply to conclude matters.

But viewpoints differ. Another IBM purchasing manager negotiating for a metal base cabinet for a high-speed printer commented:

> At your place you give the vendor an out. He can always say "I don't have that with me. I must check back." I always like to start negotiations at the

supplier's. You can sometimes invite him back to conclude them, if you don't finish everything.

One of the most important things is time. You must schedule more time than you expect the discussions to last. You mustn't be rushed.

When the General Motors steel-buying team negotiated with suppliers it held the earlier meeting in which volume allocations for the coming year were discussed at the GM Central Office in Detroit. Later visits with high-level managers of supplier companies were held in their offices. These were the discussions of longer-range pricing and steel capacity development.

Suffice it to say that location is an important psychological consideration. It is the buyer's choice, and it should be made out of an understanding for human sensitivities. Protocol, albeit unwritten, is a factor. There is also the consideration of what data resources the vendor may need and where they are available. Probably, then, choice of location may be guided by such concerns as these:

1. What information does the vendor need and is it more readily available on his home ground?
2. Is location likely to be perceived as signalling relative status and how should the choice be made to create conciliatory attitudes?
3. How can time pressures be put to work to keep the supplier's representatives focussed on the need for arriving at an early agreement?

Planning the agenda may again be an exercise in psychology. The opening item should not concern a matter of real substance, but should be useful in setting whatever tone is helpful to the buyer in that particular negotiation. It may show the buyer's willingness to be conciliatory. More often it seems to be intended to send the opposing forces into hasty retreat and to create concerns about losing the business. The buyer may ask about a range of matters, i.e., apparent inconsistencies in the bidding pattern, the possibilities for further price reductions, user-location complaints about vendor performance, changes in the production process that might jeopardize quality and service, and general market conditions. At this point, the lengthy preparations may prove to have been particularly worthwhile in the respect that they have enabled the buying team to display detailed knowledge of the vendor's operations and market climate. This serves, hopefully, to establish the fact that the buying team knows it is bargaining from strength.

The substance of negotiations is shaped to a large extent by whether prices will be arrived at largely through cost-based bargaining, or with reference to market-determined prices, or competitive-bidding negotiations. In the IBM TTL procurement, it was competitive-bidding, although market-determined prices set the back drop for discussions. As is typical of the competitive-bid model, the buyer focuses on various price/quantity combinations in an effort to move the bidder toward incremental pricing on higher volumes in return, possibly, for a contribution to overheads and an opportunity to get ahead of competitors in moving down the learning curve.

A typical and effective tactic is the item-by-item price comparison to probe for price-reduction opportunities. The seller's explanations of interprice relationships, to be perceived as being legitimate in negotiations, will typically be offered in terms of manufacturing-cost comparisons. But market prices are most often value-determined. That is some items, for reasons of differences in demand and value to the customer, command higher prices than others. Thus the item-by-item comparison in negotiations may be perceived basically as a way of moving the vendor away from value-pricing and toward cost as a basis for negotiation.

Role-playing among team members is a substantial contributor to negotiating success. For example, having technically-oriented personnel on the team allows the team leader to bring to bear a high level of expertise on design, manufacturing process, and cost questions. It, therefore, allows both sides to communicate on a technical level. In addition, there may be a more subtle factor at work: it introduces technical challenges and brings engineering values into play to shift emphasis away from price and onto ways of doing things more efficiently.

With this kind of support the purchasing manager may then play his role: to maintain a conducive atmosphere for negotiations, keep discussion flowing, work out stalemates, maintain forward progress by making appropriate trade-offs and concessions, and, at the right moment, make the deal. This last was regarded as the responsibility of the team leader alone, not to be made as a committee decision through consensus.

The usefulness in observing the IBM team at work in negotiating for integrated circuits is to gain some insights on negotiating tactics and the process itself. These are key negotiating phases:

1. Gathering relevant information, assessing the negotiating climate, and setting initial objectives.
2. Analyzing bids.
3. Setting the agenda.
4. Determining location.
5. Assigning roles to team members.
6. In the early stages of the meeting, setting the tone and establishing bargaining strength.
7. Revising target objectives.
8. In substantive negotiations, probing for price reduction opportunities through comparisons of item prices and of various price/quantity combinations.
9. Making trade-offs.
10. Clinching the deal.

Figure 3.2 *Characteristic Elements in Three Procurement Strategy Models*

	Cost-Plus	*Market-Price*	*Competitive-Bid*
Product Type	special design; often new products under development	undifferentiated commodity; often basic materials	may be standard specifications; or differentiated to meet buyer's requirements
Buyer Objectives	pay a fair price; get any cost saving benefit	assure quality; assure that no competitor gets a better price; assure long-run supply availability	get a low, fair price; assure supply availability and product quality
Seller Objectives	get a fair return; avoid cost factor risks	retain or increase market share; get the market price; avoid having any one supplier break the price; avoid Robinson-Patman Act difficulties	retain or increase market share; get the maximum price buyer is willing to pay
Buyer/Seller Relationship	high degree of technical interaction	routine technical and delivery service	some technical involvement, frequently high service requirements
Supplier Complex	often one or a very few suppliers	multisource with different suppliers playing different roles	may range from single to multisource with different suppliers playing different roles
Contract Scope and Duration	narrow product scope; short duration; specific quantity	relatively narrow product scope; volume commitments may be specific or open-ended	broad or narrow product scope; volume commitments may be specific or open-ended
Source of Buyer Negotiating Strength	engineering competence; knowledge of supplier cost factors	ability to allocate volume among multiple suppliers; large volume requirements; ability to bring in new competitors	ability to estimate supplier costs; having multiple sources available; ability to negotiate based on various price/volume/delivery combinations

This concludes the discussion of procurement strategy, in which we have examined cost-based, market-price-based, and competitive-bid-based pricing models and the four basic elements of which they are composed: procurement scope, supplier selection, price, and negotiating strategy.

Figure 3.2 suggests the combinations of strategic elements characteristic to each of the three procurement models. A procurement strategy, like any strategy, must be internally consistent to be effective. To mix strategy elements—for example, to have a large number of vendors on cost-plus contracts for the same item, or to have one supplier of an undifferentiated commodity sold at market prices—will inevitably lead to suboptimization in sourcing.

What does become apparent, however, as one studies the scheme in Figure 3.2 is that competitive-bidding strategies may vary more widely in approach than cost-plus or market-price-based procurements and are more difficult to typify. They may vary widely depending on product, nature of the supply industry, and nature of the buyer's requirements. Nevertheless, in any given procurement the strategy must necessarily be integrated and consistent.

4 Procurement Organization—The Trend Toward Centralization

As for the organization of procurement activities and the positioning of procurement functions in the corporate structure, four key observations may be made at the outset. The first is that elements of procurement are spread across all levels of organization—corporate headquarters, division, and plant. Purchasing, per se, that is vendor selection, negotiation, and ordering takes place in a variety of organizational locations. Other procurement functions such as long-range source planning, procurement-personnel development, and internal auditing are typically headquarters functions. Responsibilities for monitoring vendor performance and providing feedback to shape sourcing strategy typically rest with purchasing personnel at user-locations.

A second observation is that the locus of line buying, where purchasing actually takes place, is a function of procurement strategy. Thus, for example, negotiating with large sellers in oligopolistic industries, such as glass, or steel, where bargaining power through massed purchases is important is often carried on at corporate headquarters. Dealing, on the other hand, with a vendor in designing and building a new piece of capital equipment is typically a purchasing activity at the plant, laboratory or division level, wherever the internal engineering group that has responsibility for that development is located. The nature of negotiating processes and of working relationships with suppliers will vary considerably, depending on the type of product, the nature of the supply industry, the size of individual suppliers and the breadth or narrowness of the lines they supply. All these factors are directly reflected in where in the organization purchasing takes place and who in the organization is involved.

A third fact about procurement organization in large, decentralized companies is that it is changing. There are strong trends at work leading toward the greater centralization of purchasing, procurement policy-making, and direction. What, in fact, is happening is not to be perceived as simply a swing of the centralization/decentralization pendulum but as an adjustment of organization to changing sourcing strategies and to the needs for interfacing effectively with a changing supply environment. The structuring of purchasing activities and the distribution of procurement functions across different levels of the corporation are getting increased management attention and thoughtful delineation in the face of strong external pressures.

Fourth, and clearly related to the foregoing, a critical task for top management is to position the procurement function, overall, in the corporate structure, so as to be able to plan and carry out sourcing strategies, and to develop effective operational relationships between outside suppliers and internal groups such as engineering and manufacturing. To a large extent the problem is one of bringing about organizational change. Any efforts to centralize purchasing activities in decentralized companies fly in the face of profit accountability at the division level and cost center responsibility at the plant level. Taking away any control over purchasing at these levels is often perceived as reducing the accountable manager's control over a key factor that affects his performance. In this respect current trends in purchasing strategy and organization tend to modify the pure concepts of decentralization and profit-center management.

The discussion that follows begins by looking at the business-environment factors that seem to lie behind the trend in large corporations toward the greater centralization of procurement functions. More accurately it might be recognized as a trend away from complete decentralization because the net result is dispersion, not total centralization. That is, different elements of procurement are being centralized while others remain at the division and plant levels. Further, it will be useful to consider the trends that will continue to shape the way in which procurement activities fit into the corporate structure. There are, indeed, powerful factors working in the direction both of increasing the importance of the procurement function and leading to further change and development.

The Trend Toward Centralization

On September 1, 1974 the chairman of General Motors established a new position at the GM Central Office level, vice-president of procurement and production control. Prior to this time, procurement at GM had been almost entirely decentralized to the operating divisions. Exceptions to this pattern were the coordination of steel procurement at the headquarters level, tire purchases, and some special projects, such as sourcing for the catalytic converter. On February 20, 1975 the GM chairman then announced the establishment of a new Procurement Policy Group that would meet quarterly to review and approve recommendations from the procurement vice-president on matters of organization and policy. The Procurement Policy Group would be chaired by one of the two GM vice-chairmen. Other members, in addition to the new procurement vice-president, included GM executives at the very highest echelons in that company.

The letter of February 20, 1975 that announced the move to set up this committee stated in part:

> Coordination of procurement activities when two or more Divisions are involved will increase the Corporation's effectiveness in dealing with the many problems associated with world-wide shortages of materials, wide and frequent fluctuations in prices, etc., as will coordination between future materials availability and forward product planning.
>
> Each Divisional Purchasing Director shall continue to be responsible under his Divisional General Manager for procurement activities pertaining solely to his Division. He shall be responsible to the Executive-in-Charge, GM Purchasing Activities, in procurement matters coordinated by the Procurement and Production Control Staff in those areas approved by the Procurement Policy Group. In view of the resulting dual responsibilities, appointments of Divisional Purchasing Directors shall be made with the recommendation of the Vice President in Charge of the Procurement and Production Control Staff.

At PPG Industries, the establishment for the first time of a corporate procurement function under a new vice-president was announced in June 1972. Until this time each of PPG's four divisions had been responsible for its own procurement activities. There were procurement managers at division headquarters and at each plant location. The new corporate function would largely replace the purchasing organizations at the division level. It would directly handle the procurement of items (1) when there was a significant multiplant requirement; (2) when the procurement was a significant part of a multimaterials purchasing package; or (3) when the procurement was sensitive (a) to division operations, (b) to political considerations, and/or (c) to a high degree of purchasing expertise as, for example, commodities purchases in world markets. One or more of these criteria would apply to an estimated two-thirds (by dollar volume) of PPG purchases. Divisional staffs would be considerably reduced to serve essentially a "coordinating, planning and communicating function, integrating communications between divisional operations and the corporate centralized materials supply management." The plant purchasing-units would continue to operate, reporting to plant managers, but with a dotted line relationship to the Corporate Supply Department.

The centralization of purchasing at PPG had been studied in 1967, 1968, 1969, 1971, and 1972. A 1969 report, which had recommended centralization, listed as the first of nine advantages:

We should be able to reduce the cost of purchased materials. This would come from lower unit costs of equal quality. Also, when items are coordinated, the company is in a much better position to resist price increases. It is conservatively estimated by competent authorities that we should be able to reduce our overall purchasing expenditures by 2 percent.

A report written in 1971, however, put the above reason for centralization in second place, and gave first mention to: "Ensure adequate, dependable sources of supply for all materials, supplies, equipment and services." The list of reasons for centralizing by the time of the 1971 report had expanded to fourteen.

At General Foods a new vice-president of corporate purchasing and materials management was appointed on April 1, 1973 with responsibility for carrying out a complete reorganization so that the purchasing of raw materials and packaging would be centralized at GFC headquarters. The new head of purchasing came to this position from having served as general manager of the Post Division.

Centralized procurement had been discussed at General Foods as early as 1947. When it eventually happened, it came about as part of a major corporate reorganization in 1972 in which four of the six domestic grocery divisions were restructured as five "strategic business units," which were, in turn, consolidated into three new divisions.

Actually before that time ingredients used by more than one General Foods division, such as sugar, oils, rice, corn starch and some packaging, had been purchased by a small central group. Other procurement had been done at the plants including the purchase of wheat, meats, food chemicals, and MRO items.

Following the 1972 reorganization, the procurement of all supplies was centralized at corporate headquarters except for: (1) MRO and other nonproduct items, which continued to be purchased at plant locations, (2) coffee and cocoa beans, which remained with the Maxwell House division and the Baker chocolate business group, respectively, (3) construction materials and equipment, which were purchased by buyers at General Foods Central Engineering Services, and (4) laboratory supplies, procured by buyers at laboratory locations.

It was anticipated that the total number of buyers employed by the corporation could be reduced and some economies could be achieved through aggregating orders. It soon became evident that centralized procurement helped immensely in coping with the shortages of 1973–74. As the director of raw materials purchases in the new organization commented: "To begin with, a lot of us had doubts. But when the shortages of 1974 arose the wisdom of a centralized organization was clear. We were able to deal on a corporation-to-corporation basis. It was possible to set up a strategic allocations committee and make sure that each plant received its optimum supply of scarce materials. That would never have been possible before.''

Thus at General Motors, PPG Industries, and General Foods there were major restructurings of the procurement function in the early 1970s. In each case top management moved to establish strong central procurement functions, both for purchasing key supply items in common use among decentralized divisions and to give clear policy direction to purchasing operations at division and plant levels. At IBM, Raytheon, and Heinz USA, strong central organizations had already existed, with a broad distribution of procurement responsibilities across organization levels—corporate, division, and plant.

What factors were at work moving these companies toward increased centralization and what did their managements hope to gain? The factors that influence organizational change fall in four categories: (1) coping with supply shortages and working to assure long-term availability of needed resources, (2) responding effectively to a changing business environment, (3) seeking improved profit performance through reduced costs of materials, components, supply items, and other purchased products, (4) responding to a sensed need for increased professional development in procurement and for a more efficient use of scarce personnel talent.

The Problem of Availability. Unquestionably the shortages of basic materials and manufactured products of all types that hit the U.S. economy in the last quarter of 1973 through the end of 1974 has had a profound impact on the way purchasing is organized and carried out. At General Motors, materials shortages in 1973–74 was a triggering factor in the establishment of a strong Central Office procurement function. The divisions working by themselves had difficulty in negotiating for such critical materials as steel, zinc, aluminum, copper, polyethylene, and polyvinyl chloride. Moreover, the lack of coordination among the divisions aggravated the problem. In one instance, a GM plant purchasing agent returned three carloads (300,000 pounds) of zinc for which he had paid 30 cents a pound to his supplier because it wasn't needed in his plant. At the same time, plants in other divisions were paying as much as 60 cents a pound and had difficulty getting enough.

Lack of coordination could be a problem, as well, when two or more divisions purchased from common suppliers. The buying divisions sometimes found themselves competing, for example, for the limited capacity of small tool-and-die shops.

Bargaining by themselves with suppliers, GM plants were paying a range of prices for the same commodity, often to the same vendor and occasionally had difficulty in procuring what was needed. In 1974, the AC Spark Plug Division of General Motors, for example, was unsuccessful by itself in getting steel suppliers to reverse a decision to drop the production of tinplate in certain gauges needed for disposable oil filter shells. AC Spark Plug purchasing managers sought Central Office help in this instance and steel producers were persuaded to continue to supply the tinplate that AC needed.

The prospect of recurrent shortages also created a need for effective forward-planning of sourcing strategies. It would be important for GM to forecast supply conditions worldwide for critical materials and components, their availability and cost. Source analyses would be useful in planning the development of long-term supplier relations and also in product planning. In addition, as one of the world's largest buyers of certain basic materials, GM was in a position to help shape plans for, and encourage the development of, new capacity by its suppliers.

A factor contributing to shortages in certain areas had been government-imposed environmental regulations. As a result of EPA standards, for example, a large amount of the zinc-smelting capacity in the United States had been taken out of operation. Plant investments required to bring these refineries up to standard apparently could not be justified economically. In addition, according to GM managers, price controls imposed in 1972–73 influenced materials suppliers to seek markets where they could get higher prices, particularly export markets and energy-related industries.

Possibly the most serious supply lack to which procurement organization and strategy have responded is the fuel oil shortage brought on by the Arab oil embargo of 1973. At PPG the Corporate Supply Department was already in place by this time. The ability to cope with this crisis at PPG was recognized at the time as an unanticipated benefit of centralization. The new department was able to study PPG needs, identify alternative energy sources, negotiate for supplies, and contribute to the allocating of scarce supplies among the four divisions. Looking toward the longer run, a Fuels and Utilities group in the Corporate Supply Department began work on the development of a program for evaluating the usage of energy at PPG plants and for altering consumption patterns to assure availability and to lower costs. In addition, it began the development of data bases to forecast fuel oil, gas, and coal supply and price conditions and was actively searching for opportunities to purchase fuels in the ground. Going beyond, Fuels and Utilities anticipated tracking regulatory developments affecting energy supplies and prices and participating in regulatory activities at both the state and national levels.

What characterizes energy sourcing at the PPG corporate level is its proactive nature involving forecasting energy supply conditions, contributing to the shaping of a conducive regulatory environment, and working to evolve PPG energy-usage patterns in the light of long-term supply trends.

At General Motors, assuring the availability of critical materials, such as zinc, aluminum, and steel, involved the development of long-term relations with primary sources. In 1974, for example, it was estimated that GM lost several million dollars because it had to buy almost half of its zinc requirements from secondary sources, brokers and jobbers, at significantly higher prices than if it had been able to source from primary producers. There was a parallel situation in the case of aluminum. GM had purchased about two-thirds of its aluminum requirements from primary producers in 1965; by 1974 that was down to two-fifths. In 1971–73, GM operating divisions had been able to buy aluminum more cheaply in the scrap (secondary) market. In so doing, they disrupted the continuity of established relationships with the primary producers. By 1974, GM was paying 10.5 cents a pound on the average over primary-producer prices (about 35 cents a pound) for what it was buying in the secondary market. With its increasing aluminum requirements, GM needed to establish strong and dependable source relations with the primary producers. Its target would be 85 percent of all aluminum purchases from primary producers by 1976.

These long-range considerations seemed to be of more urgent concern at the Central Office level than in the plants. Speaking of steel buying, as an example, the executive-in-charge of purchasing activities at the Central Office commented in late 1975:

> Right now a lot of steel is becoming available and brokers are approaching plant buyers with very attractive price deals. One division purchasing manager under instructions from his plant manager bought 10,000 tons of steel at a savings of $11 a ton from a jobber. I told him that that will get back to our prime sources who have been responsive to our needs, and if they see us whacking and whittling away at our basic commitments to them we won't have any strength in future negotiations. I know, though, that when we stop the plant manager from making the best deals he can that we are affecting his measures—and that's toying with the basic guts of the GM structure.

Understandably, with strong emphasis on annual profit performance at the division level, division and plant purchasing managers would tend toward buying at the lowest available price. An important dimension of performance measurement at the division and plant level is annual cost saving. At the corporate level measures are of a different sort. They tend to be less specific, less detailed, less formal, and, most important, longer run. Thus a headquarters purchasing manager may well give greater strategic priority to long-run supply availability and low cost than to short-run purchasing costs. In other words, a key effect of centralizing purchasing decision-making for key supply items at the corporate level is to change the performance measurement environment in which such decisions are made, and in essence to bring to bear a different set of corporate priorities.

Finally, coping with shortages has involved the marshalling of purchasing power within the corporation to put negotiating strength at a single point in the enterprise. Companies like PPG Industries, General Foods, and General Motors source through suppliers who sell a wide range of products, especially materials, to a number of different divisions. By centralizing purchases at the corporate level, these companies may command attention at higher management levels in supplier organizations that are themselves large and decentralized. The nature of the supplier-customer relationship tends, then, to shift to one that recognizes long-term commitments on either side.

Commenting in April 1976, Betty Safford, a buyer at General Foods headquarters, summed up the problems she had faced in buying certain food chemicals over the previous two years:

> In March 1974, I received the news that there had been an explosion at the Beaumont [a General Foods supplier] plant. Instead of giving us 14 truckloads of sodium bicarbonate, the vendor committed 10 truckloads to us. It didn't take a mathematician to know that we were going to be in a difficult position. The timing couldn't have been worse because in the second quarter of the year our main plant is straight-out building product stocks to get ready for its seasonal spring peak. On top of that, 1974 was a boom year for us and everybody else, and the shortages really hit. The contracts we had with suppliers weren't worth the paper they were written on. Sure, they did the very best they could to give us supplies considering the environment.
>
> Then, in November 1974, the bottom fell out of the economy. Our sales were down; goods didn't move out of the warehouses and we were working off inventories; the plants cut back, and we could get all the bicarbonate we wanted. That's the way it's been through 1975—a buyer's paradise—but we know very well that the shortages could hit again and we're working hard, while there's a lull, to build new sources for the future. In fact we are in negotiations with a source of supply outside of the U.S.

At the same time, Pat Westerfeld, another General Foods buyer, was faced with problems in assuring supply availability of two other important food chemicals. Beaumont was also a major supplier of these chemicals. In late 1975 Beaumont's management announced that its plant for making one of these chemicals would be closed. Westerfeld immediately visited the executive vice-president of Beaumont's Chemicals Division and explained the consequences for General Foods of this action. An agreement was reached that the plant in question would be operated for two additional months to produce a year's supply of the needed ingredient for General Foods. Westerfeld also began immediately to cast about for supply sources to fill in the void that would be left by Beaumont's withdrawal.

In addition to the domestic divisions, some General Foods subsidiaries outside the United States were experiencing difficulty in assuring the availability of these same food chemicals. They were depending on what seemed like precarious sources of supply and turned to the GF headquarters purchasing staff for help.

Safford and Westerfeld concluded that it might be advantageous to arrange single contracts with Beaumont and other major suppliers to cover large portions of General Foods' worldwide requirements for the products these suppliers produced.

Beaumont representatives, in particular, responded favorably to the idea when it was first proposed. Several of their divisions would be involved. By late 1975 an agreement was reached. Commenting in early 1976, Westerfeld thought the new agreement had several advantages: (1) firm supply commitment, (2) price protection, (3) direct sales contact worldwide for each ingredient, (4) elimination of the need to implement emergency formulation modifications created by the supply crisis, and from a professionalism standpoint, (5) a new learning experience that added to General Foods' expertise in consolidating and managing General Foods' worldwide procurement.

A Changing Business Environment. In two important respects the business environment is changing in ways that have tended to foster the development of strong centralized procurement functions. One is the growth of multinational business operations and, as part of that, the development of large, complex multinational sourcing-systems. When, for example, General Motors began to buy significant amounts of steel from foreign sources in 1972, there was an immediate need for centralized coordination of steel procurement. Negotiating with foreign sources was difficult and time-consuming, calling for special knowledge and skills. It could not be easily handled by individual plant buyers. Negotiations with foreign sources had to be carried on for the company as a whole. A second factor influencing procurement organization is government regulations that affect purchasing activities. Government interest in fostering small business and minority-owned businesses is one example.[1] Another is the activities of the U.S. Justice Department and the Federal Trade Commission aimed at eliminating the practice of reciprocity or trade relations in industry.

With regard to reciprocity, the Antitrust Division of the Department of Justice has been successful in obtaining consent decrees from several large companies[2] in which the defendants have agreed to cease and desist from using their pur-

1. According to the U.S. Code, Title 15-Commerce and Trade, Chapter 14A, Paragraph 631: ". . . It is the declared policy of the Congress that the Government should aid, counsel, assist, and protect, insofar as is possible, the interests of small-business concerns in order to preserve free competitive enterprise, to insure that a fair proportion of the total purchases and contracts or subcontracts for property and services for the Government (including but not limited to contracts or subcontracts for maintenance, repair, and construction) be placed with small-business enterprises, to insure that a fair proportion of the total sales of Government property be made to such enterprises, and to maintain and strengthen the overall economy of the Nation." In keeping with public policy, many business firms have voluntarily introduced programs to develop sources of supply among small, as well as minority-owned, business firms.

2. Including U.S. Steel, Uniroyal, American Standard and PPG Industries. These actions have been brought under Sections 1 and 2 of the Sherman Act prohibiting contracts, combinations and conspiracies in restraint of trade. Typically in entering consent decrees, the defendants have agreed not to make any purchases from a supplier where it was understood that such purchases were conditional in any way on the supplier's buying in turn from the defendant company. The consent decrees have also called for abolishing offices responsible for developing reciprocal-purchasing arrangements. In addition, defendants are enjoined from maintaining comparative data on sales to and purchases from individual supplier/customers.

chasing power as a lever for making sales to their suppliers. The Federal Trade Commission has acted to force divestiture of acquired companies where it has been demonstrated that the acquiring company has thereby gained the power to use reciprocity as a competitive weapon.[3]

What government interest in fostering the growth of small and minority-owned business and in eliminating reciprocity have in common is that both relate to the firm's purchasing practices. Concerns in both areas lead to the exercise of centralized control over procurement activities. To encourage the development of small and minority-owned businesses as suppliers, corporate policy has typically been promulgated through centrally-issued directives and reinforced through procurement audits.

Reciprocity is also the subject of corporate policy statements and internal monitoring. But going beyond directives, there is the additional consideration with regard to reciprocity that when much of the large-scale purchasing in companies like General Motors, General Foods, and PPG Industries is done at the corporate level there is presumably more direct control over it than if important purchases were decentralized. In addition, it would be organizationally more difficult to carry out reciprocity strategies when both sales and purchasing are not under the control of decentralized, profit-centered division managements.

The essential point is that the increasing government regulation of business activities related to procurement has been a factor fostering the development of corporate procurement policy-making and monitoring functions. Government regulation has been a causal factor, as well, in moves to place the responsibility for handling large, politically sensitive purchases at the corporate level. There seems, then, to be increasing public concern with how the large firm relates to and influences its supply environment. That influence in turn has commanded top management attention and has led to the development of organizational arrangements that facilitate the exercise of top management direction over key procurement decisions.

Concerns for Profits. At General Motors, General Foods, and PPG Industries, a major objective of centralizing purchasing is to reduce the costs of parts, materials, supply items, and other purchased products. PPG studies in 1969, 1971, and 1972 all listed as a major objective of procurement centralization the maximization of purchasing power to obtain favorable terms. In addition, it was anticipated that purchasing could be accomplished with fewer, more highly-skilled personnel.

At General Motors a study was made of one of their supply items, work gloves, for which they spent more than $10 million. On one widely used type,

3. The Federal Trade Commission has based such actions on Section 7 of the Clayton Act which proscribes mergers and acquisitions where "the effect of such acquisition may be substantially to lessen competition, or to tend to create a monopoly." See F.T.C. v. Consolidated Foods Corp., 380 U.S. 592 (1965); and U.S. v. General Dynamics Corp., 258 F. Supp. 36 (1966).

canvas knit-wrist gloves, 10 GM divisions bought 843,000 dozen for use at 106 U.S. locations in 1974 and spent $4.6 million or an average of $5.46 a dozen. Seven different prices were paid in the 10 divisions for the same item, ranging from $4.88 to $5.90. One supplier alone, a broker, charged a different price for the same item to each of five divisions. The price spread in this case was $5 to $5.88. There were 95 different suppliers—manufacturers, distributors, brokers, and agents.

After the formation of the GM Central Office procurement group, managers in this unit who were responsible for nonproduct purchases negotiated contracts with six suppliers for over 120,000 pairs of gloves of one particular type, 8-ounce, knit-wrist, clute-cut large, at an estimated savings of more than 12 percent over prices paid a year earlier. With purchases of this item fragmented over a large number of buying locations and suppliers, no one location apparently had given work gloves very much attention. The opportunity for savings lay in analyzing GM's requirements, studying the supply industry, standardizing on a limited number of specifications, and negotiating with a few suppliers. In that way GM's business might be sufficiently attractive and important to each one to stimulate active price competition.

Developing and Using Scarce Personnel Resources. Clearly a factor prompting the development of centralized purchasing has been the concern for attracting competent personnel to this area and for using scarce managerial resources as effectively as possible. The range of buying assignments in a corporation calls ideally for a high degree of specialization by supply industry and by type of skill needed in dealing with external supply sources as well as internal groups. But specialization needs "critical mass." To justify the development of purchasing expertise in any product area requires a sufficient volume-base to command significant time and attention from one or more purchasing managers. That is typically accomplished by massing total product requirements across the enterprise and centralizing purchasing responsibility. The General Motors canvas knit-wrist glove illustration is a case in point.

At IBM a strong Corporate Contracts group, consisting of seven contract specialists and a group head, was responsible for negotiating contracts that accounted for a purchasing volume per buyer well in excess of the average for all industrial buyers in IBM. They were experts in purchasing a range of goods (such as office supplies) and services (such as rental cars) that were in common use throughout the IBM domestic operation.

In addition, with the growing centralization of procurement, there has developed a single point in the corporation with responsibility for fostering professional development in purchasing throughout the organization. A related benefit is the opening-up of paths of promotion across divisions. As the executive-in-charge of purchasing activities at GM commented: "Past history shows, in the majority of cases, that purchasing managers' paths of progression have been too restricted to the divisions.'' Professional development has involved, as well, the institution of formal performance appraisal systems as well as the development of training programs in purchasing management.

Sources of Resistance to Centralization

Importantly, however, increasing centralization seems inconsistent with concepts of divisional and departmental profit responsibility. Procurement clearly is a critical function affecting division performance, as are manufacturing and marketing. Thus in companies, such as PPG and General Motors, where decentralized profit-center management has been a long-standing tradition it would be natural to expect resistance to loss of direct control over the purchasing function.

At PPG, the four division managers seemed interested in the establishment of a corporate-purchasing function only to the extent that purchasing performance could be improved for materials that were common to two or more divisions. The Chemical Division general manager backed centralization of purchasing but he wasn't sure that the timing was right. He could see greater energy problems coming and felt the need for such centralization. On the other hand, he had strong plant managers who did not want to give up any control over procurement in their plants. On the whole, this general manager wanted to see a small corporate-purchasing advisory staff established as a first step. The general manager of the Coatings and Resins division was opposed to centralization. He had built up a good record of growth and earnings in his division, and he saw raw materials as the key to his success. He didn't want, therefore, to see long lines of communications develop on purchasing decisions. The Fiber Glass division general manager took the position that centralizing procurement would be timely because he did not have a well-developed purchasing function. On the other hand, the division was experiencing strong growth and he felt the need to strengthen the procurement function at the division level to serve and support his growth. The Glass Division general manager took the position that the move would be right; he was emphatic, however, that a central-purchasing group, if established, should work for him. He had already developed a centralized-procurement function within his division and it had performed well.

At General Motors, profit-center management at the division level has been the keystone in the systems for control and motivation, and management compensation at the division level is based to a significant extent on division as well as corporate profits. In good years, bonuses might represent up to two-thirds of a top manager's compensation. It was reported, nevertheless, that on the whole the new directions in purchasing at GM were being well received at the meetings with division top managements. According to one corporate purchasing manager: ''The time was right. Because of the sharp drop in GM profits in 1974, there were no bonus payments to upper management. Since nobody gets a bonus unless the total company makes a profit, there is really concern at the division level about overall corporate profitability. If we can show them that what we are doing will increase GM profits, they'll buy it.''

The timing was right. But it was evident that centralization had strong backing from headquarters management and support through the high level Procurement Policy Group. Centralized procurement outside the division structure sometimes compromises on profit-center responsibility, but the gains are perceived as outweighing any resulting complications in the performance-measurement systems.

Other organizational developments, as well, are tending to erode pure profit-center decentralization concepts in management. At General Motors, for example, one observes the gradual adaptation of old organizational principles to take advantage of modern technology in logistics and management information systems. Such an instance is the establishment in 1971 of the GM Assembly Division and the loss of division control for the most part over car and truck assembly operations.

Future Organizational Trends

There are three factors in the economic environment that are likely to cause increasing centralization of procurement functions. One would be the possibility of recurrent shortages and the concomitant development of political and business concentrations of control over supply. The corporate response to concentration of power on the supply side would be to concentrate purchasing power on the demand side and to position negotiating responsibility and authority for critical supplies at a single point in the corporation.

A second is the changing organization structure itself. As at GM, there appears to be a trend toward recentralization in industry, as management teams gain the tools to manage larger businesses effectively over greater geographic areas. It is likely that increasing centralization of purchasing will logically be a part of this trend.

The third, and perhaps most important factor of all, is the growing use of sophisticated, computer-based, management-information systems. The potential here is the increased uncoupling of the buying and using functions. At Raytheon, for example, corporate contracts are negotiated for small tools, involving approximately ten thousand items. Computer programs are developed for storing descriptive information, code numbers, and prices; for receiving orders from remote user-locations; generating acquisitions; recording receipt of the goods and generating payments to suppliers. Prices may be changed as required by entering new data in the computer program. In addition, the computer prints catalogs for use in work locations. A history of ordering activity is immediately available at any time to headquarters purchasing managers. Finally, the system requires no involvement on the part of purchasing managers at user-locations.

As has been observed, however, increasing centralization naturally generates resistance to change at division and plant levels. In companies like General Foods, PPG, and General Motors, the new directions have come about because of strong top management support. There has been extensive consultation with operating managers at the division level to determine the nature and structure of centralized procurement functions. In the last analysis, however, it seems to have been that top management concern and interest was a more weighty factor than initiatives at the division level in bringing about change. Something less than enthusiasm for centralization is reflected in the following comment of the top ranking purchasing manager at the Chevrolet Division, the director of purchases.

> Purchasing is tending to become more centralized at GM but there is a risk of its getting too damn centralized. It's important for the buyers not only to know their sources but also to know the Chevrolet using-plants intimately. The trend toward centralization will hurt purchasing's relations with the plant. They're talking about regionalizing purchasing but then the buyers won't know all those people in the plant—the master mechanic, plant engineer, material superintendent, etc. The reason for centralization is to achieve cost and manpower savings, but it will take a lot of effort, sophisticated computer systems and common codes to do the right job.

Once established, however, centralized purchasing departments have worked to gain acceptance at division and plant levels. They have established links for purposes of identifying and serving user-location needs and for responding promptly to unfavorable experiences with suppliers with respect to delivery, service, and product quality at the user level. In particular, they have sought to make initial moves that, on the one hand, showed dramatic cost savings and other gains and, on the other, would not strike at purchasing functions that would be most sensitive to division and plant locations.

Finally, a consideration that has led to the acceptance of centralized purchasing is that savings have accrued to operating divisions in terms of lower supply costs. This is evidence that division profit-performance has gained as a result.

5 The Positioning and Organization of Procurement Functions

While there have been strong pressures, mostly related to external factors, leading toward greatly strengthened headquarters-procurement activities, important buying activities have remained at the division and plant level. The organizational moves might better be perceived as structural adjustments intended to achieve some optimal positioning of different procurement functions. The intent seems to have been to place responsibilities for purchasing and other functions where they might be carried out most efficiently and with greater control on the part of corporate management. There are common patterns in the way procurement responsibilities are positioned across corporate, division, and plant levels and the way procurement functions at each of the three levels are organized.

Headquarters Functions and Structure

Although representing widely diverse industries, companies, such as General Motors, IBM, PPG Industries, General Foods, and Raytheon, exhibit common patterns in the assignment of functions to headquarters procurement departments as Figures 5.1 through 5.5 indicate. In all five companies significant purchasing activities are centrally carried out. At General Foods, General Motors, and PPG Industries—all large users of metals, chemicals, energy, plastics, and food

Figure 5.1 *Corporate Purchasing Staff Organization, 1975—INTERNATIONAL BUSINESS MACHINES*

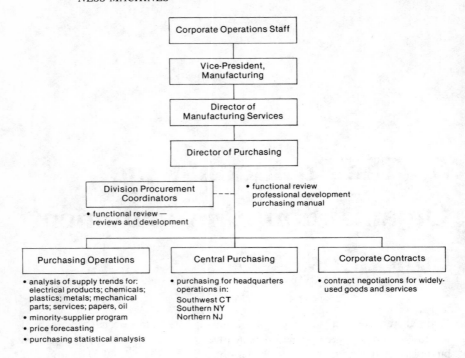

Figure 5.2   *Organization of the Central Office Procurement Function, 1975 —GENERAL MOTORS*

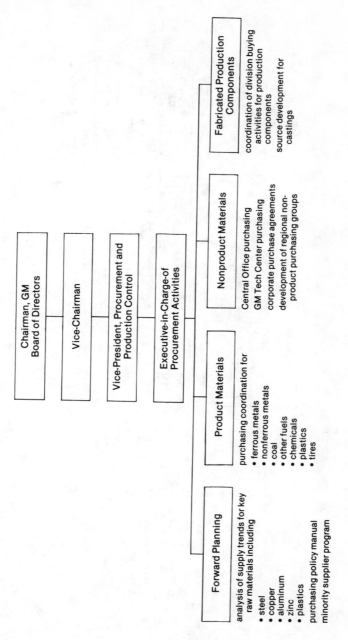

Figure 5.3   *Organization of the Corporate Supply Department, 1975—PPG INDUS-
TRIES*

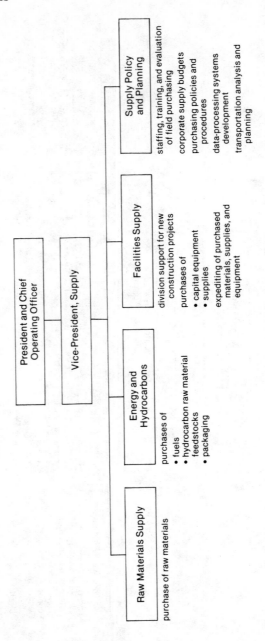

Figure 5.4 *Organization of the Corporate Purchasing and Materials Management Department, 1976—GENERAL FOODS CORPORATION*

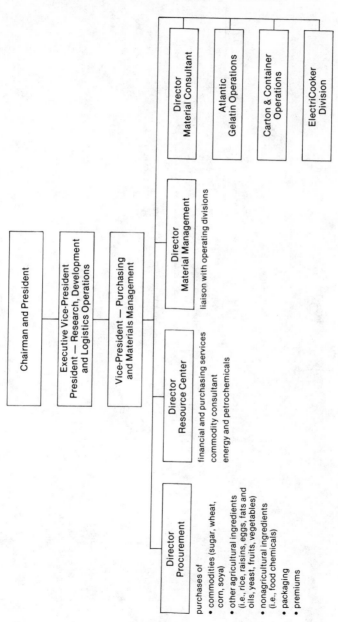

Figure 5.5 *Corporate Procurement Staff Organization, 1976—RAYTHEON COMPANY*

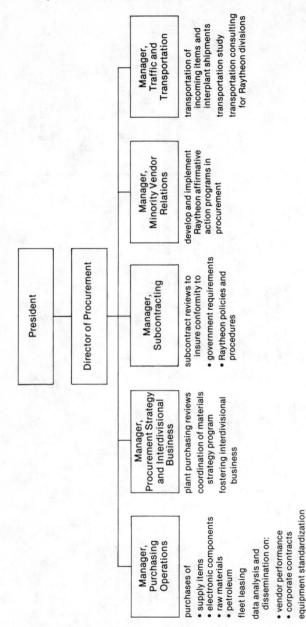

commodities—the great bulk of materials purchases is carried out at the corporate level. In addition all three engage to a greater or lesser extent in purchasing fabricated components, such as packaging (in the case of PPG and General Foods) and electronics parts (Raytheon) that will, like materials, become part of the end product. All but General Foods have undertaken to buy selected supply items, generally, those having a high degree of commonality of use across operating divisions and having a substantial total volume. At General Foods supply items are purchased at the plant level. In some instances, too, for example at Raytheon, IBM, and General Motors, the headquarters department serves as a convenient location for purchasing for all corporate departments and nearby office locations and technical centers.

In companies where extensive purchasing is done at the division or plant level, such as Raytheon, IBM, and General Motors there are nascent functions at the corporate level aimed at the coordination and development of purchasing operations at lower organizational levels. At General Motors, one member of the Central Office Procurement group was responsible for fostering the "design-coordinating division" concept in purchasing. Corporate-wide design responsibility was assigned to different GM divisions for different parts and assemblies (such as bodies, heaters, air conditioners, frames, front and rear suspension systems, and brakes). Where divisions did have design-coordination responsibility, they also had responsibility for company-wide procurement of that part or subsystem. An objective of Central Office Procurement was to further the idea of centralized procurement carried out at the division level. Admittedly, however, this approach, started at GM in the 1960s, had not been very successful. Because of the tradition of decentralization and profit responsibility as well as the jealously-guarded design prerogatives at the division level, the acceptance of design coordination across divisions has been an uphill struggle. This was in spite of the fact that the past president had recognized the urgent need to increase parts commonality across car lines and had actively championed this common design approach.

At PPG, Raytheon, and General Foods, headquarters procurement took on responsibilities for developing computer-based information systems for purchasing applications. Most important, the corporate-procurement departments were all actively involved in purchasing-personnel development, appraisal, rotation and promotion at operating levels. At IBM the Corporate Director of Purchasing indicated that a key way that he influenced the procurement function away from headquarters was through his involvement in appointing procurement managers at different buying locations. He explained:

I am consulted on most of the procurement manager appointments. At the FMRs [Functional Management Reviews] I can get to know the second-level managers (the managers who reported to the procurement manager at each location). I know who they are and what their potential is.

Although I'm consulted I don't have the final decision. That belongs to the line manager. If I take exception to a decision, though, I can take it up the line.

The point is that if you give the plant managers candidates who turn out to be good, your credibility is much sounder.

Headquarters departments have also assisted divisions in developing sources for critical materials under particularly difficult conditions. A key function of Corporate Procurement at Raytheon, for example, was working with plants and divisions on the development of materials-sourcing strategies. According to the Director of Procurement:

There are two distinct aspects of this activity. In the short term we keep a running tab on the critical markets we buy from so that we don't get surprised by inflation or shortages. In other words, we operate an early warning system. For the long run, however, we are looking ahead to Raytheon's needs in the type or quantity of material, or technology. For example, in semiconductors, our largest single category of purchased material, we try to build lasting relationships with suppliers who are pursuing the technologies we will need five years from now.

In another example, we have worked hard with the Japanese for years to obtain steel sheets to protect our supply base, because we see recurrent periods of shortage and surplus ahead. If we stay with the Japanese when steel is easy to buy, they'll stick with us when it's hard to get.

I've formalized this activity into a company-wide Materials Strategy program to bring together both staff and line personnel. I want to use the expertise of the knowledgeable people on the firing line at the plants, and have them participate in whatever strategic planning is evolved.

There are two levels to the organization of this program. First is the Materials Strategy Council consisting of five senior purchasing-executives from the divisions and three members of the corporate staff, including myself. This is the policy-making group; it determines which markets are sensitive to our needs—like semiconductors, steel, chemicals—whether volume sensitive, technology sensitive, or a "line stopper." In effect, the Council directs the research carried out by the second level of the program organization.

This level is the Commodity Subcommittee group. Each subcommittee consists of the major buying personnel of the particular commodity under study—probably 6–10 in number. The subcommittees develop forecasts of requirements, availability and price trends twice a year for short-term direction. They also assess the long-run outlook and develop strategies to assure long-term supply.

Finally, the corporate office develops short- and long-term forecasts of price inflation and reports its findings quarterly to divisions, subsidiaries and the executive office. The forecasts are used in product-material budgeting, forward pricing the material portion of contract proposals and in the negotiation of inflation protection clauses. We use one of the major economic services to support our forecasts, but tailor their forecasts to the materials and components specifically of interest to Raytheon.

The Materials Strategy Program is a major function of the corporate staff.

Typically, as at Raytheon, headquarters procurement operates to monitor the supply environment, to forecast supply, demand, and price levels for key materials, and sometimes to forecast the behavior of such basic cost elements as labor and overheads for fabricated parts. Forecasting supply conditions is an essential part of developing long-range strategies that could involve the search for substitute materials, programs to encourage the development of new capacity by suppliers, and decisions to develop internal sources rather than rely completely on external suppliers. In some cases these assessments serve another purpose: to provide data for developing target prices for negotiating purposes and against which purchasing performance could be measured.

One of the most important functions assigned to corporate procurement is the development and promulgation of purchasing policies, procedures and practices. Highly detailed, purchasing manuals cover matters of corporate policy (doing business with minority-owned companies); legal constraints (not inducing or knowingly accepting discriminatory prices; not engaging in reciprocity); conflicts of interests (not accepting gifts from suppliers or having a financial involvement with suppliers); levels of approval of contracts (dollar amounts of purchase commitments that can be made at different job levels in the organization from assistant buyer to procurement manager); bidding procedures (conduct of bidding competitions and maintenance of supporting documentation); supplier relations principles (limits on the amount of business the company may award to a single supplier as a percentage of his total workload; fairness in soliciting bids and making awards); and miscellaneous procedures (accounting for company-owned tooling and consigned stock on vendor locations; disposal of scrap and surplus; protecting proprietary information, patents, and trademarks).

Purchasing manuals serve as a vehicle for assuring that in its extensive buying operations the company follows uniform practices, that it carries out stated corporate policies; that it relates to the supply environment in a responsible way. In particular, standards of purchasing behavior seek to assure that the procurement function operates in the corporation's best interests in terms of preserving long-run supply-sources, buying at the lowest available prices consistent with quality requirements, and protecting the corporation's physical assets and proprietary technical and business knowledge.

The development and implementation of audit and review programs assures that stated policies and practices are being observed. Reviews may be carried out by the procurement department itself at buying locations. In addition, purchasing audits seem generally to be a part of the work of an internal audit department.

Like manuals, audits are highly detailed. They look for conflicts of interest, improper documentation, instances of unsubstantiated awards to other than the low bidder, purchasing commitments made by other than procurement personnel, and procedural infractions, such as failure to date-stamp bids, acceptance of late bids, and failure to obtain written confirmation of quotations received orally.

Finally, headquarters procurement may be the locus of certain miscellaneous resource functions, such as legal counsel specializing in antitrust and contract law, as at Raytheon and General Motors. Another such resource is transportation and logistics expertise both for buying transportation services directly and assisting the divisions with inbound and outbound shipping arrangements.

The headquarters function then, typically, has four broad categories of responsibility: (1) purchasing items in common use throughout the corporation, (2) developing and monitoring purchasing practices at operating levels to insure effective purchasing results and the carrying out of corporate policies, (3) forecasting the supply environment, and (4) maintaining certain specialized resources to assist line activities at both headquarters and in the field. The extent of purchasing per se done at headquarters seems to vary depending on the nature of the business. For PPG and General Foods, where the great bulk of purchases are materials, the buying activities at headquarters seem to overshadow those in the field. For IBM and Raytheon, both large users of fabricated parts, buying activities at headquarters are not as extensive as those located at field operations points. In the case of General Motors, an extensive user of both materials and fabricated parts, purchasing out of headquarters, at division locations and at the plants are all very substantial.

Division Functions

Patterns vary in procurement work at the division level. At one extreme PPG, Raytheon, and General Foods have coordinating functions. At PPG, much of the talent was taken from division procurement operations to staff the new Corporate Supply Department. Division staffs were reduced considerably to serve essentially a "coordinating, planning, and communicating function, integrating communications between divisional operations and the corporate centralized materials supply management" (1972 PPG study).

At IBM, there are divisional coordinators of purchasing reporting to the division vice-presidents of manufacturing, who act as interfaces between the corporate headquarters purchasing staff and plant and office purchasing managers. The locus for the great bulk of purchasing activity is at the plant and laboratory levels. One pattern, then, is to concentrate procurement at the corporate level and the plant, office, and laboratory locations, leaving an interface function at the division level. The manager designated to fill this role would have responsibility for relating considerations coming out of the supply environment to the development of overall division strategy. In addition, such a role carries with it the responsibility for monitoring purchasing operations at division operating-levels.

On the other hand, at General Motors the history and tradition of strong decentralized, profit-centered management combines with diversity of product lines to result in large procurement operations at the division-headquarters level. The Chevrolet Division alone accounted in 1974 for roughly half (about $8 billion) of GM's total purchases and of that amount the Chevrolet Central Office committed about $4 billion in product purchases and $1 billion in nonproduct, including construction. The $4 billion in product purchases was handled by a staff of seventy. These were purchases of fabricated parts and components that needed no further processing and were shipped directly to plants operated by the GM Assembly Division for assembly into Chevrolet cars and trucks. This group handled in excess of 17,000 part numbers and dealt with more than 3,000 suppliers including GM "allied" divisions.

Another group in Chevrolet procurement handled all construction projects over $100,000, leaving smaller jobs to the plants. In addition, there were resources for handling special tasks and problem areas, such as supplier bankruptcies, repossession of GM-owned tooling, supplier claims against Chevrolet, and the interpretation and dissemination of information on regulations affecting procurement. An activity of particular significance was the development of computerized information-systems for purchasing and inventory control.

Included in the Chevrolet organization was a general purchasing agent for raw materials, a position created in 1972 to coordinate raw-materials buying. This manager was part of the GM Central Office team that negotiated for such vital materials as steel, aluminum, and plastic.

Finally, a general purchasing manager for field operations gave functional direction to the plant purchasing agents in the eighteen Chevrolet manufacturing plants and the two assembly plants it still managed. This manager monitored adherence to Chevrolet Purchasing Policies and Procedures as well as the selection and development of purchasing personnel at the plant level. But plant purchasing agents reported directly to plant managers. A particular concern of the general purchasing manager for field operations was that plant purchasing personnel share information on the sources they were using and the prices they paid, since many used the same sources.

Thus the functions that Chevrolet procurement performed for its division were very similar to what might be found at a headquarters department, i.e., purchasing of certain categories of parts, materials, and equipment; developing and promulgating procurement policies and procedures; serving as a specialized resource center (legal; information systems; supplier relations); and the monitoring, staffing, and development of the purchasing operations at the plant level. One difference might be noted: the bulk of purchases at the Chevrolet Division consisted of fabricated parts while the GM Central Office was mainly concerned with critical raw materials. More will be said later about the rationale underlying the locus of different purchasing operations at different points in the corporate structure.

Organization and Functions at the Plant and Laboratory Levels

The discussion of procurement functions performed at this level may be relatively brief. Plant buying operations are of two types. In General Foods and PPG plant buying is concerned primarily with nonproduct supplies, MRO items purchased largely from local suppliers. These suppliers are usually distributors and not manufacturers.

At General Motors, IBM, and Raytheon a much broader range of products—materials, fabricated parts, capital equipment, and nonproduct supplies—are purchased at the plant level. What accounts for this difference between the two groups of companies is essentially the nature of manufacturing operations. Companies in the first group all operate materials-dependent process plants, with those materials purchased to a large extent centrally. Plants at GM, Raytheon, and IBM are typically job-shop or mass-production operations, manufacturing some components, buying others, and assembling these parts into end products. The purchase of fabricated parts is often, but not always, tied directly into the plant locations using those parts and particularly to the engineering groups concerned with the design of component parts. Materials purchases, on the other hand, may be uncoupled organizationally from plant locations.

In all cases, however, a key procurement function at the using-location is to monitor supplier performance and to provide feedback leading to corrective action (in the case of poor quality and late delivery) and to adjustments in purchasing strategies (changing suppliers or shifting volume from one supplier to others).

Purchasing Department Organization

The organization of line purchasing reflects first, of course, the amount of buying activity, with larger operations exhibiting a high degree of specialization by function and by type of purchase. Such an operation would be the procurement department for one of IBM's large manufacturing plants (Figure 5.6). This organization had over 200 people and processed in excess of 65,000 orders each year amounting to about $80 million, with some 14,000 vendors. The organization chart shows two purchasing groups, one for mechanical and electrical product parts and another for nonproduct items and laboratory equipment. In addition, there is an engineering interface group, Supplier Technical Assistance, and an administrative group, Plans and Controls.

Figure 5.6 *Procurement Organization—INTERNATIONAL BUSINESS MACHINES, South Bend/Mishawaka*

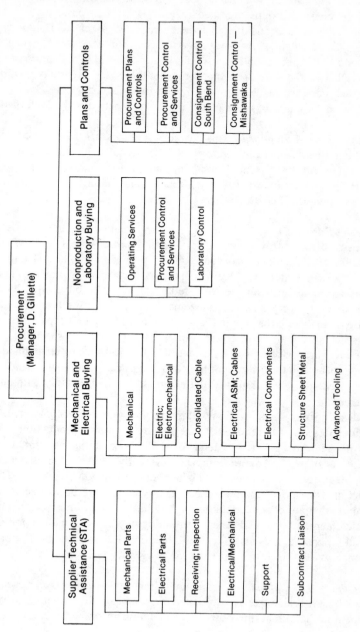

Usually, the structuring of a purchasing organization reflects the unique nature of the activity to which it is attached. But in general, the ways in which personnel in large purchasing groups are specialized reflect three basic factors: (1) the different skills needed and the experience required to buy different types of products, (2) the nature of the supply industry, of characteristic negotiating modes, and of ongoing supplier-customer relations, and (3) the nature of internal relations, that is, the kind of involvement that the buyer might have with managers in such departments as engineering and manufacturing.

In addition, at least six types of buying assignments may be identified.

1. *Product Parts—Standard*. This category includes off-the-shelf components often ordered routinely from catalogs. Knowledge of potential suppliers and of the lines they offer is essential as is an aptitude for handling high paperwork flows. Buyers have important working relationships internally with production-control personnel in manufacturing.

2. *Product Parts—Custom*. Sourcing parts and components made to user specifications is different from sourcing for standard parts. A major part of the work is managing the relations between external supplier and internal engineering groups, involving extensive development work and frequent engineering change orders, as well as stringent delivery requirements. The buyer's skills are described as being along general management lines. He or she typically develops expertise in analyzing the supplier's production facilities and capabilities as well as his financial condition and management strength. He or she needs to have mastered techniques of cost analysis and will find it useful to understand and be able to contribute to the drafting of long and complicated contracts. In addition, it may be essential to be technically skilled and to work effectively with engineering personnel.

A subcategory of specialization within this area may be subcontracts. Subcontract purchases are differentiated by degree from custom production parts purchases in the respect that they tend to be larger in dollar amount, especially schedule sensitive, and more complex. Typically, the most experienced purchasing managers are assigned to subcontracts. At the GM Chevrolet Division, for example, the most experienced buyers are assigned to items like frames and carburetors that are characterized by high dollar-volume, many engineering and schedule changes, long lead times, continuing negotiations with suppliers, high potential for cost savings or, conversely, for penalties associated with purchasing decisions, and the need to perpetuate good supplier relations.

3. *Machinery and Equipment*. As a purchasing category, this typically calls for a degree of technical expertise sufficient to establish the buyer as a qualified participant in the purchasing decision. The dominant influence is often the plant

engineer or laboratory technician. One purchasing manager at IBM commented on the job of the laboratory equipment buyer as follows:

> The labs are very demanding when it comes to response time. The buyers just have to be able to act fast. They deal with small orders and work closely with suppliers who are often model shops. The lab buyer has to be technically competent and understand mechanical sketches . . . .
>
> I think the only time when we suffer is when some lab engineer who is working at the state-of-the-art asks for a piece of equipment. It would help if we had two or three high-powered technical people who could really question what he needed. Occasionally, I suspect, we buy a Cadillac where a Chevrolet would do. A lab engineer can write specifications so that the choice of supplier is very limited. Many times he can have more influence than a manufacturing engineer in choosing a vendor.

4. *Raw Materials*. The importance of purchasing operations with heavy materials usage (metals, agricultural products, chemicals, or plastics) is recognized by assigning one or more specialists to this product area. The expertise required relates to the particular nature of the supply industry and to the nature of negotiating strategies. Nonagricultural-materials industries are typically oligopolistic in nature. Prices tend to be market-determined and negotiations focus, particularly under shortage conditions, on assuring availability of needed supplies. Supplier-relations problems relate to consistency of product quality, delivery, and obtaining technical service.

If the material is a commodity, such as sugar, for which a futures market exists, the company may be involved in buying and selling futures on the exchange. These operations are both complicated and technical, calling for considerable buyer skill and knowledge.

Materials buyers have important responsibilities for assessing the long-run technical, political, and economic trends at work in their assigned industries. Their forecasts are essential for shaping sourcing strategies, making long-term commitments, and determining the materials composition of the end products their companies produce. They, also, have an important responsibility to know the key managers in their industry companies.

5. *Supply Items*. The purchasing of the wide range of products often called MRO (maintenance, repair, and operating supplies) is an area that is often identified for procurement specialization. Included in this category are miscellaneous nonproduct electrical and plumbing supplies, cutting tools and grinding wheels, janitorial supplies, small hand tools, chemicals and office supplies, for example. Like off-the-shelf product parts, MRO buying is characterized by high order-volume with relatively low unit-value. The procurement manager at an IBM development center commented: "Systems and small orders go well to-

gether because we need a systems approach to these small orders, which individually amount to very little, but together add up to millions of dollars each year. One man in that group has already saved us $197,000 by grouping his purchases and placing larger orders with distributors.''

The task is primarily one of managing a high level of requisitioning activity and planning the product scope of supplies contracts to generate effective price and service competition among potential suppliers.

6. *Internally-Sourced Products*. In some procurement departments—GM's Chevrolet Division and Raytheon's Lowell Plant, for example—there are managers assigned especially to negotiate with internal sources of supply. The unusual difficulties of determining transfer prices and of expediting deliveries seem to warrant having purchasing managers for dealing with sister divisions. At the Chevrolet Division, the general purchasing agent in the Central Office put his more experienced buyers on purchasing from GM allied divisions because:

> . . . that's the most sophisticated form of buying, requiring the most skillful negotiating job. We don't have formula transfer prices; in most cases allied divisions don't have any outside competition; we are a captive customer. We insist that prices be supported; they refuse to provide cost data; prices are vigorously negotiated. We generally compare prices paid for similar parts last year with this year's quotations and focus our negotiations on the engineering level and component content of each, and the apparent cost differential.

In addition to the above-described buying assignments a procurement unit may also include certain support functions. For example, built into the structure of large purchasing organizations there may be personnel whose sole function is to relate to engineering units concerned with the design of parts and equipment. One such interface unit was Supplier Technical Assistance (STA) in the procurement organization at a large IBM plant (see Figure 5.6). Its role was described by the procurement manager:

> STA serves several valuable functions internally. They work closely with design engineers in the early phases and have a look at what is coming that will have to be sourced. Then sources can be developed. Being technical men, they are often consulted by the design engineers to determine the procurability of what is being designed. STA personnel also work on qualifying outside sources, appraising vendor capacity, and providing technical assistance.
>
> Another important role they have is to act as a buffer between IBM technical people and vendors. The fact that I have engineers in Purchasing considerably reduces the tendency for engineers to work directly with vendors' engineers. If we can give our engineers good service, they'll come through us.

Purchasing organizations may have their own resources for a wide range of other purposes. A plans and controls function may provide administrative services, budgeting, and financial controls. It may be responsible for monitoring purchasing work-load processing to assure that plant requirements are met on schedule. It may also maintain accounting records on parts, materials, and equipment that have been consigned to suppliers. Another responsibility sometimes given to such a control group, or to a separate unit, is cost estimating for purposes of setting purchase-price targets and appraising purchasing performance.

Procurement staffs may also include legal experts specializing on contract terms and provisions. At Raytheon, for example, an attorney in the Corporate Procurement Staff organization was responsible for legal reviews of subcontracts to assure compliance with government regulations and commercial law. In 1975, this person reviewed 730 subcontracts totaling over $625 million. Finally, among the purchasing departments studied at least two included the sale of scrap as a procurement-department function.

As in any organizational structure, procurement specialization has evolved in a way that helps purchasing to meet and cope with the challenges of the external supply-environment and the internal user-groups. It deals with a technical world and one in which skills in negotiating both externally and internally are essential to good economic performance.

The Locus of Buying Groups

As the previous section indicates, the location of the purchasing function, or line-buying, will vary tremendously depending on a range of factors. Buying groups are found at the corporate level and at use (plant, laboratory, office) locations. In addition, as at Chevrolet, they are located at division headquarters. In some instances purchasing functions are positioned in one division (the primary-user division) to serve that division and others as well. For example, Chevrolet bought frames for all General Motors car divisions. At IBM, a components procurement group in one of the manufacturing divisions was responsible for buying electronic components for other IBM manufacturing operations.

Purchasing groups may be established to serve operations in a particular geographic area. When General Motors acted to realign procurement organization, an early move was the establishment of Regional Nonproduct Purchasing—Flint Area. This operation would serve eleven GM facilities in Flint, operated by six different divisions. A buying organization of about seventy people would be responsible for supplies purchases totaling more than $500 million.

Finally, purchasing operations may be attached to particular programs. General Foods Central Engineering Services, which had responsibility for planning and constructing plant facilities and for the procurement of capital equipment, had its own purchasing function. Buyers were assigned to particular project teams to work closely with engineering personnel.

There is an inherent logic to the organizational positioning of buying units. The logic is based on purchasing strategy and the nature of the relationship between the supplier and the customer. Seven factors are relevant.

1. *Commonality of requirements* is a primary consideration. Several using-locations within or across divisions having common requirements is the basis for centralized purchasing. Relevant illustrations are packaging, sugar, and food chemicals at General Foods; steel and work gloves at General Motors; tantalum capacitors and hand tools at Raytheon; energy and hydrocarbons at PPG. Interestingly enough, at PPG a major part of the rationale for establishing a Corporate Supply Department was to gain buying economies from pooling orders of items needed by two or more divisions. Looking back on the move, however, the vice-president of supply reflected that this anticipated benefit had not materialized because there were significant differences in grade and quality required by each division for its volume purchases. Moreover, the purchasing records were not available with which to determine whether there was commonality.

By contrast, user-unique requirements tend to be satisfied by the user-location purchasing function. The base cabinet designed to go with a high-speed printer at IBM was purchased from outside suppliers by the buying group at the plant that made the printer. Buying a piece of laboratory equipment at an IBM development center would be the responsibility of procurement at that location.

The ability to standardize is a prerequisite for centralized buying. A major concern on the part of purchasing people at the division level in General Motors in setting up Regional Nonproduct Purchasing—Flint was that it would be exceedingly difficult to standardize on the wide range of supply items used at the eleven plants and to develop common codes for identification, ordering, and inventory control in a computerized information system. In fact, it would be difficult, they alleged, to gain acceptance for standardization among plant operating personnel.

Efforts to centralize seem therefore to begin with an accurate definition of requirements and preferences at user-locations and then move to develop standard specifications that may be used as the basis for the pooling of requirements. If standardization across a whole category of purchases is difficult, then a central buying-group may well settle for picking off the high-volume items, developing common standards for them, and negotiating contracts that may then be ordered on by all user-locations.

2. *Cost-saving potential* is usually a core reason, if not the full justification, for centralized buying, and clearly it is an important benefit. The potential derives from being able to support purchasing specialists who have in-depth product and supply-industry knowledge. At user-locations, small amounts of low-volume

items may not be noticed in the buying office. Speaking of work gloves, one administrator in nonproduct purchasing department in the GM Central Office noted: "To many buyers a glove is a glove is a glove. Some don't even know what sort of gloves they are buying and they have to telephone their suppliers to find out."

Cost-saving potential derives, as well, from having a large dollar base for negotiating with suppliers. And in fact, standardization offers some cost savings through economizing on inventory and spare-parts back-up and the ability to move excess supplies, materials, and equipment across department lines to fill needs in other locations.

As a political consideration, it seems to be exceedingly difficult to support moves to take away buying responsibility from decentralized purchasing-operations unless it can be demonstrated that there can be significant cost savings. As one corporate contract-specialist stated: "There has to be a clear advantage in going to a corporate contract. Otherwise it is better to leave it to the divisions and stress the local service angle and the flexibility in competitive bidding. You wouldn't win the battles up the line or with the divisions if the savings were only marginal."

3. *The nature of the supply environment* is a relevant factor in the positioning of purchasing responsibility. If, as noted earlier, the supply industry is oligopolistic in structure, it may suit purchasing strategy to negotiate with suppliers from a single point. Then bargaining takes place between countervailing powers. The buying firm develops a unified posture toward the supply industry and the individual firms that make it up. It is able to mass its purchasing power not only to negotiate favorable terms, but to get good service at user-locations, to assure long-term product availability, to encourage the development of new supplier capacity, and to influence suppliers to hold down price increases.

No such reason exists for centralizing purchases from small suppliers. Centralized purchasing managers may buy often from small suppliers, but for other reasons.

If the supply industry is such that a corporation must make substantial long-term commitments purchasing is centralized usually at the corporate level so that top management may maintain a degree of control and influence over sourcing strategy. It is relevant to note here that if sourcing arrangements are politically sensitive, as for example, in dealing with certain foreign countries, they might well be monitored at top management levels. As mentioned earlier, this has been a consideration in some of the recent moves, such as at PPG Industries, to centralize large purchases of materials at headquarters levels.

With direct purchases from U.S. steel companies amounting to roughly $3 billion in 1974, General Motors commitments to this industry would clearly be of top management concern. When GM began to source large amounts of steel from foreign mills in 1970, managers at the highest level were also involved. In late 1972, when the decision was taken to phase out foreign purchases that, again, was a matter of top corporate policy. Further, in working as they are with individual steel companies to encourage plant expansion sufficient to meet steel demand in the 1980s, and if GM purchasing managers must give even implied long-term purchasing commitments, that becomes a significant factor in GM corporate sourcing strategy. Thus, it was consistent with the need for top management inputs to strategy formulation at GM that a top level Procurement Policy Group was established in early 1975.

4. *The economic use of scarce purchasing-resources* as a major advantage is stressed in every proposal to develop centralized procurement functions or to centralize the purchase of some particular group of products. Having a broader dollar-volume base of purchases to support the development of buying expertise has already been mentioned. There are other kinds of resources that may be affordable, as well, such as engineers qualified to work as interfaces with engineering groups in user-locations to evaluate applications and then select potential sources. Another specialized resource might be a cost estimating unit that analyzes available data on suppliers' labor, overhead and raw material costs, and industry cost-price trends, for purposes of negotiating with suppliers and setting targets for buyers.

Purchasing personnel who develop a specialization in particular supply industries, such as steel, wheat, fresh produce, or soda ash tend to have long years of experience in their special fields. Apparently that is essential to developing an in-depth understanding of basic supply industries and an ability to negotiate effectively. These managers are truly scarce resources and using their competence to the fullest advantage inevitably leads toward centralization.

5. *The extent of engineering involvement in procurement decision-making* is an important determinant of the locus of line-buying activities. Engineers may be heavily involved in determining the specifications of procured parts and materials, in qualifying prospective suppliers and in working with vendors on production problems. Engineering participation in purchasing is likely to be especially intense in the design and early production stages of purchased parts and equipment, in construction projects and in the selection of machinery. Engineering involvement is also heavy where the design of the end product (and, therefore, of purchased components and materials) is continually evolving. Such would be the case, for example, for automobiles, computers, and defense systems.

In such cases, it is advantageous for purchasing to be in close organizational and physical proximity to engineering so that buyers may work closely with technical personnel in (1) the initial screening of potential suppliers, (2) the development of product specifications to reflect purchase-cost and supply-availability factors, (3) the negotiation of price, delivery schedules, and other terms, and (4) the monitoring of vendor performance.

6. The *order and usage patterns* for purchased parts, materials and supplies is also clearly an influence in where line-buying is located organizationally. In the case of a wide range of *standard supply-items delivered in small volumes,* purchasing activities seem to be at or near the user-locations. The essential requirement is that the purchase and use functions be in close geographic proximity. The reasons are several. First, the sources from which purchasing managers buy, usually distributors, typically operate on a local or regional basis. Normally, distributors are a more convenient source for such items than manufacturers because distributors usually carry wide lines of related products.

Second, usage for supply-items tends to be unpredictable and the needs immediate. Having local stocks from which quick delivery may be made is important. Purchasing managers may negotiate contracts for a range of supplies and either they or users may place orders randomly. Third, concerned as they are about community relations, plant, office, and laboratory managers will often wish to support local business.

Thus, the purchasing of supply items is typically the province of buyers at user-locations and what centralization there is seems always to be regional in nature. *High-volume standard supply-items,* however, may be purchased centrally from manufacturers or resellers who operate nationally. Usage levels are more predictable.

With regard to *product parts and materials,* the picture is less clear. The currently-accepted materials management concept would lead toward the idea that purchasing and production should be closely linked at the plant level. The materials management concept suggests that purchasing is one part of a flow system involving incoming materials, parts, and supplies; manufacturing and processing operations; in-plant inventory management, physical distribution and the maintenance of stocks of finished goods at field locations. Consistent with this idea many plant purchasing managers report to materials managers who may also have responsibility for production scheduling and control and for in-plant inventory management. Purchasing and production control proximity may be useful for making trade-offs between minimizing costs that are a function of production flows, on the one hand, and purchasing at the lowest prices, on the other. The latter would tend to dictate buying in large quantities on a regular basis. Optimizing production schedules, however, tends to lead to more small-order and cyclical purchasing in order to minimize inventory carrying costs and the risk of obsolescence. A materials manager may control this conflict in priorities, which otherwise would move up to the plant manager's or general manager's office for resolution.

A related line of argument supporting the idea that product-parts and materials purchasing should be positioned at the plant level is that the procurement function directly affects manufacturing cost-performance and should be directly controlled by the plant manager. According to the executive in charge of purchasing at the GM Central Office: "Product purchases are regular and the plant people, including both engineering and manufacturing, are much more sensitive to them. Nonproduct is not regular, is less sensitive; doesn't get so much attention."

The manager in charge of product purchases at the Chevrolet Division Central Office agreed that particular significance was attached to product purchasing because "it goes into the vehicle; continuity of production is critical; quality is important; supplier dependability is critical; more purchasing dollars are spent on product buying; more day-to-day problems of real urgency arise in connection with product purchases; there are greater risks and possibilities of strikes and disasters; and GM has very large tooling investments in vendor plants making product components, parts and materials."

Such considerations notwithstanding, the fact is that these companies seem to be moving toward centralized purchasing of product materials and of certain component parts. Apparently the advantages of centralized procurement having to do with (1) cost-saving potential; (2) ability to negotiate effectively with suppliers; and (3) the economic use of scarce purchasing-resources outweigh any loss from uncoupling organizationally the purchasing and production functions.

While there are advantages in locating product purchasing at the plant in close proximity to production control, if a choice has to be made, it seems that positioning product purchasing close to engineering is more important. In the case of the GM Chevrolet Division the great bulk of purchased parts was sourced out of division headquarters where Chevrolet engineering was located rather than at the assembly plants.

In any case, centralizing product purchasing for several plant locations may offer gains through building a fully-staffed purchasing operation with diverse skills. Having a more skillful procurement group with a broader base of purchases from which to negotiate may well outweigh any possible loss that comes from physically uncoupling the product-purchasing and production-control functions. Coordinating inflows of purchased parts with production schedules does not necessarily depend on having procurement at the plant site.

7. *The nature of the firm's relationships with its customers* is a consideration that may in some instances have a bearing on the location of purchasing. Raytheon is heavily engaged in defense contracts for the federal government and subcontractors must often be approved by Raytheon's military customer. The customer may then want a direct relationship with a procurement manager who is at the plant where the prime contract is being carried out and who is responsible for subcontracting activities on that specific project.

Figure 5.7 summarizes the factors that affect the organizational location of line purchasing activities. It suggests that in today's environment there are strong pressures leading toward increased centralization of buying in large, decentralized corporations, but that in the last analysis, organizational positioning is a matter of the type of purchase, the nature of the supply industry, and supplier-buyer relationships.

Figure 5.7   *Factors Affecting Purchasing Centralization/Decentralization*

Decentralization	Centralization
High engineering involvement in procurement decision making	High commonality of use; ability to standardize
High need to mesh purchased-parts inflows with production schedules	Concern for long-term supply availability; high corporate commitment levels
High need for local service for small quantities with unpredictable usage patterns	High need for bargaining power to secure supplies and negotiate prices
User-unique requirements	Political sensitivity
Significant customer influence over sourcing strategies and supplier selection	High procurement staffing requirements; high need for specialized purchasing skills and knowledge

6 Sourcing Decision-Making Processes: The Influence of Measurement Systems

The key decisions in sourcing are: (1) what are the product specifications, (2) will it be made in the plant or purchased from outside vendors, (3) if purchased, what vendor or vendors will be selected, and (4) what price will be paid and what are the terms of the buyer/seller relationship. These decisions, clearly, are not made by purchasing managers alone. They involve managers in the major functional areas of manufacturing, engineering, marketing, and finance. Functional area managers exercise varying degrees of influence over sourcing decisions and in different ways, depending on the nature of the product being sourced, the stage of the procurement cycle, and the extent of their interests.

Another key factor shaping procurement decisions is the whole measurement and regulatory structure within which procurement managers function. To a large extent purchasing rules, regulations, and measurement systems emanate from top leadership in the procurement function itself as a means of imposing professional discipline on day-to-day decision-making. This discipline is reinforced through internal auditing processes to assure adherence to established rules and procedures. Procurement regulations, audits and performance-measurement systems reflect values imposed on the purchasing function by corporate and division management and by functional-area management. Thus, procurement values are derived from the orientations, policies, strategies, and values of the enterprise or institution.

In this chapter the procurement performance-measurements, regulations, and audit procedures as factors influencing procurement decision-making are discussed. Chapter 7 considers the interfunctional decision-making systems within organizations, which operate in making sourcing choices.

Procurement Performance-Measures

Any system for measuring managerial performance is important, not so much because it provides a basis for rating performance, but because it imposes certain sets of priorities on the decision-making process. Managers in purchasing and in other functions, as well, will naturally behave in a way that maximizes their records of achievement in accordance with the ways they are measured.

Purchasing measures vary considerably in nature, both from one company to another, and, within companies, according to the nature of the particular operations or functions that purchasing serves. Thus, the primacy of values in any procurement group, as reflected in its goals and measures, seems largely to be determined by the missions of the operating units to which it is attached. That is not at all surprising since procurement is perceived largely as a service function.

Looking across different companies, it can be seen that purchasing measures focus largely on six areas of performance:

(1) facilitating the mission of the user-location in such ways as assuring on-time deliveries of purchased parts and materials of the required quality.
(2) negotiating acceptable prices.
(3) for individual buyers, conforming to purchasing functional area norms and expectations.
(4) conforming to corporate policies in such areas as doing business with minority-owned enterprises and with equal employment opportunity employers.
(5) managing the resources pertinent to sourcing, such as consigned tooling and materials in vendor locations.
(6) managing purchasing overhead expenses.

In any situation the first two categories are of primary importance and in that order. The third is everpresent, and the remaining three may or may not be relevant depending on the nature of the enterprise and the extent of development of its purchasing-measurement system.

Asked how he was evaluated, Robards, the glass buyer at Heinz USA, stated that one measure was Heinz's cost of bottles compared with what competitors paid. He believed that he performed well on this count, based on information occasionally supplied to him by vendors' salesmen. A second measure was the number of complaints he received from the plants about glass supplier quality and service.

More formal measures were based on the amount Robards saved in purchasing costs each year by:

(1) Negotiating prices below forecasted price levels.
(2) Bottle redesigns that result in cost reductions.
(3) Negotiated savings in inbound freight.
(4) Getting suppliers to postpone scheduled price increases.

In addition, Robards typically made commitments to his superior to achieve certain nonquantifiable objectives such as bringing in new suppliers.

Robard's immediate superior, when asked how the glass function was appraised, stated: "The most important thing is to keep the plants operating."

Adams, the vice-president of manufacturing and development, appraised the purchasing function on three criteria:

The first is *sourcing* and here we do very well. When almost everybody else was running out we did not lose half a shift. Years of painstaking relation-building paid off. The second is *price negotiation* and here we have room for improvement. We have been training our people in the art of negotiation but we still have some way to go. I want us to be opportunistic and entrepreneurial in the purchasing area. The attitude has always been "We must have top quality goods." Well, I agree with that; we must retain our reputation. I want to change the attitude though, in the buying process so that we measure quality by what comes out—our product—and not just by what goes in. If we can maintain the same quality product but use other ingredients, then we should. The third criterion on which I judge procurement is by the amount and quality of the *research* they produce. If you are to be a major buyer in any field, you must have a deep economic understanding of that field.

The following description of GM's purchasing performance measurement comes from Mann, who at the time was the director of purchases at the Chevrolet Division, the top ranking purchasing manager in GM's largest division:

The Chevrolet General Manager appraises the purchasing organization, first, on maintaining continuity of operations; it costs many, many thousands of dollars to shut an assembly plant down for a day. Second, he's concerned about integrity and business ethics; our reputation is the most important thing we have. Third, paying the market price; we have to be sure we buy competitively. Now that there is excess supplier capacity we have to be sure we go out on "general inquiry" for every part we buy. That is, we have to be sure we get bids on everything. Normally, we do this annually but when shortages hit us last year we couldn't find suppliers and we tended to extend the contracts we had simply to hold our positions with our sources.

At the buyer level, the assistant purchasing agent grades his buyers on the type of sources he develops, control of sources, negotiating skills and meeting schedules. It's all very subjective. Buyers are judged too, on the way they support their recommendations (in writing), on the contributions to GM from their suppliers, on supplier reliability and on watching supplier loading carefully.

According to MacCarter, a general purchasing agent who reported to Mann and later succeeded him, the measure of buyer performance hinged significantly on results:

Buyers are measured in terms of how their decisions have, in fact, worked out. Another factor is how they handle trouble: their ability to appraise situations; move tooling from one vendor's plant, if he's not performing, to another source without impairing production; to cultivate new sources to overcome limited product capacity. We also look at the extent of cost savings achieved through the Product Cost Review Program—this is not always a true measure as some product categories offer greater cost-saving potential than others, but it offers evidence of the buyer's ingenuity.

Other considerations: Does the buyer run an orderly office? Does he slip up? Is he responsive to late releasing—establishing competent sources to meet production schedules? Does he maintain good follow-up and handle problems in a timely manner; does he have a sense of urgency? Does he have good rapport with engineering, quality control, other departments and vendors? How well is he prepared at meetings? Are his summaries on which he bases award decisions thorough? Has he checked all aspects of a situation such as suppliers' management capability, financial status, capacity, technical know-how, equipment load, workload?

Actually, there are many things that make a good buyer. I can tell you who my good buyers are right away, but it's not easy to mechanize the evaluation, and I'm not sure a mechanized or computerized evaluation would or could measure a buyer's total performance capabilities. We go far less by the numbers and much more by the quality of the job. We evaluate performance and make appraisals all the way up the line as buying decisions move along for review and approval. We look for resourcefulness, ingenuity, responsiveness and integrity.

The manager of purchasing at one of Raytheon's large plants made this comment about buyer performance measurement:

The right source is important, the right price is important, but also the right agreement with the source is important. The key terms of agreement involve access to accounting data, to inspect plants and expedite work when necessary, and to make suggestions for improvement of the subcontractors' efforts when possible. Often the contracts are fixed price and don't provide legal provisions to grant us these rights. We must negotiate rights with vendors in order to do our job for our clients.

I evaluate buyers the same way I am evaluated. That is 1) do they keep us out of trouble in scheduling and delivery, 2) do they get good quality from the vendors they use, and 3) do they get us a good price—were many vendors solicited and was the situation as competitive as is possible and practical under the circumstances. Since we are buying many sophisticated items, a lot of our problems are ones of expediting, and we are organized to bring to light problems with vendors before they become serious.

Serving User-Location Needs. Clearly the dominant measure of purchasing performance in manufacturing locations is its ability to keep the plants running. Line stoppages for reason of vendor failure to deliver parts and materials of suitable quality on time is perceived as a cardinal failure of the purchasing function. At Heinz USA, for example, performance of glass-bottle suppliers was monitored through weekly reports that the glass buyer received from manufacturing. These reports contained information by plant, production line, and type of bottle on such matters as late deliveries, level of defects (blisters in the glass; inaccurate bottle capacity; faulty in-bound containerization) in incoming shipments based on sampling inspections and the number of breaks per million dozen on the filling lines. Suppliers were informed of deficiencies immediately and once a year each was given a summary report showing performance on quality against that of other Heinz glass suppliers, who were unnamed in the report. These reports were certainly the most important measure of the Heinz glass-buyer's performance. No other factor, including price, was likely to be more important.

By comparison, in purchasing for a laboratory such measures would not be at all relevant. To support a research and development mission, purchasing's primary goal may simply be to have specified equipment and supplies on hand when needed to meet the requirements of technical personnel. On-time delivery would, also, be a key performance measurement consideration in purchasing plant equipment since delays on one item could cause the entire construction schedule to slip.

Buying at Favorable Prices. Among the missions of user-locations that are reflected in purchasing measures is meeting end product competition in the market place. The ability to do so, of course, will depend significantly on the cost of purchased parts and materials. At IBM, the Corporate Component Procurement organization, among others, was required to make and meet five-year price commitments on purchased components. These commitments were essential in arriving at the price-to-the-market for the products IBM made and sold. At companies like Heinz and General Foods the prices of major purchased ingredients such as sugar, vegetables, fruits, and meats, as well as packaging, are significant determinants of end product prices, of margins, and of competitive strength in the marketplace.

Price considerations may weigh heavily as a measure of purchasing performance in such cases. They are less important when the purchased product is a new material, a newly designed component, or a costly piece of equipment where the possibilities as well as the costs of failure are judged by engineers, production managers, and buyers to be relatively high. Similarly, price is of lesser importance as a measure in the case of nonproduct supplies and other small overhead items while delivery may be critical.

Purchase-price performance measures, nevertheless, seem to be perceived within the procurement organization as having high value although that may not be consistent with the priorities of user-locations. The stress that procurement regulations and audits place on soliciting bids and awarding the contract to the low-bidder seeks to assure that purchases will always be made for the lowest possible cost unless there are compelling reasons to the contrary.

Purchase-price measures, however, seem at best to be measures of price acceptability rather than optimization. Did the buyer take the low bid? Was the price paid no higher than what competitors paid, to the extent that that can be determined? Was the price paid a fair one?

Purchase-cost performance may also be measured in terms of lowering purchase costs below what they might have been in the absence of certain initiatives on the part of the purchasing managers by:

- negotiating a final price below the lowest bid in a competitive-bidding procedure.
- negotiating prices at or below those indicated by independently-generated target prices based on estimates of vendor costs.
- successfully persuading a market leader to postpone or cancel a price increase, and buying below forecast price-levels.
- introducing and gaining internal acceptance for a cost-saving improvement, i.e., changing the design of a purchased part or substituting a lower-cost material.
- negotiating prices lower than those paid for goods of like quality and in like amount under a prior contract.
- negotiating to receive the benefits of a supplier cost-saving in the form of lower prices.

Measures of such achievements can be readily quantified and seem highly motivating to individual buyers whose directions come from the chain-of-command within purchasing itself.

Conforming to Purchasing Norms. So much of the evaluation of individual buyers, as the General Motors statements in particular indicate, is qualitative in nature. Basically, it amounts to an assessment of whether or not the purchasing manager reflects the values of the functional area in what he/she does. Ability to maintain good relations, for example, with both suppliers and internal groups, is highly regarded. Thoroughness, resourcefulness, initiative, integrity, and handling difficult problems with as little disruption to operations as possible are all well-respected qualities of buyers.

The ability to develop new sources has high value because of the contributions new suppliers may make to purchased-product quality, service, and lowered costs. Buyer skill is demonstrated in locating potential vendors, qualifying them, interesting them in bidding, and then persuading user-locations to try them. This last may be particularly difficult unless there is general dissatisfaction with the existing vendor complex.

Conforming to Corporate Policies. With purchasing expenditures reaching one-half to three-quarters of sales dollars in many companies, the purchasing function may be a powerful factor in shaping corporate relations and the corporate outside image. Purchasing measures will typically have the effect of charging that function with acting in a way that builds relations with local communities, national governments, and the supplier system at large. Purchasing organizations may have targets for allocating business to minority-owned companies, for contracting only with equal employment opportunity vendors, or for seeking to purchase from vendors in areas where the company markets its products. In fact, some customers, particularly U.S. government agencies, may impose these standards as a condition of buying from its suppliers. In meeting this set of measures, purchasing managers are understandably reluctant to compromise what seem to be their more important objectives: buying goods of required quality at the lowest prices. Considerable effort may then be devoted to helping a particular class of vendors to become cost-competitive and able to meet the company's requirements. At Raytheon, one manager in the corporate procurement organization is responsible for developing and implementing affirmative action programs within Raytheon operating divisions. The main purpose of the program is to encourage and develop competent minority and small business vendors who could successfully provide resources (materials, components, or labor) on a long-term basis. Among the problems with which Anderson, manager of minority vendor relations, had to cope were the following:

(1) These types of businesses often exhibited considerable passivity and reluctance in seeking business in large companies such as Raytheon, and had to be encouraged to submit bids. Many were not taking action to become aware of business opportunities.

(2) These types of businesses were often inadequately financed to handle other than small contracts, and they maintained limited inventories and small, often inadequate, facilities.

(3) Many lacked knowledge of how to submit a bid or how to estimate properly, or how to control contract costs.

(4) Several were judged to be weak in such areas as scheduling and meeting delivery dates for large purchases, or keeping to rigid specifications.

In implementing the program, Anderson encouraged plant buyers to set and to achieve goals for purchases from these types of business whenever possible. Either he, or the buyers, or both became involved in working with the vendors to overcome their problems, and to become viable competitive entities. Anderson indicated that past experience with such vendors resulted in some 70 to 75 percent repeat business. "We give them small contracts to encourage them along, but hope they will soon be able to compete on their own and become capable of performing without assistance from companies such as ourselves. If I do my job properly, I should work myself out of a job in two to three years."

Managing Resources and Controlling Expenses. If it is the practice of the company to consign tooling and/or materials to vendors, the responsibility for buying and accounting for these resources typically falls on purchasing. Purchasing may also have management responsibility for inventories of vendor-produced goods. Accountability for these assets is included in the measurement system.

Purchasing is also evaluated as a functional area in terms of its ability to control its own overheads and to stay within its expense budget. At some IBM locations, Corporate Components Procurement being one, purchasing expenses are translated into a percentage procurement burden rate. Purchasing overheads are then allocated to CCP's internal customers in proportion to the dollar amounts of goods they source through CCP. The procurement burden rate was added as a surcharge to the price paid to outside vendors, for internal accounting purposes. The use of a procurement burden rate tends to have a motivating effect on the purchasing organization to take initiatives in building its volume base (as a way of lowering the percentage rate) and, at the same time, of supporting the overheads of skilled personnel. Consistent with this idea, CCP had a New Products group in its organization that took new developments to potential IBM user-customers as a way of generating more procurement business. Using a procurement burden rate as part of a measurement system motivates the purchasing personnel to be more proactive as opposed to reacting to the demands placed upon it.

In sum, purchasing department and purchasing manager performances are subjected to a wide range of measures. The primary directions of buying behavior stem from the goals, measures, and values of the user-location the particular purchasing group serves. After that, and to the extent that purchasing is organizationally remote from user-locations, purchasing values and norms become important. Corporate policies imposed on purchasing activities is a third source of influence reflected in purchasing measures and represent "hurdle" requirements. That is, certain minimum standards must be met and purchasing procedures carried out in certain ways. Altogether the measurement system is a powerful influence on procurement choices and buyer behavior.

Procurement Regulations and Audits

Procurement audits and the rules and regulations on which they are based provide elaborate screens for reviewing purchasing activities. Audits may be performed by procurement management of its own activities or conducted as one part of overall finance and control audits by the internal audit staff of a comptrollers department.

The structure of the audit will often be based on formal procurement policies and procedures manuals that describe in great detail the regulations governing purchasing activities. Figure 6.1 is taken from a General Motors Central Office audit form that lists 37 different points for internal auditors to check when reviewing purchasing departments in the plants and divisions.

At GM, however, audits were not always so detailed. Until 1960, according to the GM general auditor at the Central Office, the policy statements governing the purchasing function at GM were very broad and general. In that year, purchasing became the focus of considerable attention at least in part because of the widespread exposure in the press to procurement irregularities at Chrysler. The Chrysler president was discovered to be placing large orders for Chrysler with a company in which he had a significant interest. After 1960, GM developed a considerably more formal and detailed policies and procedures structure that was promulgated in the 1962 purchasing policy manual. These policies were intended to put purchasing personnel firmly in charge of all buying. Until 1962 other functional areas did a great deal of purchasing: master mechanics bought machinery and equipment and works engineers contracted for construction.

A study of the range of items often covered in procurement regulations and audits suggests five broad areas of concern:

1. Conflicts of interest. To the extent possible, audits probe for situations where buyers may be taking bribes from suppliers or in any other way having a personal interest in favoring one supplier over another.
2. Assurance of competition. Regulations typically require that for any purchase over a certain minimal amount, the buyer must get bids in writing from three different suppliers and must award the business to the low qualified bidder. In the event that either of these conditions is not met for any reason, there must be documentation in the files for subsequent audit, explaining the reasons for the exception. The effort to assure competition extends, too, to laying down exact procedures for soliciting and receiving bids.

Figure 6.1 *Excerpt from Audit Form—GENERAL MOTORS*

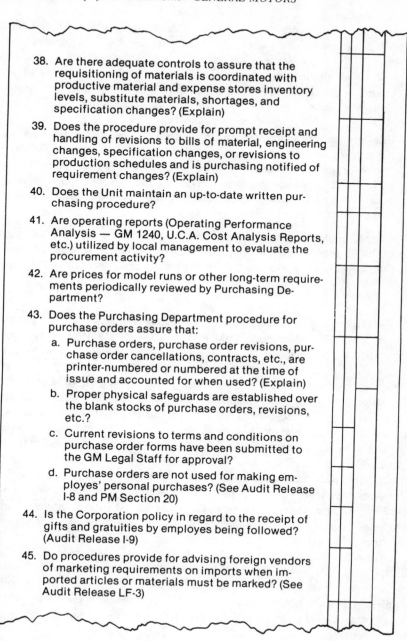

38. Are there adequate controls to assure that the requisitioning of materials is coordinated with productive material and expense stores inventory levels, substitute materials, shortages, and specification changes? (Explain)

39. Does the procedure provide for prompt receipt and handling of revisions to bills of material, engineering changes, specification changes, or revisions to production schedules and is purchasing notified of requirement changes? (Explain)

40. Does the Unit maintain an up-to-date written purchasing procedure?

41. Are operating reports (Operating Performance Analysis — GM 1240, U.C.A. Cost Analysis Reports, etc.) utilized by local management to evaluate the procurement activity?

42. Are prices for model runs or other long-term requirements periodically reviewed by Purchasing Department?

43. Does the Purchasing Department procedure for purchase orders assure that:

   a. Purchase orders, purchase order revisions, purchase order cancellations, contracts, etc., are printer-numbered or numbered at the time of issue and accounted for when used? (Explain)

   b. Proper physical safeguards are established over the blank stocks of purchase orders, revisions, etc.?

   c. Current revisions to terms and conditions on purchase order forms have been submitted to the GM Legal Staff for approval?

   d. Purchase orders are not used for making employes' personal purchases? (See Audit Release I-8 and PM Section 20)

44. Is the Corporation policy in regard to the receipt of gifts and gratuities by employes being followed? (Audit Release I-9)

45. Do procedures provide for advising foreign vendors of marketing requirements on imports when imported articles or materials must be marked? (See Audit Release LF-3)

3. Documentation. Purchasing personnel are charged with keeping complete files on each contract award or purchase.
4. Conformance to corporate policies. As mentioned earlier, the manner in which corporate dollars are spent on purchased parts, materials, and supplies immensely affects the corporation's public posture on local, national and multinational levels. Corporate managers, by means of purchasing regulations and audits, may seek to control purchasing behavior in ways that build corporate relations with outside groups (suppliers, the community, unions, governments, and public interest organizations).
5. Conformance to administrative procedures. Purchasing regulations spell out procedural systems for handling a wide variety of matters. For example, there may be regulations dealing with accounting for company-owned tooling and consigned stocks in vendor locations, scrap and surplus disposal, insurance, vendor payments, handling precious metals, and the treatment of proprietary information.

The IBM Purchasing Manual, for example, dealt with all these areas and more. It listed seventy items that were the subjects of policy definition. According to the director of purchasing the five following areas were the most important.

101. Purchasing Principles. Reference 101 began with a statement of purchasing objectives: ''The objective of IBM Purchasing is to satisfy the corporation's requirements for materials, parts, services and supplies and in doing so, to ensure both the effective expenditure of funds and a desirable company position as a worldwide member of the business community.'' It charged the IBM purchasing organization essentially with responsibility for selecting suppliers, negotiating purchase agreements, and committing funds under contractual arrangements. It acknowledged a responsibility to comply with all applicable government regulations in any country in which IBM did business and to place a significant portion of purchases with small business and with minority-owned companies in the United States. Reference 101 also covered such matters as employee's conflicts of interests (employees may not have any interests as investors or officers in outside organizations that would be in conflict with IBM's best interests); gifts (IBM employees or members of their families could not accept gifts of any type from suppliers or prospective suppliers); reciprocity (shall not be a factor in IBM procurement). There was also a section in Reference 101 on fairness to suppliers indicating that IBM would deal fairly and impartially with suppliers, recognizing their legitimate interests. IBM would extend equal opportunities to all suppliers for presenting products and services; it would seek to maintain good relationships with proven suppliers, to search for new and improved sources, and to use multiple sources.

IBM wanted to be known as a good customer. Purchasing managers believed that having a good reputation often helped in negotiations with suppliers and in encouraging potential vendors to seek IBM business. In an era of shortages, such a reputation might also be helpful.

305. Approval of Commitments. This section in the manual laid out the levels of expenditures that purchasing managers were authorized to commit on any single purchase or contract:

Procurement Manager	$60, 000 and over
Purchasing Manager	up to $60,000
Department Manager	up to $18,000
Senior Buyer[1]	up to $12,000
Buyer[1]	up to $ 6,000
Associate Buyer[1]	up to $ 1,200

1. Line buyers.

315. Supplier Quotations. Reference 315 sought to assure that IBM purchases were made at the lowest available prices, that IBM was being fair to all suppliers, and that both suppliers and IBM employees would be protected from any possibility of collusion or "unfair or improper incidents." It specified that records of purchases had to be maintained for future auditing and that procedures existed for monitoring the frequency and importance of any exceptions to basic principles (such as taking the lowest bid).

Reference 315 required for any one item over $2,000 per year or over $600 per order that a minimum of three competitive quotations be obtained. Exceptions to the requirement had to be documented by the buyer for possible management review.

If any bid except the lowest was accepted, a buyer had to file a statement explaining the reasons for the exception. The above rules did not preclude buyers from conducting further negotiations with successful bidders.

As for purchasing quantities, requests for quotations could not indicate amounts in excess of what IBM was willing to buy. Inquiries to suppliers for other than the purpose of buying (for example, to obtain manufacturing or cost information) were prohibited unless the reason was explicitly stated to the supplier. Legitimate purposes included: (1) to assist in making a make-or-buy decision, (2) to implement a proposal on a government contract, and (3) to evaluate a potential alternate source.

Finally, all incoming bids were to be received, dated and filed by someone other than the buyer and late quotations could be accepted only with the approval of the buyer's manager.

Purchasing managers were encouraged to develop and use international sources and minority suppliers if such sources were competitive. Plant purchasing managers had agreed-upon targets regarding the use of minority suppliers and tried to achieve these in developing new sources.

International sourcing is encouraged for two reasons. The first is to point out to U.S. buyers that there are efficient plants overseas that can produce items at competitive prices. It is in IBM's interest that buyers should be aware of worldwide sourcing possibilities if this leads to lower prices. The second reason is that IBM does business on a worldwide basis, both buying and selling.

322. Supplier Workload Management. IBM purchasing carefully monitored those situations where IBM orders from a single supplier location exceeded $100,000 or 15 percent of that supplier's business. Lists of such vendors and the amount of business each did with IBM in total were prepared semiannually and circulated to all buying locations. In any instances where a bidder on this list was asked to quote, competitive quotations had to be obtained from at least one other potential supplier not on the list.

IBM management's objective was that suppliers should not become overdependent upon IBM business. There was little point in building up a supplier who later went out of business because he lost a contract to another vendor who bid lower. The effect on a community if a supplier highly dependent on IBM business became bankrupt could be hard. Another reason why management wanted to avoid overdependence was explained by the director of purchasing:

> We do not tolerate problems with our buyers being offered gifts, etc. Occasionally it happens and nearly every time it does happen, it involves a supplier who is heavily dependent on IBM. That supplier gets into a position where he just has to have our business. Then he gets desperate.
>
> We want to avoid this type of problem. Sometimes it becomes necessary, especially over a short period, to have a high percentage of a vendor's business. We don't like it and we watch the situation very closely.

Corporate Purchasing Operations maintained a central file of all suppliers so that a supplier could not inadvertently become overdependent on IBM by dealing with several purchasing locations, no one of which need be aware that the vendor was selling to other IBM buyers.

521. Supplier Workload Principles. This section reiterated the principle that no supplier location should become overly dependent on IBM. It went on to state that overdependence was aggravated when: (1) the workload represented a substantial amount of money, (2) it involved technology subject to rapid change, or (3) the work had a high labor content subject to abrupt or large fluctuations. It urged the managements at IBM using-locations to support procurement managers in meeting their responsibilities for developing additional and multiple sources of supply. It required that a point of responsibility at corporate headquarters be established to coordinate buying at multiple IBM locations from an IBM supplier on the workload-control list.

Regulatory systems such as this one are an ever-present feature of the environment in which purchasing managers live and work. They exert a constant influence on procurement decision-making because they establish a certain primacy of values. Corporate interests, buyer objectivity and integrity, fairness to suppliers, and good relations with external groups emerge as high values. At the same time, the system tends to neutralize the influence on procurement decisions of biases introduced through relations with vendors, whether of a personal or business nature.

7 Sourcing Decision-Making Processes: The Involvement of Other Functional Areas

While procurement is generally regarded as the responsibility of the purchasing department, it is, in fact, a shared function in that all areas of management—manufacturing, engineering, marketing, finance and control, legal, and purchasing itself—are involved in procurement decisions. Engineers are vitally concerned with the specifications and performance of vendor-supplied components and materials used in the products they design. They are concerned, as well, with the purchase of laboratory and production equipment since they, typically, are held responsible for the proper functioning of plants and laboratories. Engineering personnel also have a strong interest in the technical competence of suppliers and in their ability to contribute new designs and new process technology to customers.

Manufacturing managers exert strong influence on procurement decision-making. Their involvement reflects their concern for the efficiency of the production process and the extent to which the quality and delivery of purchased parts and materials affects plant performance. They have a vital interest, as well, in decisions about whether particular components and materials will be manufactured in the plants they manage or purchased from outside vendors. These are make-or-buy decisions.

Marketing managers often become part of the decision-making complex when, for one reason or another, changes are proposed in the prices and/or specifications of purchased components, materials, and packaging that may affect the company's competitive posture in the markets it serves. Rising materials prices, for example, may force the company to make a choice between raising the prices of finished products or substituting lower-cost materials. The trade-off is one that may be decided by the implications for the company's marketing of taking one option over the other.

Finance and control managers see in the purchasing function an activity that significantly impacts balance sheets and cash flows. The built-up inventories of supplies waiting to go into production represent one of the greatest financial commitments most organizations make. This commitment level must be monitored and managed in accordance with forecasted sales levels, cost, availability of funds, and the supply outlook. Finance and control managers, as well, often have a voice in make-or-buy decisions and in decisions on transfer prices, the prices at which one division in a company purchases from another.

Purchasing activities must be legally sensitive to at least four areas of concern. The first is conflicts of interest, for example, a buyer accepting favors in return for placing orders with certain suppliers, or an individual buyer or the firm having interests of a financial, business, or personal nature in vendor companies. A second concern is the Robinson-Patman Act that makes it illegal for sellers to offer discriminatory prices and for buyers to induce the seller to offer such a price, or knowingly to accept a lower (discriminatory) price. The Robinson-Patman Act proscribes the practice of offering different prices to customers for goods in like amount and of like quality where the effect may be to lessen competition among those customers by favoring one with a lower price than is quoted to others. A third area of continuing legal scrutiny is reciprocity. This is the practice of using the firm's purchasing power to induce its suppliers to buy the products the firm sells as a condition of continuing to do business with those suppliers. Both the Federal Trade Commission and the Antitrust Division of the Department of Justice vigorously oppose this practice and have successfully moved in the courts to: (1) force divestiture of acquired companies where the merger has given the acquiring company significant power to use reciprocity effectively, and (2) obtain consent decrees from a number of large corporations to discontinue using purchasing power to build sales volume. Finally, lawyers, of course, have a vital interest in the way procurement contracts are drafted, especially in the terms that cover failure to perform and possible consequences for either party of this eventuality. While these are the major areas of legal sensitivity, there are others.

Procurement thus cuts across the entire enterprise, touching the nerves of many other functions and involving them in the procurement decision-making process. Furthermore, the impact on the community, the supply environment, and, international relations of the huge sums of money spent by organizations for goods and services is a matter of primary importance to top corporate managements and government officials at all levels. They, too, will seek to shape purchasing decisions in ways that best serve the broad interests they represent.

Managers in all areas act in ways that reflect the functional performance goals and measures imposed on their respective areas. And sometimes the measures imposed on the procurement function may be incongruent with those to which managers in other functions respond. Thus sourcing decisions that cut across different areas in the enterprise are often worked out through political processes.

In the discussion that follows it will be useful to consider the influences on sourcing decisions that tend to emanate from engineering, production, and marketing as well as from top corporate management. Then the factors that give procurement managers strength in the decision-making process can be considered.

Engineering Involvement

Engineering managers are often involved in determining the specifications of purchased materials and components, and in formally qualifying both vendors and the products that will be purchased from them, especially in companies making highly technical products such as computers and missile systems. Their influence tends also to dominate the processes of defining specifications for new capital equipment and making the final purchase decision.

Product assurance (the testing of purchased parts and materials) and vendor qualification are often long and expensive procedures. Their sole purpose is to insure the ultimate performance of the end product. It seems important, then, to preserve the objectivity of the qualification function by not subordinating it to manufacturing, marketing, and purchasing considerations at that stage. The qualifications process, however, becomes the initial screen in source selection, and in effect determines how many and which vendors the procurement manager may count on for bidding and negotiating purposes.

In the purchase of capital equipment, engineering tends to be responsive to production interests in having trouble-free manufacturing processes. Engineering will therefore favor suppliers whose products have performed satisfactorily in the past, and avoid those vendors whose products have posed service and operating problems. As for the latter, engineers seem to have long memories! Engineering personnel involved in equipment purchasing also will favor suppliers with whom they have built up smoothly-working technical relationships. Inevitably, there is a high level of technical interchange with suppliers on design and service matters in equipment purchasing.

Delivery is also a major consideration in vendor selection. An equipment purchase is often made as part of a larger project, such as an expansion of plant capacity or the construction of a new facility. Delivery schedule on a particular piece of equipment is then related to the schedule for the overall project. Delays in the receipt of one machine may easily cause a stretch-out of the overall project at considerable cost.

Regarding price sensitivity, as a general rule, engineers do not seem to be price-buyers, giving much greater priority to delivery and assurance of good performance. This assurance comes from prior experience with the supplier or knowing the vendor by reputation, or even from having had an involvement in the equipment-design process. While price considerations may be the deciding factor between two or more equally-qualified suppliers, more often one supplier is favored for reasons of the superiority of product, service, delivery, and technical support. Price then becomes a matter of what is acceptable: Does the price fit within the project budget? Is it reasonable as compared with the vendor's last price for a similar piece of equipment? Is it as low as what the vendor would charge some other customer? Or sometimes, subjectively, does it seem fair?

Consider, for example, a situation in one company involving the purchase of six large reactors for chemical processing. The orders were placed individually over a one-year period for these units that cost in the range of $50,000 to $85,000 each. At the direction of engineering managers responsible for planning and installing new plant facilities, each of the six orders was placed with the same vendor, Smith Company, although this supplier was never the low bidder. Smith Company, however, had supplied almost all of this customer's reactors in the past. Needless to say, procurement management working on this series of orders had difficulty in getting suppliers to respond to successive RFQs for the reactors.

In commenting on why Smith Company had been chosen, the engineering manager noted that his concerns were mainly 1) how well the equipment performed, 2) whether new facilities came on-stream within schedule and budget commitments, and 3) the extent of start-up and debugging problems. Price was not a governing factor, he believed, if the total cost of a new manufacturing line or new plant fell within the authorized budget. If it did not, then usually the whole project was scrutinized and often redesigned. However, if any bid but the lowest was accepted on a particular order, he had a routine letter prepared for the files, documenting the reasons for making the award as he did.

The engineering manager recalled an instance twelve years earlier in which the reactors were inadequately designed and constructed:

> The first reactors had dimpled jackets. We took the lowest bidder, a small "shade tree" shop in New Jersey, and we had nothing but problems. Almost from the time they were installed they began leaking and we got in a local welder (ASME [American Society of Mechanical Engineers] approved). He must have come in more than a hundred times in that first year. We had to shut the plant down each time because we were handling highly flammable materials and using a welding torch was risky. We lost a lot of reactor time. And we couldn't get good welds. Then we discovered that the fabricator had done a

lousy job, even using below-standard materials on the inside where it didn't show. After bringing in a consulting metallurgist, we decided to scrap those units and buy new ones. It actually cost us more to take out those first reactors than they cost in the first place.

  Replacing a reactor is a horrendous job. There's so much piping and a lot of auxiliary vessels around the main reactor. A relatively minor difference in original cost is peanuts.

And finally, the engineering manager expressed his views on the increased difficulty experienced by procurement management in getting potential suppliers, competitors of Smith Company, to respond to RFQs for chemical reactors:

I'm not greatly disturbed by the lack of bidders as long as we think we're getting fair prices. I would be upset if I thought we were locked in and the vendor was getting fat profits. Actually there is a tendency to go back to the same supplier once you've developed a rapport and you know from experience that his work is good. It's reassuring from an engineering point of view. You don't have to be so exacting with the specifications. Sometimes you can even pick up the telephone and say "Send me another unit like the one you sent me last time." And you can be in constant communication while the equipment is being built.

Production Influences on Sourcing Decisions:
The Make-or-Buy Choice

As the earlier discussion on purchasing performance measures indicated, production needs and values assume high priority in procurement decision-making on product parts and materials. Production influence tends to be less in the case of nonproduct supply items simply because this category of purchase is not so directly linked to production schedules and end product quality. On product parts, production's continuing feedback to purchasing on vendor performance is very likely to be reflected in the allocation of business among suppliers, and in decisions to discontinue poor performers. Production needs will influence the order pattern as well. In the interests of minimizing investments in materials and parts inventories, the production-control function will tend to let orders placed with vendors move up and down with fluctuations in production schedules. While purchasing would normally prefer stable order levels in the interest of minimizing vendor costs, production interests tend to dominate.

  The make-or-buy decision is another important area in which production interests exert considerable influence on sourcing. There are two kinds of make-or-buy decisions. The first concerns the utilization of existing facilities to make something currently being supplied by outside vendors. The second relates to decisions to build new capacity to make something that might otherwise be sourced outside.

Utilizing Existing Capacity. Decisions to bring work into a plant or leave it with outside vendors brings into play a range of conflicting considerations. On the one hand, corporate policy may give high priority to work-force stability, level employment, and the preservation of cadres of skilled employees. Hence, when economic activity is at a low ebb, a common response on the part of plant, division, and corporate managers is to bring work in-house. Purchasing managers, however, typically resist. Their concerns include:

(1) preserving a healthy supplier complex.
(2) avoiding the unfavorable effects on vendor costs that come from production cutbacks and the subsequent sharp build-ups that reflect economic cycles.
(3) in some companies, preserving the purchase-volume base to support procurement overheads and to maintain skilled purchasing personnel.

As among these various considerations, maintaining work-force stability weighs heavily in make-or-buy decisions. Make-or-buy analyses, for example, often seem to compare the out-of-pocket costs of making some component in-house with external vendor prices, thus giving the ''make'' option a comparative advantage. The validity of using variable costs for make-or-buy analysis rests on the fact that fixed overheads would continue whether the plant capacity was utilized or not.

In any case, decision-making typically involves representatives from manufacturing, purchasing, perhaps engineering, and perhaps finance; the process itself is political in nature. Below is the process at the General Motors Chevrolet Division as described by Schaefer, a member of the GM Procurement Staff.

According to this manager, make-or-buy decisions in General Motors were made at the division level. As a result, practice varied somewhat from division to division. In a survey that Schaefer made of eight divisions shortly after joining the GM Procurement Staff, he found that in five out of eight cases the make-or-buy committee included one representative each from the manufacturing, purchasing, and financial departments. In two large divisions make-or-buy decisions were made by manufacturing managers. Reflecting functional interests, these two managers tended in their decisions to favor keeping their division plants busy with work most suited to plant skills and resources, and to rely on outside vendors for the remainder.

Just prior to joining the GM Purchasing Staff, Schaefer had been on the financial staff at the Chevrolet Division. One of his responsibilities was to represent the financial staff on the make-or-buy committee of the Chevrolet Division. He believed that Chevrolet had an effective make-or-buy decision-making process. Its success, in his opinion, was due to the fact that the committee had three strong members representing their respective functions well (''If you don't, one man will snow the other two!''), meeting weekly (''If it meets infrequently, you know a lot of make-or-buy decisions are being made unilaterally outside of meetings.''), and making post-audits, usually after a year, of each decision. In each case, the committee compared quotations on price-per-piece and tooling from GM allied divisions and outside vendors with the cost to manufacture at Chevrolet, including variable factory cost and other expenditures that might be incurred, such as tooling, plant rearrangement, machinery and equipment, and land and buildings. Some products, such as engines, axles, and transmissions, were always manufactured by the Chevrolet Division. The procurement of other components, such as plastic parts, wheels, stampings, propellor shafts, and exhaust systems, might go either way and could be sourced from Chevrolet plants, from allied divisions, or from outside suppliers. Buyers were charged with making make-or-buy analyses and submitting recommendations to the committee. A summary sheet, in each case, showed quotations from outside suppliers and allied divisions, including charges for freight and any special tooling, and cost estimates, both variable and full cost, from Chevrolet plants. An additional consideration in make-or-buy decisions was whether a Chevrolet plant had excess capacity and needed the work to maintain employment and cover overheads. On the other hand, considerable weight was also given to the past performance of outside suppliers, particularly to contributions they may have made in engineering design.

Schaefer spoke of his role on the Chevrolet make-or-buy committee:

As a member of the financial staff, it was my job to see that decisions were made in the overall best interests of the corporation. At GM there's a *very* heavy dotted line between the division comptroller and the corporate financial staff, and so my responsibility was not limited to the division.

At the first meeting I attended I said that we would be conducting post-audits. That is, if we took work inside, my department would compare actual costs after it was well into production with the cost estimates presented by Manufacturing at the time we made the decision. We'd allow, of course, for escalation in direct labor, burden and material costs to the extent that any outside vendor's cost would have been similarly affected. If we made the decision to go to an outside vendor, we'd do the same thing: check actual costs against the original quotes.

Using post-audits does a lot to improve the quality of the original data. What you want is to have Manufacturing come in the first time with a sharp-pencil figure, and not come back after seeing outside quotes and say, ''Well, maybe we can shave a little here or a little there.'' And you want to be sure, too, that you're working with identical specifications from vendors and from the inside source and include shipping costs.

As for sourcing from allied divisions, one comptroller has the right to call the comptroller in another division who may have submitted price quotations on a particular part and ask for their costs. I would do this if the make-or-buy decision was to make sure that the job was sourced in GM's best interests.

While Chevrolet had a very good make-or-buy decision-making process, that didn't mean that the decisions all went easily. Inevitably there were some real debates. I remember one situation where Manufacturing wanted to bring inside a key component. It had been sourced from three outside vendors as well as one of our own plants. What made it difficult was that the engineering design work was being done by the outside vendor instead of Chevrolet engineering. If we took a much greater percentage of the work inside then we'd have to do our own design work. The purchasing representative and I after studying the cost data thought the work should stay mainly with outside vendors. But it was an important battle for Manufacturing, and they were prepared to appeal it all the way to the top. Well, we finally agreed that Manufacturing could keep a portion of the work inside for a two-year trial period. Then if they couldn't meet their cost targets, it would all go outside. I don't like having the engineering design function with the outside vendor because this permits him to tailor the design to fit his manufacturing facilities and not necessarily ours.

The role that the finance representative plays on the make-or-buy committee at Chevrolet is worthy of comment. This member seemed to serve as a balance wheel and in his relations with the manufacturing and engineering representatives he worked to "keep them honest." It would be easy, for example, for manufacturing to develop favorable cost estimates to support claims for taking work in. A post-audit system would make that more difficult.

In addition, he brought to bear the broader corporate interests on make-or-buy decisions thus tending to offset manufacturing's overriding interest in work-force stability and procurement's concern for preserving the health of its vendor complex. His ability to play this role reflects some degree of detachment from division performance measures stemming from his strong link to the corporate financial staff. At General Motors, division comptrollers are appointed, rotated among divisions, promoted, and compensated under the direction of the corporate financial vice-president.

Building New Plant Capacity. The make-or-buy decision in which the make option entails adding new facilities is different from decisions involving the utilization of existing capacity. Fundamentally it requires full-cost calculations, rather than out-of-pocket, to assess the relative advantages of sourcing internally or externally. More important, however, than cost-price comparisons are these questions:

(1) Is the product something that the company typically makes and for which it has the technical expertise?
(2) Is there concern about the long-run viability of external sourcing arrangements?
(3) Are supply-industry dynamics and product technology such that the company should seek to preserve its flexibility in using different sources?
(4) Is it important to develop and preserve manufacturing capabilities in certain technically-strategic areas?

(5) Is it important to make rather than buy in order to protect proprietary knowledge?

Gillette, a plant procurement manager at IBM, explained current practice:

When it came to resource planning we used to stumble over ourselves doing things at which we are noncompetitive. What we now try to do is to take the whole workload and divide it into strategic and nonstrategic parts. We then do the strategic part and send the rest out.

Strategic items are defined as those that satisfy one or more of four criteria:
(1) Contain proprietary information that we do not want to go outside.
(2) The work is necessary to maintain or develop key skills.
(3) We need to make them to control quality.
(4) Cost is higher to buy.

Gregory, director of Corporate Component Procurement at IBM, was not satisfied with the way make-or-buy decisions were made:

It's important to be conscious of when make-or-buy decisions are actually being made. Whenever you add plant, equipment or people, you've actually made a make-or-buy decision. But managers don't think of it that way. They see it as adding capacity to meet market demand. Rarely does anybody examine the "buy" option before adding capacity. So when you come up to a make-or-buy choice as we normally think of it, a "given" is that you already have the capability in place.

In the same way, we never consider the possibility of developing a part inside and releasing it for manufacture to an outside vendor. It's automatically released to an IBM plant, but we should ask from the beginning, "Is the item vendorable?"

There is a certain list of products we always make because we have the capability and a certain list of products we always buy because we don't have manufacturing capability and we're not interested. Those two lists amount to 85% of the total. That leaves 15% that could go either way and the percentage is shrinking.

Manufacturing says that the more we make the more we have to cover overheads. The problem is that it is a self-fulfilling prophecy. In the long run you can't work like that. You must use full-costing. At the moment, if a new piece of logic is needed it is sent to the Development Center and if they want to make it, they do. Cost was seldom discussed. That's slowly changing and we have some tug-of-wars between us. We argue that we can arrange for its development and manufacture outside at a far lower cost. But the issues and rationales are not of the level you would expect in a sophisticated operation.

From purchasing's point of view it takes a lot of work to challenge all the opportunities that might exist for buying at a lower cost outside. Having the resources to do this would build up the purchasing burden-rate.

These comments reflect the realities of make-or-buy decision-making. In fact, often the make-or-buy question is not directly considered. If market demand increases, plant capacity will be expanded to make those items that manufacturing has traditionally made. New products developed by engineering tend to be turned over automatically to manufacturing. The manufacturing role in the make-or-buy decision seems to dominate; it has a "right of first refusal" for all practical purposes. It may elect to make, and will normally do so if it has the manufacturing technology and available capacity. If not, then purchasing assumes the responsibility for sourcing externally.

The IBM purchasing managers' comments suggest that there may be attractive cost-saving benefits in taking work from the plant and placing it with outside vendors. But to take the initiative in identifying and analyzing these opportunities requires procurement resources that are not usually available, given the day-to-day demands of purchasing work to meet production schedules.

By contrast, decisions to make something that has traditionally been purchased from outside suppliers and that involves new and unfamiliar manufacturing processes are not typically made by default. Between 1972 and 1974, for example, Heinz USA managers extensively studied the possibilities of manufacturing ketchup bottles. Ketchup bottles represented over 40 percent of the company's total glass purchases. According to one manager's calculations, the cost savings could amount to a 27 percent annual cash-flow return on an investment of $12 million. Moreover, interest in making glass containers was stimulated by the fact that one of Heinz's major competitors was successfully making its own glass bottles, and Heinz itself operated its own can-making lines.

Nevertheless, the proposal was rejected for reasons that reflected the great uncertainties attending a move into new manufacturing technology. According to the purchasing manager responsible for buying glass:

> In general I was not in favor of it. There were too many unanswered questions. It didn't go far enough. Some of the figures couldn't be true. The glass industry isn't a 12% after-tax industry. It's a 3 to 4% industry. [The report] didn't look at backup suppliers or the fact that we would have to provide our own storage facilities. We'd have to move ketchup production out of two plants and consolidate it so that our glass plant could operate economically.
>
> This could complicate our price negotiations with suppliers. We would have our own glass plant making the high-volume items and we would probably have to pay vendors higher prices for what we didn't make.

In addition to the business risks so well articulated, there is a clear undertone of personal risk in these comments. Rommel, the new general manager for production control, stood to lose in his relations with other managers, both superiors and peers, if shutdowns in the glass bottle plant disrupted ketchup production. Robards, the glass buyer, would lose bargaining power in negotiating for glass bottles and for requirements that Heinz continued to source from outside vendors. If lower purchasing volumes meant having to pay higher prices, the measures by which Robard's performance was appraised would suffer. As for Adams, the new vice-president of manufacturing and development, sponsorship of a multimillion dollar investment that was something less than completely successful certainly could not help his career. He had little to gain and much to lose.

Marketing's Influence in Procurement Decision-Making

When procurement decisions affect marketability of the company's products for reasons of product design, promotability, serviceability, or price, the marketing function becomes an interested and involved participant in sourcing decisions. As the authority on the impact of product design and price decisions on sales volume, it may carry much the same weight as manufacturing does on make-or-buy decisions and engineering on product specifications.

At Heinz, for example, a proposal to redesign the ketchup bottle[1] to save money "touched a marketing nerve" and was strongly resisted for three years in spite of potential cost reductions totaling over $1 million offered by the change. There would be savings in the cost of the ketchup bottle and freight both in-bound and out-bound. Savings would also accrue in the bottle-filling lines because of the greater operating speeds that would be possible, as well as reduced downtime for reasons of glass breakage. But the Heinz ketchup-bottle design was well-known, easily identified, and believed to be a factor contributing to Heinz's leading position in the U.S. ketchup market. Moreover, the design was a long-standing tradition. The bottle redesign had been proposed by Heinz USA's major glass supplier in response to a breakage problem that developed briefly in one plant in the summer of 1972.

According to the ketchup product manager in retail marketing: "My initial reaction was 'you've gotta be kidding.' You don't fool around with that sort of thing. If you lose even 1 percent of sales it wouldn't be worth it." He went on to indicate that while the Marketing Division wanted to make savings, it was not prepared to take unnecessary risks: "We've already had a change with the bottle caps. For seventy years every cap had 'Heinz' in red letters printed on it but when Manufacturing Development said we could save $70,000 a year if we took

1. The existing bottle design, the one long associated with Heinz ketchup, was octagonal in shape in the bottom half with scallops on top where the flat side panels met the rounded, tapered top portion of the bottle. The new design, by contrast, was round but the scalloped configuration was retained at the point where the bottle began tapering down in circumference. The new design had several advantages. It would require less glass and, at the same time, would be stronger than the present bottle. It would permit a smoother flow of molten glass into the mold to result in consistent, high quality production, and reduce breakage in glass-manufacturing, glass-shipment and glass-filling operations. Further, inspection procedures could be automated and made considerably more precise and accurate.

the 'Heinz' off we did so. We did it in a spirit of cooperation. It's not going to hurt us. There's a big difference between that and a round bottle. We'll save the battles for the ones we care about.''

Like the proposal to construct a facility for making glass ketchup bottles, the bottle-redesign issue can be best understood in terms of gains and risks, both business and personal. Manufacturing stood to gain through lower production costs, fewer line interruptions, and reduced rejection rates on incoming bottles. Purchasing could score a major cost reduction thereby enhancing its performance according to the way it was measured. Marketing had little if anything to gain. The redesign was certainly not likely to increase sales volume and might possibly reduce it.

Marketing's strength in the continuing discussions over three years concerning the bottle redesigning proposal can be attributed to the fact that it was the authority on the effect of any design changes on sales. Its judgment would have to be weighted heavily, particularly since there was a paucity of hard data on the potential gains and risks.

General Management as a Factor

General management may exercise a strong influence on sourcing decisions. This influence emanates largely from concerns of a strategic or policy nature. For example, at General Foods, the vice-presidents of the Food Products Division and the Beverage and Breakfast Foods Division, the executive vice-president to whom they reported, and the vice-president of Corporate Purchasing and Materials Management met weekly to decide on and monitor strategies for buying sugar. Sugar would naturally represent a major and volatile element of cost for these two divisions.

General management's influence is felt especially in broad policy matters involving the company's relationships with the supply environment. Top management involvement in steel-sourcing decisions at General Motors reflects a long-run concern for having enough steel-making capacity in the United States to meet the demands of the automotive and other steel-using industries at the same time. GM top management was also involved in sourcing for the catalytic converter. The reason, in that case, was in part the tremendous scale of commitments that had to be made to outside vendors. (Another reason was GM President Cole's own direct interest in the engineering challenge of designing and building the new device.)

Another dimension of general management concern having a very direct and pronounced effect on sourcing decisions is maintaining stability of employment. Here is a statement by the Chairman of the Board in the IBM 1975 Annual Report that illustrates the importance that the company's top management ascribes to its responsibilities for maintaining employment.

> IBM has instituted a number of programs in the past year to respond to opportunities in the marketplace and uncertainties in the economy. Retraining and voluntary relocation have created new career opportunities for some 3,800 IBMers worldwide, while another 1,900 people in the U.S. have left the company under provisions of a special opportunity program through which employees with 25 years of service may leave voluntarily, with up to four years of special compensation. As a result of these and other measures, the company has been able to avoid lay-offs, *in keeping with our long tradition of full employment.* [italics added]

A possible implication of this concern for full employment at IBM is that in periods of economic uncertainty, purchasing will be busy pulling work back into the factory. A corollary of the full employment tradition at IBM, however, is a concern for monitoring and controlling systematically the amount of work placed with each vendor. The purpose is to avoid, if possible, having IBM orders represent such a large percentage of any one vendor's workload that its loss would seriously affect that supplier's operations. The company's policies reflect a sense of responsibility for the health of supplier organizations and for employees in their communities, as well as a concern for IBM employment levels.

Finally, top management directives and monitoring procedures impose discipline on procurement practices to ensure conformity with the law and public policy, and to avoid conflicts of interest. In recent years, for example, eliminating reciprocity has been a matter of particular concern.

General management influence, in sum, comes to bear on matters having to do with (1) product price and marketability in a competitive environment, (2) the long-run preservation of a healthy sourcing system, (3) making large, long-term purchase commitments, (4) the impact of fluctuating levels of economic activity on individual suppliers and the communities in which they are located, and (5) assuring conformity with legal requirements and public policies.

Procurement, Itself, as an Influence

Procurement seems to be the dominant function in purchasing decisions made in a steady-state condition, that is, when the design of the purchased part is established and vendors have been qualified. At this stage in the purchasing cycle, price as well as long-run supply availability may be the primary concerns.

In the same way, purchasing dominates procurement decision-making when there are intensive long-term supplier relationships having to do with management problems, as opposed to technical-engineering matters. This would be true of subcontract work in particular. A useful example is the work of the leaf-spring buyer at Chevrolet: once he had set up his supply complex, his main efforts were focused on planning vendors' production schedules to mesh with Chevrolet production-flow requirements.

The procurement function tends to dominate, as well, when the critical expertise in effective sourcing is knowledge of and skill in dealing with the supply environment—the steel industry at General Motors, or the sugar market at General Foods, for example. Under conditions of repetitive buying over long periods, purchasing tends to build up technical expertise in the product, a knowledge of supply-industry dynamics, and relationships with individual suppliers that far surpass the expertise that may be found in other functional areas. Purchasing then fills the authority role.

Balance of Power in Procurement Decision-Making

This discussion of the relative influence of general management and of such functional areas as engineering, manufacturing, marketing, and purchasing on procurement decision-making suggests a series of interrelated propositions. Such a scheme might be useful to division and corporate managements in shaping the overall administrative system through which procurement decisions are made. In the context of this discussion, the administrative system includes functional area performance measures, corporate policies, information flows, organizational structuring, and staffing relevant to procurement decision-making.

Proposition 1: There tends to be a high degree of interfunctional involvement in decisions relating to purchased-product specifications and vendor selection (1) in the early stages of the procurement cycle, (2) on matters involving basic changes in the sourcing system and (3) on large, nonrepetitive purchases. This is self-evident in the respect that the traditional responsibilities of the basic functional areas carry over into procurement matters on questions of product design, process design, quality assurance, and make-or-buy decisions. In routine and repetitive purchases in the latter stages of the procurement cycle, however, procurement decision-making may be relatively uninfluenced by functions outside of purchasing as long as the supplier complex meets performance expectations.

Proposition 2: Under conditions of goal conflict among functional areas, procurement decision-making is essentially an internal political process. When it is difficult to quantify costs and benefits of different solutions and when any one solution may not be optimal for all those concerned, an outcome may be reached through an interplay of forces inside the company. The outcome may then seek to accommodate different interests through a process of compromise. Alternatively, it may reflect the primary interests of the dominant party among those involved. In this process, directions emanating from general management may be an important factor increasing the relative power of one or more interest groups but not necessarily determining the outcome.

Proposition 3: The functional area or group recognized as having the relevant authority role will dominate the decision-making process. Where the authority resides in any case will depend on the nature of the issue. For example, in the case of the proposed ketchup-bottle redesign at Heinz, marketing was the recognized authority. On the selection of a vendor for an expensive piece of production equipment, engineering will usually fill this role. In each instance, engineering or marketing judgments, as the case may be, are respected in recognition of the experience, technical proficiency, and responsibilities of the functional managers.

Proposition 4: The directions set by the recognized functional authority will be determined largely by (1) the goals and measures imposed on it or self-generated, and (2) the perceived gains and risks of possible outcomes for the individual decision-makers. In the case of engineering and manufacturing, these measures often seem to stress such values as continuity of production, minimal maintenance, high end-product quality. To the engineering manager concerned with purchasing reactors, a modest savings in original cost was negligible compared to the penalties in having the equipment go down.

The perception of gains and risks from the individual decision-maker's viewpoint is normally congruent with functional goals and measures. But it goes beyond that to be influenced by some subjective factors, i.e., how secure is the individual in his or her position; will conceding in one situation gain an advantage on some other, more important issue; what are the relative personal rewards and penalties for low risk/low gain versus high risk/high gain opportunities.

Proposition 5: When the outcome is significant to a nonauthority functional area, it will seek coalition support if its goals are in conflict with those of the authority area. If there are significant cost-saving gains to be made by a modification in product specifications, purchasing may seek reinforcement from any other potential interest groups. It may be that, together, they can build an authority base and a critical mass of gains to offset the dominance of the authority function. In some cases, purchasing may even seek the support of a favored outside vendor to bring pressure on a recalcitrant authority group.

Proposition 6: The balance of strength of authority and nonauthority roles may be significantly influenced by the existence of some critical mass of hard data and the effect that may have in generating general-management support for one position or the other. This proposition simply states that a convincing case, based, preferably on quantified data, must be made to bring about basic change if that change goes counter to the conventional admonitions of the relevant authority group. It goes farther: a critical mass of evidence may swing the balance only if it draws general management support to the side of the issue the evidence favors.

Proposition 7: The behavior of the purchasing function in procurement decision-making reflects the goals, values and short-range measures of that group with which it is most closely associated. The farther removed organizationally from the user-locations it serves, the more its behavior responds to long-range basic purchasing concerns. This proposition is based on the difference between short-range measures and long-range purchasing concerns that cannot be sharply drawn as a practical matter. Admittedly, both purchasing functions closely tied to user-locations and those organizationally set apart exhibit high sensitivity to such basic supplier performance factors as product quality, delivery, and technical service. The difference comes in other ways. Purchasing units tied directly to plant, laboratory, and office operations may be more greatly influenced by user-brand preferences, individual-user assessments of vendor service, and short-range procurement-cost performance. Purchasing functions tied to engineering groups charged with designing and buying equipment seem to respond to such measures as ability to work effectively with engineers and project managers, effectiveness in getting on-time deliveries, finding new supply sources, and "beating the budget"—usually in that order.

Centralized procurement operations, by contrast, show a sensitivity to long-run source development and long-run procurement cost performance, as opposed to short-run cost minimization.

The Relative Strength of Purchasing in Procurement Decision-Making

Given the quasi-political nature of the environment in which purchasing operates, it is useful to ask what factors tend to give the procurement function strength in internal negotiations. At least four can be identified: (1) its level of technical and managerial resources, (2) its access to relevant information, (3) the extent of general management support it has, and (4) its own status as an authority in particular procurement areas.

Technical and Managerial Resources. The effectiveness of purchasing in negotiating both internally and externally will depend greatly on whether the department has technical competence and credibility. Engineering personnel in the purchasing organization may work effectively in a liaison capacity with product- and process-design engineers to contribute ideas about procurability to the design process. They can also work between internal technical personnel and vendor engineers in the early stages of the procurement cycle.

In some instances, procurement groups have the resources to search out cost-saving opportunities that might come from buying a part rather than making it.

Access to Information. Information is power. In negotiating internally, purchasing managers need information to help them in assessing procurement cost and product benefit trade-offs. Purchasing gains strength, as well, to the extent that it has a total overview of the supply industry and individual suppliers while the other parties involved have only fragmentary knowledge.

General Management Support. The extent to which top management takes a direct interest in and supports the integrity of purchasing bears directly on its internal functional strength. At General Motors the formation of a Procurement Policy Committee composed of top officers of the company gave a measure of "muscle" to that function, which hadn't existed before. It signalled top management's serious concern that purchasing be a strong functional area serving the long-run needs of the company.

Top management support may also flow through policy statements and routine audit procedures. The point is illustrated in a speech made in 1972 by the GM General Auditor at the Central Office to GM purchasing officers:

> Although there has been substantial improvement in recent years, we continue to find instances where the Purchasing Department has abandoned its responsibilities in areas where it feels that it does not have the best expertise. We find special tooling purchases being made by the Tool Engineers; we find machinery and equipment purchases being made by Production or Equipment Engineers; we find advertising and promotional items and programs being negotiated and contracted by marketing personnel; plant repair, rearrangement and minor construction purchases are authorized by Master Mechanics, all without sufficient participation by Purchasing.
>
> We do not consider statements such as "Purchasing reserves the right to approve the selected source," "Purchasing reserves the right to solicit additional sources" or "Purchasing will approve the sources invited to quote" as being sufficient participation by Purchasing.
>
> When shortcomings in these areas are called to attention, we generally are told that these procurements are technical and the Purchasing Department does not have qualified technical personnel in these areas. Bear in mind that the Departments which take over negotiation and contracting for these procurements usually do not have any purchasing expertise. The Corporation has been most emphatic in stating that it wants the procurement of facility-type items, advertising, promotions, etc. kept under the control of the Purchasing Department which is free to solicit all the technical assistance it may need from engineers, marketers, etc. Far too many billions of dollars are being spent in our annual construction programs to allow any relaxation in observance of the strictest controls. The Corporation has had too many unhappy experiences with some of its construction contractors and sales promoters. We know we

are often dealing with firms which are capable of deceiving our sharpest purchasing experts and they can certainly pick our engineers clean.

These words are not meant to be critical of engineers and other non-purchasing employees but, remember, engineers are interested in getting machinery in place, in getting the tooling trial runs made, etc. Their primary interests or talents are not directed toward costs and other purchasing controls which are the hallmark of the professional buyer.

Authority Status. As noted earlier, purchasing may be cast in the authority role when the essential knowledge is that of the supply environment, and in cases where repetitive buying makes the purchasing manager technically competent as well. Often purchasing moves into the expert role when there is an authority vacuum. This will be particularly true in the purchase of office supply items and equipment, small tools, and expendable plant operating supplies, in which no other functional area has the time or interest to develop product expertise.

In conclusion, it would seem that procurement can be a powerful contributor to corporate growth and profitability. It may make important contributions, as well, in the long-run development of supply lines. But the procurement function has been subordinated largely to other functions—production, engineering, and marketing—and its role, for the most part, has been confined to serving their immediate needs. To fill a larger purpose, procurement might usefully become a more proactive function, taking the initiative on opportunities to source more favorably from outside vendors, rather than to make, and to foster the development of external supply capacity. If this is to happen, there are four necessary conditions: that procurement gain increase status through reporting at higher management levels and through greater top management support; that it be given the necessary resources; that it be staffed with competent personnel compensated at salary levels competitive with those in other management functions; and that the measures imposed on it reflect greater expectations regarding its role and responsibilities.

Appendix A

THE LITERATURE OF PROCUREMENT

An introductory review of some of the major texts in procurement serves the purpose of positioning this study in the literature of the field.

Essentially, procurement literature falls into three categories. There are the books that describe purchasing's role and the techniques of doing the work of buying and procurement management. Another part of the literature focuses on the behavioral aspects of the buyer's job and considers the nature of the influences at work in shaping individual, as opposed to corporate, buyer behavior. It would seem that the primary purpose of these studies is to help sellers understand buyer interests, motivations, and internal relationships so that the sellers can relate effectively to their customers as people. A third part of the literature treats the negotiating process specifically. It considers the bargaining processes through which prices and terms are set. Its purpose is to suggest strategies, techniques, and tactics to help both buyers and sellers in dealing with each other. There follows brief reviews of six of the major books (there are others[1]) in the field of procurement. The purpose of these reviews is to present the scope of what has been written.

1. Among the texts in procurement are the following:
Lee, Lamar Jr. and Dobler, Donald W., *Purchasing and Materials Management: Text and Cases,* (McGraw-Hill, New York, 1965).
Heinritz, Stuart F. and Farrell, Paul V., *Purchasing: Principles and Applications,* 5th ed., (Prentice-Hall, Englewood Cliffs, NJ, 1971).
Miles, Lawrence D., *Techniques of Value Analysis and Engineering,* 2nd edition, (McGraw-Hill, New York, 1972).
Fallon, Carlos, *Value Analysis to Improve Productivity,* (Wiley-Interscience, New York, 1971).
Dowst, Somerby R., *Basics for Buyers: A Practical Guide to Better Purchasing,* (CBI Publishing Company, Inc., Boston, 1971).
Combs, Paul H., *Handbook of International Purchasing,* 2nd ed. (CBI Publishing Company, Inc., Boston, 1976).

Purchasing Management, Materials in Motion by Westing, Fine, and Zenz[2] falls in the first of the three classifications. It describes the objective of purchasing as buying "materials of the right quality, in the right quantity, at the right time, at the right price from the right source with delivery at the right place." Underlying this general goal are a set of more specific objectives, designed to:

1. Achieve continuity of operations.
2. Maintain adequate standards of quality.
3. Avoid duplication, waste, and obsolescence.
4. Maintain the company's competitive position.
5. Enhance suppliers' image of the company.
6. Develop harmonious internal relationships.

In dealing with the way purchasing may be organized, Westing, Fine, and Zenz give particular attention to the *materials management* concept which would position purchasing in close organizational proximity to production functions at the plant level. The organizational integration of production and purchasing would then facilitate the making of optimal trade-offs affecting both functions. To quote:

The term *materials management* came into common usage and practice in business during the 1960s. Its essential significance is that it highlighted for management the fact that there were economies to be gained by coordinating the related activities of production planning and scheduling, purchasing, shipping, storing, handling, and controlling of materials put into the manufacturing process.

In large part, Westing, Fine, and Zenz concern themselves with procedural aspects of purchasing, such as the handling of small orders and negotiating CPAs; with "stockless purchasing," or buying on consignment;[3] with supplier-evaluation techniques and price-cost analysis ("the analysis of all factors that enter into price, and the attempt to ensure that the final price is a reasonable one in terms of the use to which the material is to be put and the competitive situation faced by the buying and selling firms"). Finally, Westing, Fine, and Zenz consider the evaluation of purchasing performance and suggest a range of criteria that may usefully be applied. For example:

· Quality—number of rejections of incoming shipments.
· Quantity—"downtime" resulting from material shortages and number of emergency and rush orders.
· Price—purchased materials as a percentage of the selling price of finished goods.

---

2. Westing, J. H., Fine, I. V., and Zenz, G. J., *Purchasing Management, Materials in Motion*, 4th ed. (John Wiley and Sons, New York, 1976).
3. Under consignment purchase arrangements the vendor maintains a stock on the buyer's premises (or in some cases on the vendor's premises) and is paid as the stock is used.

· Time and Place—actual delivery dates versus promised dates.
· Workload—number of orders processed, salesmen interviewed, etc.

In several important areas *Purchasing Management, Materials in Motion* makes useful contributions to the literature of procurement:

1. The description and assessment of materials management as a useful current approach to managing the flow of materials throughout the organization.
2. The presentation of approaches and procedures for dealing with routine purchases to reduce operating cost as well as the purchase price of these items.
3. The description of techniques for evaluating supplier performance as an element in the supplier-selection process.
4. The value of price-cost analysis as a tool in the determination of the "right" price, whether for negotiations or for comparison with other potential suppliers.
5. The necessity for establishing multidimensional criteria of purchasing effectiveness to evaluate performance. The purchasing function's contribution to the success of the firm can be significant; its potential should not be ignored or left to chance.

Purchasing and Materials Management by England and Leenders[4] is similar in approach. It begins with a description of purchasing's role in the organization and stresses its problem-solving aspects. Thus:

To solve problems, procurement managers employ a variety of purchasing strategies. These strategies are sets of decision rules designed to solve particular problems within acceptable limits of risk and resource allocation. Because this problem-solving activity occurs in a social context, it requires both analytical skills and skill in interpersonal relations.

England and Leenders give particular attention to the role of computer-based management information systems for enhancing the effectiveness of the purchasing function. The four basic benefits they identify are:

1. The mechanized handling of procedures reduces clerical manual effort to a minimum.
2. Information from records becomes available almost instantly.
3. Control over operations is improved, not only by the timely availability of the information for sound decision-making, but also by the flexibility afforded by the ease of handling vast quantities of detail, thus providing new tools for the buyer and manager.

4. England, Wilbur B. and Leenders, Michael R., *Purchasing and Materials Management,* 6th ed., (Richard D. Irwin, Inc., Homewood, Ill., 1975).

4. Operating performance is improved by the availability of information and the improved control of operations.

Another distinguishing feature of this book is its comprehensive perspectives on the functions, forms, and management of inventories. These purposes of carrying inventories are identified:

1. Transit—arising from the need to transport inventory from point A to point B.
2. Cycle—management's attempts to produce in economic lot sizes.
3. Buffer—arising from decisions regarding risk.
4. Anticipation—stemming from expected changes in demand, supply, or price.
5. Decoupling—desiring to separate dependent production centers.

The authors then relate the three commonly recognized forms of inventory, raw materials, work-in-process, and finished goods with the five functions described to define a matrix of fifteen form-function inventories. This new perspective has some significant implications, as follows:

Because we are now dealing with up to 15 different kinds of inventories, the problem of control becomes a little more complicated. First, we should recognize that the behavior of inventories is the direct result of diverse policies and decisions within a company. Marketing, production, finance, and purchasing decisions directly influence the level of inventories throughout the organization . . . .

Second, not all inventories are equally controllable for other reasons. Long-term marketing commitments in terms of distribution networks may render transit finished goods inventory levels quite inflexible, whereas the relatively shorter term production scheduling plans may provide a great deal of flexibility in the control of decoupling work-in-process inventories. Consider another case. Short-term production scheduling may provide a great deal of flexibility in work-in-process cycle inventories; relatively longer term supplier development and purchasing commitments may result in rigid raw material cycle and transit inventories. How often has the total value of inventories risen due to the unavoidable accumulation of raw materials as production schedules and product demand drop rapidly? To be effective inventory control managers must recognize the controllability of each kind of inventory in the short and long run.

Third, why haven't EOQs [Economic order quantitites] worked? Very simply, EOQs are cycle inventories and may be only a small part of the total inventory picture. Managers who produce only in EOQs are ignoring the potential benefits of transit, anticipation, and decoupling inventories. Often the production in noneconomic order quantities may be more profitable.

In concluding their discussion of inventory control, the authors make the following observation:

> The control of inventories is complex because of the many functions and forms. Inventory levels are the result of many short- and long-term decisions and policies of all functional areas (i.e., production, marketing, purchasing) within the organization. The control of inventories represent a shared responsibility and must be viewed as such.

Describing the selection of supply sources as "purchasing's most important responsibility," England and Leenders give particular attention to describing what buyers should look for in suppliers.

> A good or preferred supplier should be one which does the following for its customers. It provides the quality specified and delivers on time as promised; has an acceptable price; reacts to unforeseen needs such as suddenly accelerated or decelerated volumes of business, changes in specifications, service problems, and any other legitimate requests. The good supplier takes the initiative in suggesting better ways of serving customers and attempts to find new ways of developing products economically. The good supplier will warn ahead of time of material shortages, strikes, and anything else that may affect their operations. It will provide technological and other expertise when requested by customers. It will remain competitive on a continuing basis.

An important facet of supplier selection that has been explored in depth by this book relates to the range of benefits that may derive from sound long-term working relationships:

> The purchaser is aware that benefits will accrue to both the supplier and the purchaser, benefits of which the supplier may not be aware. These benefits may be limited to the particular order at hand, or they may include more far-reaching results, such as technical, financial, and management assistance; future business from the same purchaser as well as from others; training through learning about new manufacturing processes, skills, or quality levels; reduction of marketing effort; use of long-term forecasts permitting smoother manufacturing levels and a minimum of inventory; and so on.

As in any basic textbook, the principal contribution of *Purchasing and Materials Management* lies in identifying and presenting in an organized manner the fundamental structure of the field. England and Leenders have accomplished this objective and at the same time have provided some conceptual advances worthy of further consideration.

1. The role of purchasing as a problem-solving activity, thereby emphasizing the strategic context of purchasing decisions.
2. The identification of the role computerized systems can play in relieving the purchasing function of many routine clerical activities, while emphasizing opportunities for improved decision-making and control.

3. The recognition of the 15 cell form-function inventory matrix and its implication for the development of more sophisticated inventory control tools.
4. The identification of an enlarged opportunity for supplier development actions and their influence in establishing and maintaining "good suppliers."

Dean Ammer's book on *Materials Management*[5] has as its unifying theme the concept that to be effective purchasing should be conceived of as being one function in the flow of materials into, through, and out of the organization. In describing the scope of materials management, Ammer notes:

> With the exception of receiving [and] inspection, materials management embraces all other functions concerned with ordering, storage and movement of material. In the typical company, it would embrace the activities performed by the following major departments: purchasing, production control, stores, traffic, and physical distribution . . . .
>
> Materials Management is concerned with the flow of materials to and from the manufacturing departments. The materials manager regulates this flow in relation to changes in demand for finished products, actual or predicted prices of materials, supplier performance on quality and delivery, availability of materials, and other variables. He bases his decisions on information from other departments within his company, suppliers, and other sources, including news in business periodicals. In its simplest form, most of materials management consists of learning how to get what, when, and from whom.

Materials management in large part involves the process of making trade-offs among conflicting goals that have traditionally established priorities at different stages in the materials flow. In arguing for a materials management approach to sourcing, manufacturing, inventory management, and distribution, Ammer contends that the traditional organization structure acts as a deterrent to the optimization of the flow process. According to Ammer:

> *Basic principle.* All materials objectives are interrelated . . . a gain in one objective means sacrifice on other objectives. In materials management you never "get something for nothing," you may, however, be getting something you do not really want or need. If an organization does not identify its material management objectives and develop a program to achieve them, it may be giving undue attention to some objectives and neglecting others.
>
> In the organization where materials management objectives are not consciously identified, one objective, low-operating cost, tends to be concentrated on to the exclusion of all others. In fact, top management often is not really aware that any other objectives exist (although it may be conscious also of the continuity-of-supply objective). In such organizations, $1 may be saved in operating cost at the cost of a $5 saving in purchase prices or inventory

5. Ammer, Dean S., *Materials Management,* 3rd ed. (Richard D. Irwin, Inc., Homewood, Ill, 1974).

carrying costs. The objective in all too many organizations is to manage materials as cheaply as possible instead of as profitably as possible.

Organization limits. In many cases, organization structure inhibits achievement of a proper balance of objectives. When materials management functions are scattered throughout the organization, each materials subfunction tends to develop objectives of its own which may not be consistent with company objectives. For example, if a purchasing manager is made subordinate to a marketing manager, he begins to take on marketing objectives rather than those of materials management. Every subordinate tries to please his boss. And, in this case, the boss-pleasing effort might cause him to pay undue attention to secondary objectives like reciprocity and relatively little to more fundamental materials management objectives.

The wrong objectives get undue emphasis even in cases where the boss does not interfere. For example, a purchasing agent may give undue emphasis to the price objective and all but ignore the equally important objectives of continuity of supply, inventory, and quality. Similarly, a production control manager may be so conscious of the need for continuity of supply that he all but ignores the inventory objective. Materials objectives are most likely to be balanced in a rational fashion when responsibility for achievement is clearly delegated—preferably to a materials manager who has authority to do the job. Even then objectives are not static. The materials manager must always reevaluate them when business conditions change or when they are affected by top-management decisions.

Ammer divides the material cycle within an organization into seven stages: design, sourcing, production planning, ordering, receiving, inventory control, and final stages.

He identifies four aspects of the materials flow as being critical to success in managing the process. These are: (1) forecasting and planning; (2) inventory control; (3) supplier relations; and (4) cost reduction.

Forecasting and Planning. After identifying a variety of sources where materials managers may obtain guidance in forecasting the demand, supply, and prices of supply items, Ammer nevertheless stresses that forecasting is to be perceived as an art, not as a science:

Investment decisions are based not on current activity but on businessmen's estimates of future activity. Business forecasting is the art of anticipating future business decisions. Analyzing current statistics is not enough; the forecaster must predict how businessmen will react to these statistics and the forecasts on which they are based. If he has a knack for it, the materials manager is in a much better position to do this than the professional economist is. Economists can be expected to catch swings in business sentiment only when they show up in news releases and business statistics. The materials manager, on the other hand, is in daily contact with leaders of the business community—his suppliers. If he is an intelligent listener, he can sense changes that will not be reflected in GNP statistics for months to come.

Inventory Control. There is probably no element of the materials management process where the conflict of objectives, discussed earlier, is more clearly visualized than in inventory control. Ammer focuses on this issue both in his description of inventory control and in his discussion of various control systems. He summarizes his perspective on the significance of this conflict as follows:

> Thus, as in all the other phases of materials management, there is a conflict of objectives in inventory management. The objective of high inventory turnover conflicts with the objective of continuity of supply and other objectives (discussed in Chapter 3). Of all business assets, inventories are the least stable and most difficult to control. Unfortunately, both for their profits and for the economy as a whole, American corporations do a rather bad job of inventory management. Their inventories tend to be high when they should be low, and vice versa. Bad inventory planning has been one of the major causes of almost every business recession.

In the review of available control systems, he covers order-point and periodic control approaches as well as classical statistical techniques for analyzing and smoothing random variations in material demand. The traditional analytical methods for determining the EOQ and safety stocks are presented in great detail.

Supplier Relations. Like England and Leenders, Ammer stresses the importance of the benefits that come from nurturing the firm's complex of suppliers. His summary comment:

> Why do they go to the trouble? Suppliers not only can use a company's products but they also may become some of the company's biggest boosters if they are sold on the company as a customer. More important, suppliers can be an important source of cost-reduction ideas.

Cost Reduction. On the subject of cost reduction Ammer discusses in some detail break-even analysis, learning curves, and negotiating tactics as one approach to achieving savings; on the other side, he emphasizes value analysis, standardization, and operations research methods (e.g., linear programming and simulation). Ammer emphasizes the importance of this area in the following way:

> The most basic materials management objective is low prices, which have a more direct effect on profits than any other factor . . . if the average manufacturing company can reduce materials costs by just 2 percent it can boost its profits by 10 percent.

Ammer's *Materials Management* makes significant contributions in four areas:

1. It forcefully and logically presents the rationale behind the materials management concept and lays out clearly its scope and substance.
2. It focuses attention on the basic conflicts that exist among materials management objectives and shows how these are frequently translated into organizational clashes among various departments.
3. It identifies the vital role played by forecasting in all materials management activities and decisions. It presents the forecasting problem not as a mechanistic exercise, but as an art in which the forecaster applies experience and sensitivity to the available data, while at the same time offering a variety of analytical tools that can be used.
4. It presents a sound general overview of the field and, at the same time, describes in sufficient detail a wide range of techniques, strategies, and methods to provide value to the most operationally oriented managers.

In striking contrast to the operational perspectives of the purchasing texts, *Organizational Buying Behavior* by Webster and Wind[6] presents a behavioral viewpoint on the buying activity occurring within an organization. It is necessary to recognize that their point of view is that of marketers seeking to understand the process so that they may more effectively interact with the organization to influence buying decisions. Nonetheless, the integrated conceptual framework that is defined in the book is valuable to purchasing and materials specialists as well as to marketers.

Webster and Wind offer the following definition of organizational buying behavior:

Organizational buying behavior is therefore defined as the decision-making process by which formal organizations establish the need for purchased products and services, and identify, evaluate, and choose among alternative brands and suppliers. "Decision-making" is used here to include information-acquisition and -processing activities, as well as choice processes and the development of goals and other criteria to be used in choosing among alternatives.

As the foundation for presenting their own conceptual model, the authors briefly describe a number of alternative models of organizational buying behavior drawn from the literature of economics, purchasing, and marketing. The authors' position on these perspectives is that each "has concentrated primarily on one set of variables to the exclusion of others. Each illuminates a portion of the organizational buying process for our viewing and leaves the other parts in darkness." They therefore argue for and propose a more comprehensive and integrated model of the total process.

6. Webster, Frederick E. Jr. and Wind, Yoram, *Organizational Buying Behavior* (Prentice-Hall, Englewood Cliffs, New Jersey, 1972).

The Webster-Wind model is shown below in Figure A.1. In describing organizational buying behavior, Webster and Wind recognize the complex interactions that take place within an organization in response to buying needs that are perceived by the organization. In the first place, several individuals are involved in the buying decision process. These direct participants are members of the buying center and have certain specific roles to fulfill in carrying through the decision process. These roles have been identified as *deciders, influencers, buyers, users,* and *gatekeepers.* Any individual may play more than one role, and more than one individual in the buying center may be associated with each role.

Four groups of factors have been identified as the determinants of organizational buying behavior:

1. *Individual Factors*—The "set of needs, goals, habits, past experiences, information, attitudes and so on which each individual applies in each specific situation."
2. *Interpersonal Factors*—The interactions of members of the buying center based upon their roles in the process as well as the history of the group's previous interactions and social experiences.
3. *Organizational Factors*—The "objectives, policies, procedures, structure, and systems of rewards, authority, status and communication that define the formal organization as an entity and significantly influence the buying process at all stages." The organization's objectives also define the existence of a buying need in the first place.
4. *Environmental Factors*—In addition to the marketing stimuli of potential suppliers, the technical, social-cultural-political, and economic characteristics and institutions of the society exert an influence on the buying process.

Each of these four determinants has two subcategories. These are described as task elements and nontask-related elements, which, though probably self-evident, are defined below:

1. Task—"Those that are directly related to the organization's buying problem as defined by organizational objectives."
2. Nontask-Related—"Those that are not directly related to the buying problems."

In the balance of the book the authors present a detailed description and analysis of each of these four principal factors affecting organizational buying.

Environmental Influences. In their discussion of the environmental influences, Webster and Wind make the following observation:

Environmental influences are subtle and pervasive. They are hard to identify and describe, and they provide the context within which organizational, interpersonal, and individual factors in turn exert their influence. One way of

Figure A.1 *The Webster-Wind Model of Organizational Buying Behavior*

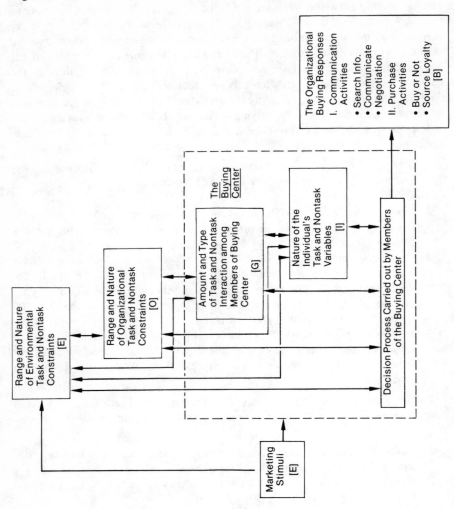

conceptualizing environmental factors is as a set of contraints on the organization—a set of predetermined boundaries beyond the control of the organization and its members. In another sense, the environment is a source of information which the organizational buyer takes into account in his decision-making behavior. The reckoning may be *explicit,* as is the case when one considers the significance of anti-trust regulation for a given decision, or it may be *implicit,* as is the case with basic cultural values and political beliefs.

As an aid in understanding the scope and level of these subtle influences, the authors provide a model of environmental effects on the organizational buying process, as seen in Figure A.2.

This model distinguishes between the types of influence (physical, technological, economic, etc.), the social institutions through which these influences are exerted, and the ways in which these influences impinge on buying decisions. The authors define this last relationship as follows:

As can be seen in this figure [see Figure A.2], environmental factors influence the buying decision process in four rather distinct ways. First, they define the availability of goods and services to the buying organization. Second, they define the general business conditions within which the firm must operate, including the business cycle, the political climate, the legal environment, and the availability of monetary resources. Third, they define the values and norms (for the society as a whole and for subgroups within that society) that provide an important set of criteria against which to evaluate alternative buying actions. Finally, the environment provides a flow of information to the buying organization and its members concerning both task and nontask communication on the availability of goods and services, general business conditions, and values and norms.

Organizational Influences. In presenting this facet of the process, Webster and Wind draw heavily on the research and concepts of organizational behavior. Using Harold Leavitt's[7] structural definition of organizations as the framework, they describe the effects of each of his four sets of organizational variables on buying behavior:

tasks—the work to be performed in accomplishing the objectives of the organization;

structure—systems of communication, authority, status, rewards, and work flow;

technology—problem-solving inventions used by the firm, including plant and equipment and programs for organizing and managing work;

people—the actors in the system.

In addition, the authors present a schematic representation of the influence of these factors on the organizational buying process (see Figure A.3).

7. Harold J. Leavitt, "Applied Organization Change in Industry: Structural, Technical, and Human Approaches," in William W. Cooper, Harold J. Leavitt, and Maynard W. Sheely, II, *New Perspectives in Organization Research* (John Wiley and Sons, New York, 1964), pp. 55–71.

Figure A.2 *A Model of Environmental Effects on the Organizational Buying Process*

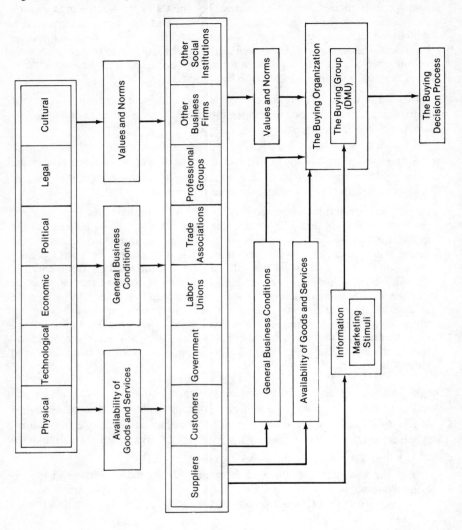

Figure A.3   *A Model of the Buying Organization*

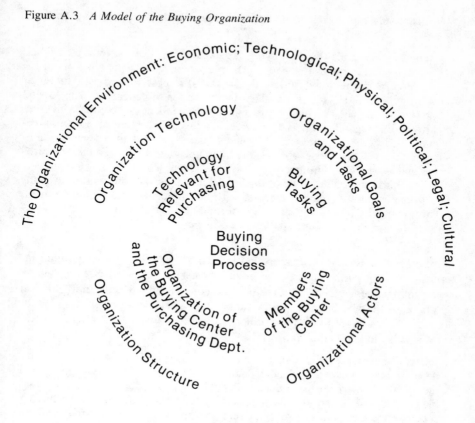

In discussing this pictorial model, the authors make the following observations:

> Implicit in the model of the buying organization . . . are several assertions. First, the model implies that each of the four elements of the buying organization (people, technology, structure, and tasks) is best viewed as a subset of each of these four sets of variables in the larger organization. The logical corollary of this view, which stresses the interdependency of buying with other parts of the organization, is that understanding the buying organization requires understanding the larger organizational system of interdependent elements. Second, the model stresses the interdependency between the organization and its larger environment.
>
> The third important feature of this model is that each of the four subsystems of organizational variables interacts with and influences each of the others. The people influence the structure, technology, and tasks; technology influences people, structure, and tasks; and so on.

Interpersonal Influences. Interpersonal influences, based on the continuing interaction among participants in the buying center, play a vital role in shaping organizational buying behavior. The buying center is defined as the individuals in an organization who interact during the buying decision-making process. Webster and Wind have divided the functions of the buying center into several specific roles indentified as follows:

> There are several distinct roles in the buying center: users, influencers, buyers, deciders, and gatekeepers. Understanding these roles will help one understand the nature of interpersonal influence in the buying decision process. It is quite likely that several individuals will occupy the same role within the buying center (e.g., there may be several users) and that one individual may occupy two or more roles (e.g., buyer and gatekeeper). All members of the buying center can be seen as influencers, but not all influencers occupy other roles.

In order to relate these roles to the various stages of the buying decision, Webster and Wind have developed a matrix (see Figure A.4).

The buyer in this network of relationships is described as follows:

> . . . the person in the organization with formal authority for the selection of sources of supply. Although this authority may be constrained in many important ways, it is in many cases the key *terminal* position of organizational responsibility for the buying decision. In other words, the buyer (or purchasing agent) is the final decision-maker, so that when other members of the buying center attempt to exert influence, their efforts are directed toward him with the intention of constraining or otherwise influencing the choices available to him.

In a summary comment on interpersonal factors in organizational buying behavior, Webster and Wind note that:

Interpersonal influences in the organizational buying decision process reflect the many different viewpoints of those organizational members who perceive that buying decisions are important to their performance within the organization. Users, influencers, deciders, buyers and gatekeepers interact to determine the outcome of the decision. Although the buyer has formal authority for the buying decision, his actual influence on the outcome of the decision process may be significantly reduced as the result of the influence of others at earlier stages of the buying process which defines the constraints on the feasible set of buying actions.

Buyers who are ambitious and wish to extend the scope of their influence will adopt certain tactics and engage in bargaining activities in an attempt to become more influential at earlier stages of the buying process. These tactics or bargaining strategies define the nature of the buyer's relationships with others of equal organizational status and structure the social situation that the potential supplier must face in dealing with the buying organization. An understanding of the nature of interpersonal relationships in the buying organization is an important basis for the development of marketing strategy.

Figure A.4   *Decision Stages and Roles in the Buying Center*

	User	Influencer	Buyer	Decider	Gate-keeper
Identification of Need	X	X			
Establishing Specifications and Scheduling the Purchase	X	X	X	X	
Identifying Buying Alternatives	X	X	X		X
Evaluating Alternative Buying Actions	X	X	X		
Selecting the Suppliers	X	X	X	X	

Individual Behavior. The detailed review of the various elements influencing organizational buying decisions concludes with the role of individual behavior, defined as follows:

At the heart of the organizational buying process, then, is the individual—a person both influencing and influenced by the other persons around him and by the organization and its various subsystems. Imbedded within these various influences (which, as we have seen, have both task and non-task dimensions), the individual makes his unique contribution to the workings of the organization. To understand organizational buying behavior we need to understand also the behavior of the organizational buyer as an *individual*.

In some respects, the individual buyer (or decider or influencer) within the organization is similar to the individual consumer or household purchaser. Certainly, the same basic mental processes—motivation, cognition, and learning—are basic psychological processes that must occur in all buying behavior.

In other respects, the buying behavior of individuals within the context of the organization is different from all other forms of buying behavior. As a member of the organization, the individual's behavior is influenced by the extent to which he accepts the goals of the organization as his personal objectives. He is also influenced by organizational members and structure, as we have seen. . . . Furthermore the organizational buyer is in a unique position by virtue of the information structure available to him within and through the organization. He may be exposed to a particular variety of information sources only because he is a member of that buying organization.

Thus, Webster and Wind draw together in one broad conceptual framework concepts from the behavioral sciences in order to describe and explain the organizational buying process. The usefulness of their study rests on three major contributions:

1. They have provided marketers with insights into the multidimensional character of organizational buying decisions and have suggested communications strategies for dealing with this complex process.
2. They have given purchasing managers a much clearer picture of the behavioral underpinnings of purchasing activities so that they may better manage the purchasing function.
3. They have presented a conceptual model that may serve as the foundation for further research. Since their model was published, a significant number of studies have used it as a conceptual framework. There is now solid empirical verification of the model; by providing an integrating framework, the model has contributed to the development of a body of knowledge about the procurement function.

Another study of purchasing behavior written for industrial marketers is Levitt's *Industrial Purchasing Behavior: A Study of Communications Effects.* [8] In comparison with the more recently written Webster and Wind book, Levitt focuses on aspects of individual buying behavior and does not take account of organizational, interpersonal, and environmental influences in purchasing decision-making. In particular, the Levitt study identifies two important variables that influence purchasing decisions: the *source effect* and the *presentation effect* of the seller's sales message. The first refers to the general reputation of the company the salesman represents. The second has to do with the quality of sales

---

8. Levitt, Theodore, *Industrial Purchasing Behavior: A Study of Communications Effects,* (Division of Research, Harvard Graduate School of Business Administration, Boston, 1965).

presentation: its substance, its clarity, and its relevance with regard to meeting the particular needs of the organization the buyer represents.

The research on which this study was based led the author to conclude that the relative impact of source and presentation effect varied depending upon whether the recipient of the sales message was a more technically sophisticated engineer or a less technical-minded but professionally competent purchasing agent. According to Levitt, source effect tends to have more influence on the former.

> The research found that the power of source effect (company reputation for credibility) varies by the character and "competence" of the recipient of a sales message. Thus, there is some indication that, in the case of complex industrial materials, purchasing agents, who are usually highly competent as professional buyers, may be less influenced by a company's generalized reputation than are technical personnel, who are presumably less competent as buyers but more competent as judges of a complex product's merits. In first appraising complex new materials on the basis of sales presentations made directly to them, technically sophisticated personnel seem to be influenced by the seller's reputation to a point that is unexpectedly higher than the influence of that reputation on such technically less sophisticated personnel as purchasing agents. In short, technical personnel are probably influenced far more by company reputation than has been widely assumed, and certainly more than such technically less sophisticated people as purchasing agents.

A second set of variables that affect the relative weight of source and presentation effect on buying decision relates to the degree of risk associated with a particular purchase. A *high-risk* decision might be a decision to adopt some new material or component the use of which could conceivably alter the end product and/or require production-process adjustments. A *low-risk* decision, by contrast, might relate to a routine purchase of items familiar to those who will use them, or a decision to undertake a further evaluation of some new product rather than reject it out of hand. The higher the risk, the more influence sales presentation has on the less technically oriented buyers. But the higher the risk, the more technically sophisticated personnel fall back on their own technical appraisals rather than trust the sales presentation. Thus:

> While all audiences seem to be influenced by the quality of the sales presentation, important differences apparently exist between purchasing agents and technical personnel. In the lower-risk decision situation of whether to give a newly presented complex new product a further hearing, technical personnel are more powerfully influenced by the quality of a direct sales presentation than are purchasing agents. Put differently, on low-risk purchasing decision, the technically less sophisticated purchasing agents seem to rely less heavily on the quality of the sales presentation than do the technically more sophisticated personnel in making their decisions. But on high-risk decisions (whether

actually to buy the product) the reverse is true: that is, the greater the risk, the more favorably purchasing agents are influenced by good sales presentations, and the less favorably technical personnel are influenced by such presentations. The greater the risk, the more likely technical personnel are to rely on their technical judgments about a new product's virtues rather than on the quality of the sales presentation in favor of the product. But purchasing agents, being technically less sophisticated, seem forced, in high-risk situations, to rely more heavily on the seller's presentation.[9]

Contrary to popular belief, the Levitt study demonstrates that industrial-buying behavior is not strictly guided by economic considerations but is powerfully affected by more subjective factors, not the least of which is the personal character and background training of the decision-maker. Translating his analysis into conclusions useful for industrial marketers, Levitt makes these observations:

It seems clear that company reputation is a powerful factor in the industrial purchasing process, but its importance varies with the technical competence and sophistication of the customer. The quality of a sales message and the way it is presented are capable of moderating the influence of this source effect, but again it varies by audience. Generally speaking, it pays for a company to be favorably well known, and perhaps especially among customers having some degree of technical sophistication, such as engineers and scientists. But superior sales messages and well-trained salesmen can help less well-known companies to overcome some of the disadvantages of their relative anonymity. A well-planned and well-executed direct sales presentation can be an especially strong competitive weapon for the less well-known company. Moreover, the greater the riskiness of the purchasing decision the customer is asked to make, the more likely it is that a good sales presentation will produce a customer decision in favor of the direction advocated by the source.

A third category of procurement literature views purchasing as essentially the art of negotiation—what happens when buyer and seller meet face to face and bargain about prices and other terms of a contractual relationship. A leading author of books on negotiation, and particularly well known in the purchasing fraternity, is Chester Karrass, who has written both *The Negotiating Game* and *Give and Take*.[10] His purpose in these books is to contribute to the understanding and to aid in the development of negotiating competence on the part of both buyers and sellers. In this respect, the Karrass books are essentially skill- or technique-oriented.

In *The Negotiating Game,* Karrass describes the personality traits, based on opinion surveys conducted among professionals, that tend to be characteristic of successful negotiators.

9. Theodore Levitt, "Communications and Industrial Selling," *Journal of Marketing,* Vol. 31 (April 1967), pp. 15–21.

10. Karrass, Chester L., *The Negotiating Game* (The World Publishing Company, New York, 1970), and *Give and Take* (Thomas Y. Crowell Company, New York, 1974).

Those who know most about negotiation, the professionals, have spoken. They collectively believe that the following seven traits are most important:

—Planning skill
—Ability to think clearly under stress
—General practical intelligence
—Verbal ability
—Product knowledge
—Personal integrity
—Ability to perceive and exploit power

From my experience and reading I would not quarrel with these findings except to add a few that I consider essential. A negotiator must think well of himself. This feeling of self-worth should come from a history of getting things done satisfactorily and faith in one's ability to understand and resolve the fundamental values being negotiated.

The ideal negotiator should have a high tolerance for ambiguity and uncertainty as well as the open-mindedness to test his own assumptions and the opponent's intentions. This requires courage. Finally, in every good negotiator there must be an inner desire to achieve, to aspire, to take that sensible but extra measure of risk that represents a commitment to one's strivings.

Karrass contends that of all the elements in the negotiation process aspiration level influences the outcome more than any other. He describes this factor in these terms:

An individual's level of aspiration represents his *intended* performance goal. It is a reflection of how much he wants—that is, a standard he sets for himself. *It is not a wish but a firm intention to perform that involves his self-image.* Failure to perform results in loss of self-respect.

Further, he relates aspiration level to certain personality traits, which he summarizes as follows:

In the light of recent experimental findings we may draw some conclusions about the relationship of personality to aspiration level. The achievement-oriented person is attracted to tasks that involve skill. Unlike the gambler, he prefers to take mid-range risks and tends to be realistic. He likes to do a job well for its own sake, and he is a persistent striver who believes that hard work pays off. This type of person tends to approach ambiguous situations with confidence of success, enthusiasm and optimism.

Achievement-oriented persons take a long-term view of life. They plan and direct their energies to projects that take time to complete. They are problem-solvers and obstacle-removers, patient, determined and competitive. When they have a job to do and need help, they choose experts. On the job they tend to talk about business rather than other matters. They have a lesser need for closure and black-and-white solutions than those who are not achievement-oriented.

The achievement-oriented person expects success and therefore sets his aspiration level high. He succeeds because he is realistic, persistent and receptive to feedback.

A second key element in the negotiating process is the relative degree of power held by buyer and seller. The successful negotiator develops, often intuitively, a sense of what power is and how it may be used most effectively. Karrass observes:

> For practical purposes power may be defined as *the ability of a negotiator to influence the behavior of an opponent*. The eight principles listed below are applicable to most transactions.
>
> *First,* power is always relative. Rarely if ever does a buyer or seller enjoy *complete* power.
>
> *Second,* power may be real or apparent. The fact that a position is supported by logic, justice or force does not guarantee success. A seller may be in a preferred position, but if neither he nor the buyer perceives the advantage, he has none. Conversely, the seller may be in a weak position due to lack of business, but if the buyer does not perceive this, the buyer's power is not enhanced.
>
> *Third,* power may be exerted without action. If an opponent believes that action can and will be taken against him, it may be unnecessary to act.
>
> *Fourth,* power is always limited. Its range depends upon the situation, government regulations, ethical standards and present or future competition.
>
> *Fifth,* power exists to the extent that it is accepted. A buyer who insists that he will not be exploited by a monopolistic seller is less likely to be victimized. Some people are simply less willing to be dominated than others and would rather do without than be exploited.
>
> *Sixth,* the ends of power cannot be separated from the means. One cannot hope to develop a loyal customer by using exploitive tactics. Several years ago we did business with a ruthless supplier because it was to our best interest to do so. The supplier, an aggressive conglomerate, was aware of its bargaining position and took the occasion to be uncompromising and disrespectful to our people. It was a short-lived victory, for it is now distrusted by industry and government buyers alike.
>
> *Seventh,* the exercise of power always entails cost and risk.
>
> *Eighth,* power relationships change over time. The balance of power moves as the balance of benefits and contributions from the parties change.

If these are the principles relevant to the use of power, what are its sources? That is, what factors constitute the power base from which one bargains? Karrass identifies nine sources of power:

> 1. BALANCE OF REWARDS. Rewards may be of a tangible or intangible nature. Financial rewards need not be expressed in profit alone but may come about as a result of goals associated with cash flow, liquidity, borrowing power, partial

coverage of fixed costs, maintenance of specialized productive resources or return-on-investment targets. Rewards may also be long run—that is, a result of expanded markets, products or channels of distribution.

2. BALANCE OF PUNISHMENT OR NONREWARD. One of the first lessons we learned as children is that parents can punish as well as reward. A seller can punish a buyer by circumventing his authority or by harassing him with minor changes. A buyer can punish a seller by threatening to remove him from a bidder's list or by rejecting a product for minor quality flaws irrelevant to its end use. Deadlock is an interesting form of punishment that leaves both parties in an unpleasant state of uncertainty.

3. BALANCE OF LEGITIMACY. No other source of power is so hypnotic in its effect as legitimacy. We have learned to accept the authority of ownership, tradition, appointment and laws to such an extent that we fail to question their applicability in changing situations. It is the attack on legitimacy by militant blacks and whites that so disturbs our society. Legitimacy is a source and symbol of power.

4. BALANCE OF COMMITMENT. Commitment, loyalty and friendship are benchmarks of power. Those with teenage children are aware that one of the strong bases of parental authority is associated with companionship rather than material rewards. Managers often learn that a mediocre worker who is committed to company objectives may be more effective than a talented but less dedicated man.

5. BALANCE OF KNOWLEDGE. Knowledge and the control of information is power. The more a negotiator knows about an opponent's objectives and bargaining position the stronger he is. Knowledge of product, marketplace, legal phraseology and regulations is also a source of strength. By the same token, a thorough understanding of the theory and practice of professional negotiation is an essential ingredient of power.

6. BALANCE OF COMPETITION. Competition has an important effect on bargaining power. The seller who can keep his plant busy on other work and the buyer with multiple sources are in a strong bargaining position.

7. BALANCE OF UNCERTAINTY AND COURAGE. Security is a goal that humans cherish. We share a desire to avoid risk wherever possible. The person who is willing to accept a greater burden of uncertainty with respect to reward or punishment enhances his power.

8. BALANCE OF TIME AND EFFORT. Time and patience are power. The party that is most constrained by time limits provides the opponent with a base of strength. It is for this reason that purchasing executives stress the importance of lead time and early-warning inventory systems.

9. BALANCE OF BARGAINING SKILL. Bargaining skill is power, and that's what this book is all about. The ability to plan, to persuade, to manipulate perceptions, to mobilize bias, to analyze power and decision-making, to select effective people to understand the theory and anatomy of negotiation constitutes a base of power available to buyer and seller alike. Can anyone afford to relinquish this source of strength?

Finally, in his analysis of negotiation, Karrass describes the bargaining process as taking place at five levels: (1) share bargaining; (2) problem solving; (3) attitudinal bargaining; (4) personal bargaining; and (5) in-group bargaining. The first relates to issues involving the division of benefits arising from the negotiations, that is, money and property as well as power or status. At this level, what one may gain the other will lose. By contrast, the problem-solving level is that phase in which each party can help the other to achieve certain goals at no expense to themselves. To do so requires that each understand the problems of the other and work openly toward mutual and acceptable solutions.

Identifying attitudinal bargaining as a level of negotiation recognizes that each party inevitably starts with preconceived beliefs, opinions, and biases about the other and ideas about how to approach the interchanges. Satisfactory outcomes are contingent upon mutually modifying attitudes and preconceptions so that the problem-solving and share-bargaining processes may take place.

Personal bargaining is the label Karrass gives to the struggle within the individual negotiator to reconcile his own personal goals, values, and aspirations with the facts of a realistic and acceptable outcome. In-group bargaining goes beyond the individual to take account of the conflicting goals and performance measures of all of the actors on one side or the other. According to Karrass:

> In a strict sense, organizations do not have objectives, but people within them do. Each member of a decision-making coalition has his own level of aspirations and a personal definition of the critical issues. The negotiator is but one member of the coalition that establishes group goals. Furthermore, each of the participants has an individual value system and represents a different degree of power, status and bargaining skill. What we normally call bargaining objectives is really an outcome of the in-group process.
>
> Conflict within an organization is the result of differences in facts, goals, methods or values among members. The variations cause group members to look at issues in a personal way and to search for group solutions that provide as much safety and satisfaction as possible to themselves. In such cases, the negotiator is faced with the uncomfortable task of reconciling a bewildering number of in-group demands. Unfortunately, the opponent is not inclined to be helpful.

Overall, Karrass contributes significantly to an understanding of that skill which is at the heart of procurement as a professional pursuit. His discussions of aspiration levels and of the sources and uses of power as elements in purchasing negotiation are particularly useful. His recognition that the bargaining process goes beyond dividing benefits and risks between two parties and that it also involves mutual problem-solving and conflict reconciliation on each side is an enlightened perception of one of the world's oldest rituals.

Thus, the literature of procurement ranges in its foci from purchasing techniques, to negotiating skills, to broad descriptions of buying behavior. At one level, it deals with the tasks, tools, and techniques of line purchasing. At another, it focuses on procurement as an organizational process and describes it in the language of the behavioral sciences.

Given the great magnitude and scope of purchasing activities, and given their importance to the success of any business or nonprofit institution, as well as their impact on economic, political, and social systems, the supporting body of writing is relatively sparse. Compared with the literature of marketing, for example, it is thin indeed. The contributions of a limited number of authors, including those described above, have carried a considerable burden of representing the field to students, academicians, and business practitioners.

Appendix B

CASE PROBLEMS IN PROCUREMENT STRATEGY, ORGANIZATION, AND DECISION-MAKING

LIST OF CASES

GENERAL MOTORS (1)

Sourcing for the Catalytic Converter

It was December 9, 1969 and Tom Hustead, chief engineer at GM's AC Spark Plug Division, was on a company plane flying to a meeting in Rochester, New York.

George Chestnut, general manager of AC, was in the back with GM President Ed Cole. Suddenly George came forward and said, "Tom, you better come back here. Ed Cole is talking about having AC develop and manufacture seven million catalytic converters a year."

Gee, I thought, I can't even spell "catalytic"!

Mr. Cole had been at the White House with other industry leaders in November to review the proposed HEW[1] emission standards for 1971, 1975 and 1980. He reported that GM believed it was technically feasible to develop systems to meet the then proposed 1975 standards (but there were just no technological answers for the 1980 standards). Then in January, at a meeting of the Society of Automotive Engineers in Detroit, Cole stated that GM, beginning with its 1971 models, would lower the compression ratios of its engine to prepare for the day when the lead would go out of gasoline and the converter would go in. Excerpts from Mr. Cole's speech are included in Exhibit 5.

In September 1970 amendments proposed to the Clean Air Act were introduced in Congress which, in effect, moved the previously proposed 1980 standards up to 1975–76. The passage of the amendments catapulted the auto industry into crash programs to meet what seemed at the time to be impossible demands. The allowable emissions levels for 1975 were now one-fourth of what they were previously.

At GM, the AC Spark Plug Division (AC) was assigned the task of developing and manufacturing a converter through which engine exhaust gases would pass to remove carbon monoxide (CO), hydrocarbons (HC), and oxides of nitrogen (NOx). AC was the division at GM which manufactured a wide range of automotive parts such as oil filters, air filters, spark plugs, switches, and instruments. It supplied these components, both to its allied divisions (Chevrolet, Buick, Oldsmobile, Pontiac and Cadillac) and through distribution to the automotive aftermarket.

Although responsibility for the converter rested with AC, Mr. Cole personally devoted a significant amount of his time working with Hustead and AC engineers on the design of a new catalytic converter and made important contributions.

---

1. U.S. Department of Health, Education and Welfare.

All quantitative data not publicly available, names of vendor companies, and names of GM personnel (except those of Messrs. Cole, Hustead and Chestnut) have been disguised.

Cole had come up through engineering at GM and had always maintained an active professional interest in this function, even as president. At the outset, the engineering team was divided about the design of the catalyst system. One group favored the so-called 'monolith', the core unit of which would be a cylindrical ceramic substrate, molded like a honeycomb and coated with a catalyst. Others believed that the substrate should be small ceramic beads rather than a single cylinder, to provide a large surface area over which exhaust gases would pass. As for catalyst materials with which to coat the ceramic surface, GM engineers initially focused their search on base metals. It became clear following EPA hearings in the spring of 1972, however, that base metals would be inadequate for meeting the emerging emissions control requirements. The search then shifted to the noble metals including platinum, palladium and rhodium as the only possible materials for surface-coating the ceramic carriers. In addition, it was apparent from the outset that the catalytic converter could work only with unleaded gasoline. Exhaust from leaded gasoline would quickly cover the catalysts with a lead coating and render any exhaust emissions control system inoperative.

Although GM President Cole strongly favored the monolith design, the decision was made to undertake parallel developments of both types of converters. AC engineering teams were assigned to design a monolith and a bead converter and a search was begun for outside suppliers who would build plants to make both types of catalysts initially.

By 1973, tests seemed to indicate the superiority of the beaded substrate and thereafter developmental work was focused on this concept. The GM catalytic converter as designed is shown in Exhibit 1. It consisted of an outer cover and an inner shell of aluminized stainless steel with a layer of ceramic-fiber insulation in between. The catalyst was carried in a louvred retainer made of a special chrome stainless-steel. There were input and output tubes through which the exhaust passed. A removable plug was built into the converter through which the catalyst could be removed and replaced, although the system was designed to last for 50,000 miles without a changeout. It would go on all 1975 GM cars and light trucks (up to 6,001 pounds gross vehicle weight). Two sizes were planned, one which would take 175 cubic inches of catalysts (the "175") and one which would contain 260 cubic inches (the "260"). The converter would be positioned on the underside of the car at a point below the front passenger seat (see Exhibit 2).

Sourcing for the catalytic converter was a mammoth undertaking. It involved:

(1) Locating and contracting for sources of platinum and palladium.
(2) Developing sources for making and coating the catalyst substrate.
(3) Arranging for large supplies of a special grade of stainless steel.
(4) Building and equipping new AC manufacturing facilities to make the outer

cover, the stainless-steel inner shell and the louvred retainer and to assemble the converters. Working closely with outside suppliers of catalyst and stainless steel to design and construct dedicated facilities.
(5) Establishing outside sources for the input and output tubes, the plug, rivets and the ceramic fiber insulation.

This case describes the sourcing history for catalyst materials and stainless steel. It describes as well the difficult problems which GM faced in mid-1975 because (1) demand for automobiles had fallen far short of what had been anticipated when sourcing arrangements were made for the catalytic converter and (2) the Environmental Protection Agency (EPA) and other organizations had raised questions about dangers that might possibly be associated with the use of the catalytic converter and (3) there was great uncertainty regarding the acceptable levels of emissions that would be legislated in California for that state and by the Congress for the United States as a whole.

Developing Sources for the Noble Metals.

In May, 1972, Ed Cole called me into his office and said he wanted me to find out about the world supply of platinum and palladium. I contracted with Arthur D. Little [a consulting firm] to make a study, and they did a very thorough job in a very short time.

These were the recollections of Mr. Tom Christian who at the time was GM staff director of procurement, reporting to the executive-in-charge, production control, procurement and logistics in the Central Office.

The ADL study indicated that palladium and platinum were very limited in supply and that significant new production capacity would have to be developed to satisfy the new automotive emissions control requirements. Relative to existing production of platinum and palladium, these needs were considerable. Mr. Cole estimated that by 1975 GM alone would have to have 300,000 troy ounces[2] of platinum yearly for the catalytic converter and 120,000 troy ounces of palladium.

Shortly after receiving the ADL report, a GM negotiating team[3] held discussions with potential Russian sources, but an early decision was made, however, to focus sourcing efforts on South African mining companies instead. According to Christian:

Buying from Russia could be risky in the long-run. Availability of supply would be uncertain and we didn't feel we had any protection against drastic price changes.

2. One troy ounce = 1.097 ounces.
3. The GM team included Mr. Christian and Mr. Fred Eustis, a member of the GM legal staff as well as the GM staff manufacturing vice president, and an assistant controller on the GM financial staff.

As recalled by Fred Eustis:

The Russians held themselves out as ready, willing and able but the whole discussion foundered on price.

In South Africa platinum and palladium came from the Merensky Reef area near Johannesburg and was found in a vein that ran southwest to northeast and averaged three feet in thickness. This vein outcropped on the earth's surface at the southwest end and was about a thousand meters below the surface at the other end. The proportions of different metals coming out of this source were as follows according to the ADL report:

platinum	60%
palladium	27
ruthenium	5
rhodium	2.7
iridium	.7
osmium	.6
gold	4
	100%

Inquiries were mailed to seven possible sources in South Africa with great care being taken to time-stamp and register the letters and put them in the mail at the same time. Well before this time, GM lawyers instructed all those who had any knowledge of the sourcing program for the noble metals not to deal in the stocks of the mining companies or in the futures markets for these metals. As was expected the prices of platinum and palladium rose sharply when news of GM's inquiry became known. Prior to the inquiry, platinum had been selling at $135 a troy ounce. Its price on the futures market reached over $300 when it became known that GM would be negotiating for a supply of platinum and palladium.

Responses to GM's inquiries served to narrow prospective suppliers to two South African mining companies, Ibis and Van Horne. Representatives of both concerns came to Detroit for initial discussions but further negotiations with both were conducted in Johannesburg. The Van Horne proposal emerged as the more attractive one to the GM team both for reasons of overall cost and because it embodied several features not advanced by Ibis.

To meet GM's anticipated requirements, Van Horne would invest approximately $75 million to cover sinking new mine shafts and adding refining capacity. A major part of the investment, as well, would go into building a town to house and care for 10,000 additional workers.

The initial prices which were negotiated were $110 a troy ounce for platinum and $60 a troy ounce for palladium. The platinum price included 35 rands[4] per troy ounce for each ounce below 300,000 troy ounces of platinum. Thereafter

4. At that time one rand = $1.25

prices would be adjusted annually based on mutually agreed-upon economic indices. To be acceptable to both parties the price adjustment arrangement would (1) provide for objectively determined revisions without involving the auditing of the vendor's internal accounts, (2) not take away from his incentives for cost reduction, and (3) maintain reasonable price stability for the buyer. The base, therefore, selected for price adjustment purposes was the platinum and palladium producers' prices as reported weekly in *Metalworking News*. Van Horne consented to including a "most favored nations" clause in the contract: it would sell noble metals to no other customer for emissions control applications at a price lower than the one charged to GM. The mining company also agreed to set up a three-months buffer stock, part near the mine in South Africa and part in London.

In addition, the GM/Van Horne contract provided that GM would pay cancellation charges if it wanted to reduce or withdraw entirely from its contractual commitment. Its liabilities under these clauses of the contract would increase rapidly as Van Horne built up its investment in new facilities between October 1972 and December 1973, before any deliveries were made. Cancellation liabilities then would decline gradually as investment was amortized in the price of delivered metal.

The contract would be for ten years. As seen by GM team members, this term represented a compromise between the desirability of preserving maximum flexibility in the light of future uncertainties and the opportunity to pay for the amortization of Van Horne's investment over an extended period in order to minimize unit cost.

After working out the terms of a contractual arrangement with Van Horne, the GM team did not then return for further negotiations with Ibis for two reasons. Ibis representatives had indicated early on in the discussions that they didn't want to be in a position of being whipsawed. In addition, the GM team anticipated the possibility that needs in excess of the then foreseen requirements might call for a future second source, logically Ibis. Van Horne representatives had been skittish about committing to amounts as great as 300,000 troy ounces of platinum and 120,000 troy ounces of palladium.[5] They were particularly concerned that the noble metals might be obsoleted for reasons of technical development as catalysts in emissions control applications.

Developing Catalyst Capacity. Concurrent with efforts to establish sources for noble metals, GM managers worked on finding outside manufacturers to make catalysts. It would be necessary to find sources for the substrate, either in pellet or monolith form, and to have it coated with a solution made from platinum and palladium. There were tremendous uncertainties. At that time the form of the substrate, pellet or monolith, was one. The material from which the substrate

5. As it developed subsequently, GM's needs never reached these amounts. Car demand declined and a smaller amount of catalyst per car was required than had been originally anticipated.

would be made was another. The proportions of the metals in a coating solution and the thickness of the coating that would be applied to the substrate were also unknowns.

But time was short and Cole moved quickly to assure that GM would be ready to meet the 1975 emissions standards. Christian recollected:

> Mr. Cole told me to get in touch with Reade & Co. and 'get something on paper.' He had talked with one of Reade's top executives and was persuaded, first, that Reade could do the job and, second, that it would need at least 20 months lead-time.

In the meantime technical development work was proceeding on the substrate and the solution. The most suitable material for the former was found to be alumina. As for the coating, it was determined that the most suitable proportions of platinum and palladium would be about the same as the ratio in which these two metals came out of the ground in South Africa.

In August 1972, two companies, Reade and Cox, were given letter agreements authorizing each one to proceed with the simultaneous development of engineering designs for plants to make the monolith catalyst carrier as well as pellets. (Both companies were known as leading suppliers of catalysts for a wide range of industrial manufacturing processes.) Although persuaded that the monolith was superior, Mr. Cole had compromised with the opinions of others, including Hustead, that the pellet concept was better.

The letters of intent committed GM to paying on a monthly basis for investments in engineering work and plant and equipment. When the supplier began delivering acceptable catalysts to GM, it (the supplier) would repay GM and then amortize the investment in the cost of the product.

Tom Christian, AC engineering managers and Mr. Bob Beall of AC purchasing had also been working on locating potential catalyst manufacturers. They identified and screened more than 60 companies, narrowing the list down, including Reade and Cox to seven by July 1972. These seven were thoroughly evaluated on such factors as their tentatively proposed price per cubic foot of catalyst, engineering competence, quality control procedures, management depth, financial stability and "housekeeping." As shown in Exhibit 4, these factors were rated on a one-seven scale (with one the top rating in any case) and then the ratings were weighted to reflect the relative importance of each factor. Price (cost per converter) was given the most weight (six), and quality control procedures the next (four). Production control (ability to meet fluctuations in schedules, and general production control procedures) was also weighted four.

In November 1972, Carney Chemical was given a letter agreement authorizing this company to begin work on designing a facility to manufacture catalysts in pellet form. Carney had been using a ceramic substrate manufactured by a large

British firm, Catalyst Carriers Ltd. (CCL), for experimental purposes, and immediately contracted with CCL for its total output.

In March 1973, the judgment was made to go with the pellet concept in the catalytic converter, because the surface area to which emissions would be exposed would be much greater using pellets as opposed to the monolith honeycomb and because of the greater physical strength of pellets. By June 1973, AC engineers had tested extensively the samples submitted by the seven major candidates and others. They concluded that the catalysts made by one firm, Fulmer, met GM's tentative specifications while the samples from three other companies, while not yet meeting GM's specifications, were sufficiently promising in quality to warrant GM's making formal contractual arrangements. They were Reade, Carney and Regal Scientific.

In November 1973, Cox, to which a letter agreement had been issued, was terminated and received cancellation charges of $5.75 million. The pellets it had produced crumbled in the steel retainer in certain test modes. In the meantime, in August 1973, even before AC engineering had officially qualified them as GM suppliers, AC purchasing negotiated contracts with the four most promising firms because deliveries would need to begin in April 1974. The contracts were for three years. Price was stipulated in each contract to take effect as of August 19 and would be adjusted on May 1, 1974 for the 1975 model year. Price escalation was based on any increases in the price of the ceramic substrate, the vendor's cost of fuel, wage increases provided for under the vendor's labor contracts, and increases in the cost of other materials based on the Industrial Chemicals Commodity Price Index in the *Survey of Current Business*. Prices for the 1976 model year (beginning May 1, 1975) and the 1977 model year would be redetermined based on the seller's actual costs for the previous year. And, according to the contracts:

> In the negotiation of a fair and reasonable catalyst price, the parties agree that such catalyst price shall not be measured solely by cost, with profit being a percent thereof, but that the parties shall also consider in their pricing philosophy the aspect of a fair return on investment.

The contracts also stipulated cancellation charges based on the vendor's build-up in investment. In the case of Carney Chemical, for example, GM's exposure would be $12 million on September 1, 1973, $14.7 million on April 1, 1974 and $13.2 million on July 1, 1974 (assuming that delivery of acceptable product began on schedule on May 1). In addition, GM was committed to pay for ending inventories of catalysts up to a limit of 30,000 cubic feet in the event of final cancellation. For purposes of price redetermination and possible cancellation settlements, GM had the right to audit vendors accounting records.

Price calculations did not include the cost of platinum and palladium. GM would sell this metal to the catalyst supplier and would, in effect, buy it back when it received finished product.[6] The contracts also included a provision requiring the catalysts suppliers to assume 25% of the cost of an automobile recall (up to $225,000) if the reason for the recall was failure of the catalyst to conform to specifications. Another contract provision stipulated that the benefits of any "value engineering" contributions made by the vendor would be shared 50/50 with GM in redetermining price.

As it subsequently developed, a particularly important contract provision was the one which required the four firms to share process technology at no cost and allowed GM to require anyone to take technology from another. On the other hand, a supplier would not be liable for failure to perform to GM specifications if the reason related to the fact that it could not achieve satisfactory results having been required by GM to adopt another technology. Exercising its rights under this provision, GM asked Reade to adopt Fulmer technology and Carney to use processes developed by Regal Scientific.

From May 1972 to September 1973, according to Christian, he and Bob Beall and Ray Jones from AC purchasing spent nearly all their time working on the catalyst contracts:

The contracts were complicated and we were delayed waiting for approvals from AC engineering.

By September 1973, three of the four suppliers had been approved by AC engineering. Reade, however, had been unable, using Carney technology, to make catalysts that would last for the required 50,000 miles.

Stainless Steel Sourcing. The catalytic converter would require an estimated 55,000 tons annually of a special grade of stainless steel for the converter itself. An additional 32,000 tons would be required by the Chevrolet Division for connecting tubes. That amount altogether would increase the demand on U.S. stainless steel producers by 25% for this particular grade at a time when steel of all types was in very short supply. With considerable reluctance three suppliers agreed to commit a total of 31,000 tons a year. One large steel supplier was persuaded to build new capacity to produce 38,000 tons annually. GM entered into one-year contracts with the first three and a three-year contract with the steel company which constructed new stainless steel capacity. GM's total contractual commitments in the first year amounted to $64 million even though the great bulk of the steel would be purchased not by GM itself but by its suppliers. Normally, purchasing managers were unwilling to enter into contracts with materials suppliers, in effect, on behalf of their (GM's) parts suppliers. In this instance,

---

6. Elaborate security procedures were established by GM and Van Horne against the possibility of theft or hijacking, since GM owned the metal when it left South Africa.

however, steel company representatives had expressed a strong preference for dealing directly with GM. They wanted stainless steel requirements emanating from a single point and they wanted GM itself to assume the contractual responsibility in what they regarded as a risky venture.

The contracts provided for price escalation. Adjustments would be made quarterly based on a formula which took account of the price of chrome, labor rates in the steel industry and the U.S. wholesale price index.

The Situation in 1975. From the beginning the catalytic converter program had been fraught with uncertainty for both GM and its suppliers. There were the inherent difficulties of estimating the demand for automobiles in 1975 and beyond. There was the risk that the particular design concept developed by GM engineers for controlling automotive exhaust emissions could be technically obsoleted. Then there was the ever-present possibility that the EPA, the Congress, or the state legislature in California could significantly change the requirements being imposed on the automobile industry. As of mid-1975 these uncertainties still remained.

A particular problem that troubled GM was the large contractual commitments it had made to suppliers in the face of sharply declining demand for automobiles. In July 1972 when GM purchasing managers had requested quotations from catalyst suppliers, the estimate of GM car production for the 1975 model year on which they made their plans was 6.3 million cars. A year later the forecasts for 1975 for planning purposes had to be adjusted downward to 5.25 million cars. GM volume in the 1975 model year was actually 4.25 million cars. In mid-1975 the planning volumes for the 1976 and 1977 model years was 4.15 million cars in each year. In 1975 only 165,000 troy ounces of platinum had been taken against the original commitment with Van Horne for 300,000 troy ounces and 120,000 troy ounces of palladium. Fortunately, no penalties had to be paid because the producer could sell the output elsewhere. Moreover, in late 1974, GM renegotiated with Van Horne to adjust the minimum contractual amounts on platinum to 200,000 troy ounces and on palladium to 80,000 troy ounces although Van Horne was still obligated to supply metal at the original commitment levels if GM required it to do so. The reduction of its commitment in the amount of 100,000 troy ounces of platinum and 40,000 troy ounces of palladium cost GM approximately $18 million in an advance cancellation charge. This amount could be recouped in whole or in part in the form of lower prices for amounts taken by GM in excess of the minimums. The requirement for platinum was estimated to be 165,000 troy ounces for the 1976 model year and possibly 190,000 troy ounces in 1977 based on projected car sales.

As for stainless steel, although GM's contracts provided in total for a supply of 69,000 tons a year, it used only 43,000 tons in the 1975 model year. As of mid-1975 the one-year contracts had not been renewed; the largest supplier's new plant had been shut down for four months and there was a $12 million stainless steel inventory at the AC catalytic converter plant in Milwaukee.

The sourcing of catalysts from the four suppliers posed a particularly troublesome problem in the face of declining car volume. Contracts had been signed for 750,000 cubic feet of catalyst but GM had only been able to take 530,000 cubic feet from its suppliers and was liable for penalties for amounts not taken. Each of the four suppliers posed somewhat different problems for GM.

Regal Scientific. In the 1975 model year, Regal Scientific had delivered 155,000 cubic feet of catalyst to GM and had been a satisfactory supplier. Its price after providing for escalation factors had been $92.33 per cubic foot. In continuing negotiations with GM, this company had offered volume price reductions for the 1976 model year as follows:

155,000 cubic feet	$104.11 per cubic foot
200,000 cubic feet	97.27 per cubic foot
300,000 cubic feet	90.48 per cubic foot

The reasons for these volume discounts related to manufacturing economies of scale as well as volume price reductions from Catalyst Carriers, Ltd. for the substrate. Commitments for any volume above 155,000 cubic feet would not have to be made at the beginning of the year. Instead year-end price adjustments could be made for actual amounts taken. The penalty for taking less than the minimum volume would be $56.17 a cubic foot.

Fulmer. Fulmer had delivered 147,000 cubic feet of catalyst in the 1975 model year. Based on escalation its price had risen from $61.29 to $66.08 over the year. Under price redetermination its price for the 1976 model year would be $100.93 for a comparable quantity. The difference of $34.85 from its 1975 price was accounted for by increased costs of alumina, a higher usage of platinum and palladium than was originally contemplated, and underestimating other cost factors originally. In addition the 1976 price included $14 per cubic foot toward amortizing of a $3 million loss on the catalyst project in 1975. The exact amount had been a matter of prolonged negotiation. GM's contract with Fulmer was not explicit on the extent of GM's obligations to make up these losses. While the contract had recognized the principle of compensation based on a fair return-on-investment and provided for price redetermination, GM negotiators didn't feel GM should be liable for a supplier's inefficiencies.

Carney Chemical. This supplier had accounted for 175,000 cubic feet of catalysts received by GM or 25,000 cubic feet over the minimum for which GM had contracted. Carney's price had been $92.68 for the 1975 model year. For the 1976 year, Carney and GM had negotiated the following schedule of prices:

150,000 cubic feet	$98.23 per cubic foot
250,000 cubic feet	93.15 per cubic foot
300,000 cubic feet	90.67 per cubic foot

Reade and Co. Catalyst samples submitted by Reade did not pass GM qualification tests and this company had not, therefore, supplied any catalyst to General Motors. The product met physical specifications but it could not pass the 1000-hour accelerated-life test designed to determine whether or not the catalyst would last for the required 50,000 miles. Engineers from Reade and GM, working together, had been unable to determine the cause of the problem. They did not know whether the difficulty was with the substrate, the preparation of the catalytic solution or in the coating process. Combinations of substrates and catalytic solutions from the three other GM suppliers were being tested in the Reade plant. According to the contract, however, GM was liable to Reade for $15 million for not taking the 243,000 cubic feet for which it had contracted in 1975. Reade representatives claimed that failure to perform was due to the fact that Reade had been required by GM to take technology from another supplier, namely Fulmer, and had to invest an additional $8.5 million in plant over the $10 million already invested. If GM was to terminate Reade completely as of the end of the 1975 model year, the penalty would be $25.3 million.[7] Reade negotiators had proposed that GM pay Reade $2 million on April 1, 1975 as interest on the amounts Reade had invested over a two-year period. In addition they wanted payments of $700,000 a month to cover depreciation on facilities ($450,000), operating expenses ($150,000) and interest ($100,000).

The prices which Reade quoted for 1976 were as follows:

250,000 cubic feet	$112 per cubic foot
150,000 cubic feet	142 per cubic foot
100,000 cubic feet	180 per cubic foot

The price for 250,000 cubic feet would be lowered to $106 per cubic foot if GM paid Reade the $2 million in interest that Reade claimed.

7. This amount was calculated as follows:

Capital expenditures	$19.7 million
Start-up costs	2.3
Fulmer royalties for alumina substrate technology	.8 million
Shut-down costs	.5 million
Interest on capital investment	1.7 million
Engineering work on plant design	.3 million
	$25.3 million

For the 1976–78 model years the four suppliers had indicated the following penalties, on a cubic foot basis, for failure to take minimum amounts under contract in any year:

Fulmer	$52.66
Reade[8]	64.26
Carney	59.50
Regal	60.72

If GM should elect to terminate any of the four suppliers at the end of any model year, 1975 through 1978, it faced the following cancellation payments:

	1975	1976	1977	1978
Fulmer	$3.7 million	$3.4 million	$2.7 million	0
Reade	25.3	26.1	16.2	$6 million
Carney	12.7	9.6	5.6	0
Regal	8.3	6.7	3.7	0

These penalty payments were calculated to include unrecovered capital expenses and start-up costs, interest on investment and shut-down expenses. One supplier, Carney, claimed that in addition GM would owe it an amount for return on investment in the event of termination.

The Longer Term. Planning for the catalytic converter for the longer term was particularly difficult. EPA representatives and some public groups had gone on record as questioning the desirability of using this design for emissions control. For example, Eric O. Stork, the EPA's chief mobile-source pollution control officer, told a luncheon audience[9] in Detroit on June 10, 1975 that the catalytic converter was a potential fire hazard.

In certain failure modes and during extended idling periods, catalysts get hot enough to ignite combustible materials with which they may come in contact, and one of the most important things that can be done is to give the motorist warning . . . . It's not a tricky thing to install an overheating sensor of some kind. It's a Mickey Mouse kind of a problem.

Although believing that such a warning device was essential, Stork did indicate that the problem may have been over-publicized and its magnitude exaggerated.

8. The schedule of penalties for Reade was based on the assumption that the contract could be extended to four years rather than the original three.

9. A session of the Automotive Electronics Conference and Exposition. Mr. Stork's speech was reported in the *Detroit Free Press* of June 11, 1975, page 9-C.

We have been working with the U.S. Forestry Service on the problem, and one of the troubles in investigating it is finding such fires.

A potentially more serious problem was the fact that the converter, while controlling carbon monixide and NOx emissions, gave off sulfuric acid. Cars with converters gave off about 35 times as much sulfuric acid as those without converters, according to EPA representatives. Accordingly in March 1975 EPA Administrator Russell E. Train announced that new EPA standards covering sulfates emissions would soon be issued for the model year 1979. As reported in a *Business Week* article in the March 24, 1975 issue:

. . . according to the automakers, there is no practical way to remove sulfates from exhaust. The likely result of Train's action, therefore, will be the removal of the converters. "At the levels EPA is talking about (.001 to .01 gm/mile of sulfuric acid), we will have to meet the standard without a converter," says Donald A. Jensen, director of Ford Motor Co.'s emissions office.

Ironically, Ford and GM suddenly are defending converters. "EPA threw us a curve," says Ernest S. Starkman, GM vice-president of environmental activities. GM, says Starkman, had counted on the converters to meet President Ford's goal of 40% mileage improvement by 1980.

While Train gave the converter high marks for fuel economy—with them, 1975 cars average 13.5% better mileage—he insisted he was forced to curb their sulfuric acid emissions. At some point, he said, more effective converters might do more harm than good. GM and Ford disagree. Says Jensen, "We don't think EPA should be establishing standards until they know what sulfuric acid levels the standard would result in."

Only Chrysler embraces the EPA decision. "I'm very pleased," says Charles M. Heinen, Chrysler's director of vehicle emissions and long-time foe of catalytic converters. His pleasure stems largely from Chrysler's plans to meet present standards without converters. By 1977 the company hopes to equip most of its cars with a "leanburn engine," which, with an electronically controlled spark, meets present emission standards with a 5% fuel economy improvement. And with higher octane leaded gasoline, compression can be boosted adding another 4% gain, Heinen says. GM and Ford have been exploring similar engines but apparently have not matched Chrysler's success.

GM argued strongly in public statements that the catalytic converter be retained and based its case not only on the converter's effectiveness in controlling emissions but also on the fuel economies it made possible. Efforts to control emissions before 1975 when catalytic converters were used had resulted in engine modifications that achieved some reduction in the levels of undesirable emissions but reduced miles per gallon of gasoline as well. GM also argued publicly that the 1975 emissions standards for 1975 should be continued in order to help the company meet public goals on gasoline economy. Tighter emissions standards could only be achieved in the short run, it was contended, at the cost of fuel efficiencies.

In its publicly issued *1974 General Motors Report on Programs of Public Interest* (dated April 1975) an article on "Vehicle Emissions, Fuel Economy and Air Quality Standards," GM said in part:

In August 1974, GM submitted a comprehensive document to the Federal Energy Administration projecting GM automobile fuel usage in terms of miles per gallon. President Ford, in his television address of October 8, 1974, requested auto manufacturers to achieve a voluntary 40% improvement in average fuel economy by the 1980 models, as compared with 1974 models. GM's response was not only to agree with the President's improvement program, but to commit GM to an all-out effort to achieve the goal, assuming a continuation of emission and safety standards at the 1975 levels. . . .

GM's 1975 models have demonstrated significant gains over 1974—about a 29% improvement on the basis of the Government's proposed measuring procedure. This is because the catalytic converter has allowed engines to be retuned for more efficient operation and because rear axle ratios have been changed. Some additional progress is expected in 1976. Added improvements will result from the lighter, more fuel-efficient 1977–1980 model GM vehicles, provided Congress amends the Clean Air Act to allow an extension of the 1975 emissions standards through 1980, as GM has requested. By 1978, which is as far as definitive product plans are projected at this time, it is anticipated that average fuel economy for GM cars will be at least 18.1 miles per gallon, a 48% improvement over 1974. With reasonable improvements, the 18.7 miles per gallon goal (53% improvement) should be within reach by 1980. . . .

As shown in Exhibit 5, The Federal exhaust emission standards currently being met for hydrocarbons (HC), carbon monoxide (CO), and oxides of nitrogen (NOx) are 1.5, 15 and 3.1 grams per mile. These represent very significant emission reductions of 90%, 83%, and 38% from uncontrolled cars. The standards for California are more stringent and are set at 0.9, 9 and 2 gpm. The next scheduled Federal emission standard change will be in 1977, at which time the NOx standard will be tightened to 2 gpm, a 60% reduction from uncontrolled cars.

On March 5, 1975, the EPA Administrator delayed for one year the previously scheduled imposition of tighter standards in 1977 for HC and CO. As a result, the stringent levels of all three pollutants as required by the Clean Air Amendments of 1970 are now scheduled to apply to 1978 models. In announcing the one-year suspension, the EPA also recommended against imposition of these stringent levels in 1978, and recommended to Congress that the law be amended to allow continuation of 1977 emission levels through 1979 (see bottom portion of [Exhibit 4]. The EPA Administrator called for further reductions in 1980, but proposed that the ultimate statutory standards of 0.41 grams per mile for HC and 3.4 for CO not be imposed until 1982. EPA further recognized the overly-stringent requirement of 0.4 gpm for NOx (because of errors made initially when measuring NOx in the atmosphere), and proposed that this requirement be held at the 2 gpm level at least through 1982.

General Motors believes the EPA Administrator's recognition of the importance of stabilizing automotive emissions standards for the next few years is in the public interest. However, the 2 gpm NOx standard for 1977, rather than continuation of the current 3.1 gpm standard, will cause a decrease of about 5%-10% in GM's projections of fuel economy . . . .

If 1975 standards were retained through 1980, as GM has requested, substantially better fuel economy would result as a consequence of weight reductions, aerodynamic and other improvements, without the extra cost for more complex emission control equipment. At the present level of emission control, the auto industry will be able to design and adjust its engines for maximum efficiency to promote effective use of our fuel supply. The 40% overall improvement in auto fuel economy then could be achieved by product modification to decrease engine size, by adopting more economical axle ratios, improving transmissions, and reducing weight, rolling resistance and air drag . . . .

In its recent decision to delay 1977 emission standards for one year, the EPA indicated that, for the first time, a sulfuric acid emission standard would be proposed to apply no earlier than the 1979 models. This decision was reached in order to avoid the possibility of a sulfuric acid-related health problem which might possibly occur sometime in the future.

GM agrees with the EPA's assessment that sulfuric acid emissions from catalyst-equipped cars do not pose any present public health hazard . . . .

Automotive sulfate emissions result from the combustion of an unessential element—sulfur—which occurs naturally in the fuel. While GM is actively working on after-treatment systems, including sulfate traps to remove sulfates from the exhaust, the imposition of an emission standard for sulfuric acid may require discontinuing the HC and CO-oxidizing catalytic converter. The problem is that the catalytic converter does its job of oxidizing so well, that some of what previously left the exhaust pipe as sulfur dioxide now is further oxidized to sulfur trioxide and sulfates.

General Motors also addressed the catalytic converter issue in the public press. A typical example of the message it sought to convey is shown in Exhibit 6, an advertisement which appeared in the July 7, 1975 issue of *Business Week*.

Strongly convinced that the catalytic converter had made substantial contributions to environmental protection and to the nation's goals on energy conservation, General Motors representatives based their planning for the foreseeable future on the assumption that the catalytic converter would continue to be a mandatory component in automotive vehicles. If that planning assumption turned out to be inaccurate, the penalties of shutting down the program could be considerable. In addition to writing off a substantial part of its $100 million investment in the Milwaukee plant, it would be liable for cancellation fees to vendors in the following amounts:

	As of 7/1/75	*As of 1/1/76*
To catalyst suppliers	$ 45.4 million	$ 29.6 million
To steel suppliers	0	0
To Van Horne (for noble metals)	$ 87.0	$ 73.0
	$132.4 million	$102.6 million

As of June 1975, purchasing managers at AC Spark Plug had defined four possible options for the future sourcing of catalysts:

Option 1: Cancel a portion of the commitment to Reade and pay $6.9 million in penalty charges in each of three years, 1976–1978. This might be the lowest cost solution except for the fact that GM's assumed cost-of-money was 8½%. In addition, it would mean idling significant capacity at Reade.

Option 2: Terminate Reade and pay $26 million. Cost-of-money was a major consideration here, too. Based on present value, the cost of this option to GM could be figured at about $33 million. Furthermore, it would eliminate a significant amount of capacity that might be needed if car sales trends turned up markedly.

Option 3: Retain Reade but terminate Fulmer at a cost of $3.4 million. The main objection to this option was that GM would be terminating a reliable, highly qualified supplier and retaining one that as yet had not produced catalysts of acceptable quality.

Option 4: Keep all four suppliers and allocate orders approximately as follows:

	1976 MY	*1977 MY*
Fulmer	167,000 cu. ft.	130,000 cu. ft.
Reade	130,000 cu. ft.	165,000 cu. ft.
Carney	140,000 cu. ft.	140,000 cu. ft
Regal	80,000 cu. ft.	80,000 cu. ft.

This option was calculated to cost $9.7 million in failure-to-take penalties in the two years.

Exhibit 1
GENERAL MOTORS (1)

Catalytic Converter

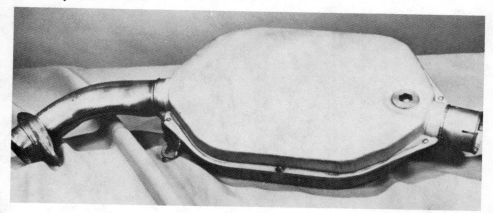

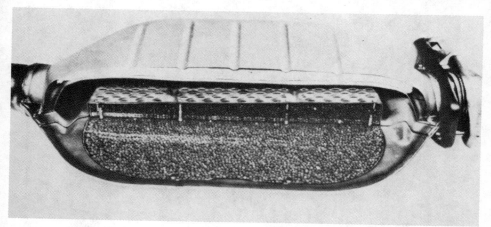

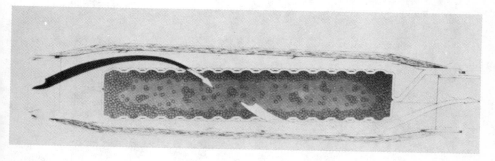

Exhibit 2
GENERAL MOTORS (1)

Positioning Of The Catalytic Converter In The Automotive
Exhaust System

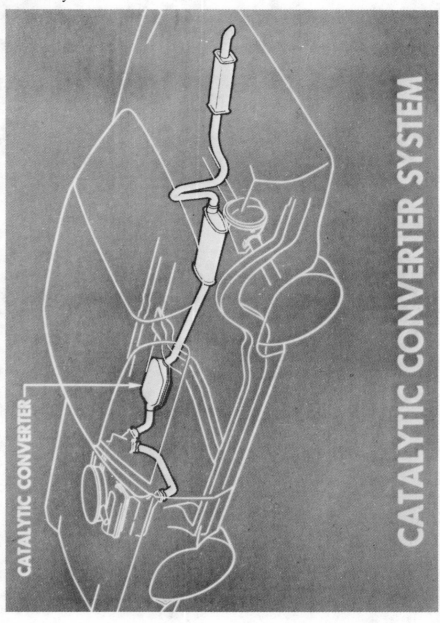

Exhibit 3
(GENERAL MOTORS (1)

Maximum Available Platinum And Palladium In The Free World For All Applications (Thousands Of Ounces)

Platinum	1970	1972	1974	1976	1980
Canadian Production	185	185	185	185	185
South African Production	960	750	1,750	3,500	4,400
Miscellaneous Production	65	65	65	65	65
Imports from USSR	400	300	300	300	300
Free World Total	1,610	1,300	2,300	4,050	4,950
Palladium					
Canadian Production	185	185	185	185	185
South African Production	385	310	790	1,710	1,980
Miscellaneous Production	40	40	40	40	40
Imports from USSR	1,370	1,295	1,300	1,300	1,300
Free World Total	1,980	1,830	2,315	3,235	3,505

Projected Net Free World Purchases of Platinum and Palladium for Non-Automotive Uses (thousands of ounces)

Platinum	1972	1974	1976	1980
U.S. and Canada	380	470	500	690
Japan	490	395	330	185
Western Europe	380	430	500	675
Others	50	60	70	90
Free World Total	1,300	1,355	1,400	1,640
Palladium				
U.S. and Canada	725	820	905	981
Japan	660	750	822	926
Western Europe	415	533	619	765
Others	30	32	34	38
Free World Total	1,830	2,135	2,380	2,710

Source: Arthur D. Little report prepared for General Motors

Exhibit 4
(GENERAL MOTORS (1)

Ranking Of Potential Catalyst Suppliers, July 1972

Weights placed on criteria.—Ranking based on 1 thru 7 points with "1" being the Best. Therefore, the lower the total number of points, the better the ranking. (Multiply weight times rank to get T or total points for that criteria)

Criteria	Weight	Elkart Rank	Elkart T	Reade Rank	Reade T	Carney Chem. Rank	Carney Chem. T	Regal Sci. Rank	Regal Sci. T	Fulmer Rank	Fulmer T	Cox Rank	Cox T	Galper Rank	Galper T
Cost per Converter*	6	7	42	6	36	3	18	5	30	2	12	4	24	1	6
Prod. Cont.															
1) Ability to Meet Fluc. in Sch.*	3														
2) Gen. P.C. Procedure	4	1.25	5	2.25	9	3.25	13	5.5	22	5.87	23.5	5.12	20.5	4.75	19
Gen. Q.C. Procedure	4	1	4	3	12	4	16	2	8	6	24	5	20	7	28
Engineering Ranking*	2	1	2	3	6	4	8	6.5	13	6.5	13	2	4	5	10
Mgmt. Depth	2	1	2	3	6	4.5	9	2	4	6	12	4.5	9	7	14
Manuf. Exp. of Cat.*	2	7	14	1	2	3	6	5	10	2	4	4	8	6	12
Fin. Stability															
1) Fin. Analysis*	½	1	.5	6	3	5	2.5	4	2	2	1	7	3.5	1	.5
2) Dol. Sls. Vol.*	½	1	.5	2	1	6	3	3	1.5	4	2	5	2.5	3	1.5
FOB*	1	1	1	5	5	4	4	7	7	2	2	6	6	7	7
Facilities	1	2	2	4	4	6	6	1	1	5	5	3	3	3	3
Sales Rep.	½	3	1.5	1	.5	4	2	7	3.5	6	3	5	2.5	6	3
Housekeeping	½	4.5	2.25	7	3.5	3	1.5	1	.5	2	1	4.5	2.25	6	3
Total			76.75		88.0		89.0		102.5		102.5		105.25		107
Ranking			1st		2nd		3rd		4.5th		4.5th		6th		7th

Exhibit 5
GENERAL MOTORS (1)

Auto Exhaust Emission Regulations
(1975 Federal Test Procedure)

	GRAMS PER MILE (49 States)		
	Hydro-carbons	Carbon Monoxide	Oxides of Nitrogen
Prior to 1960 (average level)	15.0	90.0	5.0
1968	6.3	51.0	—
1970	4.1	34.0	—
1972	3.0	28.0	—
1973	3.0	28.0	3.1
1975 Interim	1.5	15.0	3.1
1977 Interim	1.5	15.0	2.0
1978	0.41	3.4	0.4

California 1975 standards: 0.9 HC, 9.0 CO, and 2.0 NOx

	Hydro-carbons	Carbon Monoxide	Oxides of Nitrogen*	Sulfuric Acid
EPA Recommendations:				
1978	1.5	15.0	2.0	—
1979	1.5	15.0	2.0	Standards to
1980–1981	.9	9.0	2.0	be announced
1982	.41	3.4	2.0	by the EPA

*NOx standards require further study.

Exhibit 6
GENERAL MOTORS (1)

GM Advertising Message On The Catalytic Converter
Business Week, July 7, 1975

Exhibit 7
GENERAL MOTORS (1)

Excerpts From A Speech By Edward N. Cole, President Of General Motors.

January 14, 1970—Annual Meeting Of The Society Of Automotive Engineers (Detroit, Michigan)

GM Committed to Solving Problem

We have said before, and I repeat it here tonight: We are committed to eliminating the automobile as a factor in the nation's air pollution problem at the earliest possible time. We will have no hesitation in using a power source other than the internal combustion engine if it will solve the automobile's part of the pollution problem and meet the needs of our customers at a price they can afford to pay for automotive transportation.

Our research into alternate power sources has been going on for many years and has included just about every possible competitor to the gasoline internal combustion engine. In the long run, we recognize that new power sources may be required. But in the desire for a quick solution, let us be careful not to give up the highly-developed, efficient internal combustion engine for a power plant of unknown and unproved qualities. We could be creating more problems than we cure.

Development of a new power source for automobiles is not a simple assignment. Considerable work must be done and technological breakthroughs must be achieved before an alternative power plant can be ready for passenger car use. Extensive research in this area is now going on in the automobile industry.

In the meantime, there are a number of avenues by which we can further reduce the amount of pollutants from the conventional gasoline engine. These include modifications in engine design, improved control systems and possibly fuel injection for more precise air-fuel ratios. The key questions are: How far can we go in cleaning up the gasoline engine, and what will be the national clean air requirements of the future?

Future Auto Emissions Goals

Based on information from several sources, it appears that the U.S. Department of Health, Education and Welfare plans to issue shortly proposed new automotive emission goals for 1975 and 1980 model vehicles. If these proposed goals go into effect, here is how the 1975 model cars would compare emission-wise to the non-equipped cars of 1960.

During this period, emission of hydrocarbons would be reduced 95 percent, carbon monoxide 85 percent and oxides of nitrogen 75 percent. And while there is no accepted means at this time of measuring the emission of particulates (which are solid materials in the exhaust), it appears that the 1975 specification would require the elimination of about 50 percent of the present particulate matter from exhaust emissions.

The proposed HEW goals for 1980 would require that the allowable emissions in each of these categories be reduced by more than 50 percent compared to 1975.

Achievement of these proposed levels of auto emissions will be no easy assignment. But in my opinion, the quickest, most effective way of moving toward goals of this type is to seek every possible means of reducing the levels of pollutants from the gasoline internal combustion engine.

The automobile companies have spent many millions of dollars in attempting to control automotive pollutants—both through improved engine combustion efficiency and emission control systems. And this work will continue extensively. The petroleum companies, too, are concerned with this problem and have strong programs designed to seek contributions from the third major element in the emission triangle—automotive fuels. We must not neglect any area of potential improvement as we escalate the war on air pollution.

For example, reductions in gasoline volatility could have a major effect on the amount of hydrocarbon vapors emitted from carburetors and fuel tanks of cars which are not equipped with evaporative emission controls. The reduction of gasoline volatility levels would be particularly important because it would bring immediate reduction of emissions in all cars—new and used.

Adjustments in the molecular structure of gasoline could also prove highly beneficial. We know that smog is caused by a complicated interaction of sunlight, nitrogen oxides and certain hydrocarbons. Because olefinic hydrocarbons have a particularly high photochemical smog reactivity, a reduction of these substances could have marked benefits—particularly with respect to evaporative emissions.

Effects of Lead in Gasoline

The potential gains which might be realized through removal of tetraethyl lead from automobile gasoline should be evaluated. Our research indicates that after several thousand miles of driving a car using fuels without lead, there is a reduction in hydrocarbon emissions of about 40 to 100 parts per million compared to a car using leaded gasoline.

Even more important to long-term reduction of pollutants, however, is the fact that within the present state of the art, lead presents problems with respect to the life of possible advanced emission control concepts. Research indicates that without lead in gasoline, long-life exhaust catalytic converters would become technically feasible. Exhaust manifold reactors also would have increased life. The same is true of exhaust gas recirculation systems to control oxides of nitrogen. We need these advanced concepts to reach our 1975 and 1980 objectives.

There is another important factor to be considered. Proposed federal goals are expected to call for substantial reductions of auto exhaust particulates by 1975 and virtual elimination by 1980. Most of the particulates in automotive emissions are lead compounds derived from tetraethyl lead in the gasoline. It is important to emphasize that—if stringent control of particulates becomes a federal goal as we expect—we know of no way presently that such control can be accomplished with lead in gasoline.

Contributions of Leaded Gasoline

The introduction of tetraethyl lead in gasolines in the early 1920's was considered a major advance in fuel technology. At that time, the use of additives was the only known way to increase the octane levels of gasoline. In later years, as fuel chemistry became more sophisticated, petroleum scientists developed new refining processes and learned how to alter the molecular structure of gasoline. This resulted not only in improving anti-knock characteristics, but also increasing overall fuel performance. In World War II, for example, leaded gasoline played a vital role in the production of high performance fuels for military vehicles and aircraft.

In the meantime, our society was developing at a rapid pace. The automobile industry was faced with increasing demands for better, higher performance vehicles with which people could travel expeditiously and safely— both in city traffic and also on the highspeed turnpikes which were spanning the nation. To meet these requirements, more efficient engines with higher compression ratios were needed and this meant development of even higher octane gasolines. Because it was still the least expensive means of boosting octane ratings, tetraethyl lead became a universal ingredient in virtually all automotive gasolines produced in this country.

In short, tetraethyl lead permitted the petroleum industry to increase the octane rating of its gasolines and improve their anti-knock characteristics. This allowed the auto companies to boost compression ratios which resulted in improved engine efficiency and customer benefits—either in terms of economy or performance.

The use of tetraethyl lead, therefore, has made a significant contribution over the years in increasing the efficiency of our modern internal combustion engines. Today, however, we are dealing with a new set of requirements.

Must Reevaluate Engine-Fuel Relationships

The inter-relationships involving octane levels, compression ratios, use of lead and costs, must be reevaluated in light of the increasingly serious air pollution problem. For example, use of unleaded fuels as a means of reducing pollutants from exhaust emissions would result in a loss in engine efficiency because of the lower compression ratios required. However, it is possible that this loss in efficiency could be recovered through improved fuels and fuel systems and engine modifications.

It is urgent that those most concerned with these problems—the government, the automobile manufacturers and the petroleum refiners—give top priority to the resolution of these issues. It is particularly vital that efforts be made as quickly as possible to establish specifications for fuels with reduced pollutant characteristics which would be available for automotive use at some future date—such as 1975. This is a critical requirement if the petroleum companies are to have adequate time to make necessary changes in the composition of motor fuels and the automobile companies have sufficient time for design, testing and tooling requirements of modified power systems which can operate satisfactorily on these new fuels.

The common goal is to find the best possible solution for maximum reduction of pollutants in the soonest practical time frame and at the lowest cost to the consumer. Achievement of this objective no doubt will require additional modifications in engine design, as well as improvements in control systems and fuels.

Seek Pollution-Free Engine

We have already demonstrated in our laboratories that these improvements are technically feasible. As a result, it is my opinion that the gasoline internal combustion engine can be made essentially pollution-free in the hands of the public. This is what must be done to meet suggested future federal emission goals. This is a goal to which General Motors is devoting extensive resources and we are confident it can be achieved.

Ten years from now, the choice of automotive power sources will not be predicated on small differences in the emission of pollutants, in my opinion, because the levels of emissions will be about the same for all power plants. Rather, the choice will be made on the basis of which engine—or engines—will provide the greatest overall benefits to the American car owner.

As engineers and managers, it is important to recognize the vital need for providing sound leadership for progress in these and similar areas. The automobile industry obviously is equipped with the technical resources and know-how to provide such leadership.

But we must be highly aggressive in taking action and, equally important, in getting credit for our accomplishments. And getting public credit for what we do has been extremely difficult in recent years. But if we don't provide strong leadership and have this fact recognized, we must accept continuing public criticism and perhaps even government regulations which might be unsound. Most damaging of all, lack of leadership on our part could result in misguided national policies which would not advance the cause of safety or cleaner air but also could be extremely detrimental to our customers and the mobility of our economy and thus seriously affect our business.

Long-Range Standards Necessary

It is also important that the Federal Government and the automobile industry cooperate closely in developing more stable, long-range standards and test procedures for both safety and auto emission controls. Frequent changes in standards and test procedures—either in terms of specification requirements or general goals—and insufficient advance notice of changes, could impose severe burdens on the automobile companies and be a disservice to our customers and the public as well. We need sound, long-range planning of national goals in these and other critical areas—goals developed cooperatively by industry and government on realistic time schedules. This is necessary to minimize wasted effort and to maximize the combined resources of our nation which in the long run will provide the greatest gains in the shortest time and at the lowest cost.

In seeking maximum utilization of total resources toward the resolution of this problem, much work is to be done. The automobile industry, over the years, has done extensive research and development work in advance power sources and emission control systems. The results of this work have been made public through various presentations to technical societies and through publications.

If the Federal Government desires to finance research in the vehicular pollution field, we believe it could be most effectively utilized in areas where new data and technological breakthroughs are badly needed by the automobile industry—rather than duplicating work already accomplished or now being done by the automobile industry. Areas of greatest potential for new research activities which might be funded by the Federal Government, for example, would include studies designed to develop new and improved materials for components of advance power plants and for exhaust reactors, with particular emphasis on catalytic materials for exhaust control systems.

Important Engineering Challenges

In focusing major attention on the problems of automotive safety and air pollution, it was not my intention to minimize the importance of other areas of challenge to the automobile engineer. To place these critical assignments into proper perspective, let me summarize my remarks tonight with what I consider to be eight of the most important challenges or areas of greatest potential for the automotive engineer in the next decade or two.

One is the need to develop a more effective systems approach to design which encompasses all of the essential requirements of the automobile during its lifetime of use. Obviously, attention must be given to such essentials as emission control, safety, performance, utility, economy, convenience, durability and sales appeal. However, equal consideration must be given to other factors involved with long-term transportation value of the vehicle. Of major importance are buildability, serviceability and repairability.

Challenge number two is to develop better concepts of space engineering. As the customer demands more and more of his automobile, we must seek new ways of maximizing the use of space available both in exterior dimensions and under the skin of the car. Important considerations are basic performance, safety, roominess, convenience, protection against property damage, but with definite limitations imposed by such vital factors as highway and parking space. We cannot expect any more space to work with; but we could have less.

Increased Use of Electronics

Our third area of opportunity is increased use of electronics—and more specifically solid state devices. It is conceivable that the car of the 1980's will contain an efficient in-car computer which would serve as a processing center for information about various operational parameters. This would allow us to simplify many auxiliary functions and reduce space requirements for many separate electrical sensing and control systems. Other probable areas of application for electronics include fuel injection, ignition, braking systems, driver communications, as well as devices to monitor or control other functions vital to safety. I also expect much more extensive use of electronics as aids to manufacturing quality and service diagnosis.

Our fourth major engineering challenge will be to develop new materials and fabricating processes. The next few decades will see the birth of new alloys and non-metallic materials with performance far surpassing that of traditional metals—and, hopefully, at lower costs. These advances should open broad new avenues for improving the automobile, encompassing both design and propulsion.

The fifth important challenge is to improve maintainability of auto designs during their lifetime of use—particularly in the areas of safety and air pollution. This involves further improvements in basic quality by a closer correlation between design and manufacturing practicalities. We should seek new design concepts and materials which provide extended durability and trouble-free operation. In addition, we need to develop a truly effective systems approach to the diagnosis of mechanical problems—both as a part of basic design and as a foundation for improved field service.

The sixth challenge is to develop a system for disposing of junk motor vehicles—a system which would be economically feasible within our free enterprise system and without the need for government subsidy. New advances in processing methods would represent a substantial contribution toward this goal.

The Engineer as an Innovator

Our seventh major area of challenge relates to the continuing basic responsibility of the engineer as an innovator—as a prime creator of constructive change. This requires particular emphasis on development of new or improved designs, materials or concepts as a means of providing increasing value in our products which are so fundamental to our way of life.

Our eighth major challenge concerns the effects of the engineer's work both on society and the physical environment. This involves not only automotive safety and air pollution, but also such other major challenges as automobile thefts, industrial pollution and urban transportation, including parking requirements.

It is particularly vital that we—as engineers and managers—provide leadership in anticipating, directing and helping to create the forces of change for the greatest overall progress. We must learn how to manage change more effectively than we have in the past so that we are the beneficiaries rather than the victims of change. We must learn how to manage accelerated change so it can be more effectively assimilated into our business and into our society.

Never in the history of our nation has the engineer been given such great responsibilities. Never has his role in the future been more vital. Society has great confidence in engineers to help solve the major problems of our times and create a fuller, more enjoyable life for all of us in the years ahead.

Let's roll up our sleeves and get on with the job!

GENERAL MOTORS (2)

GM Regional Non-Product Purchasing—Flint Area

On the recommendation of Mr. Don Lindsay, vice president of the Procurement and Production Control staff in the Central Office, the Procurement Policy Group at its first meeting in February 1975 had approved a plan for establishing 7–10 regional non-product purchasing organizations. Each such buying group would serve plants, laboratories, and offices in a geographic area on purchases of supplies, machinery and equipment, and construction. The procurement of most components and raw materials for manufactured products would remain with the individual plant and divisional buying organizations.

The Flint area was selected by Messrs. Lindsay, Cowan and Beall[1] as the first one in which non-product purchasing would be centralized. There were 11 GM facilities in Flint, operated by six different GM divisions.[2] The Central Office Purchasing proposal provided for a buying organization of about 70 people headed by a GM purchasing coordinator who would report to Mr. Beall at the Central Office. All personnel would be on the GM Central Office payroll. At least 11 of the buyers in this organization would be located in the respective facilities to serve in a liaison capacity and to buy items that were unique to a particular plant. GM Regional Non-Product Purchasing—Flint (RNPP–F) would be responsible for about $550 million of purchases in its first year.

Having received approval to proceed with RNPP–F from the Procurement Policy Group managers in the Central Office, Purchasing staff moved toward refining the definition of the new organization's structure and implementing it. Mr. Beall, who was directly responsible for carrying out the regional non-product purchasing program, then initiated a series of eight meetings in the Spring of 1975 with 11 representatives of the six divisions having facilities in Flint that would be affected. To plan and carry out these meetings, Mr. Beall requested assistance from Dr. Alfred Elliott, a specialist in organization development in the Central Office.

At the first meeting, Mr. Beall described the broad outlines of a regional non-product purchasing concept and said that the group would take as "givens" that (1) it would be a regional program, (2) it would have a manager and (3) hopefully, some of the basic elements would be in effect by year-end. Division representatives had been made aware, before the meeting, of the regional pur-

1. Mr. Cowan was executive-in-charge of procurement in the GM Central Office and reported to Mr. Lindsay. Mr. Beall reported to Mr. Cowan.
2. Four Chevrolet plants, three Fisher Body plants, one plant each for Buick, AC Spark Plug, and GM Parts, and the GM Institute (a company school).

chasing idea and a representative of one of the larger divisions had already prepared a position paper in opposition to it—which he was not permitted to read. Other reactions, too, to the proposal were largely negative. After general discussion, Messrs. Beall and Elliott divided the 11 purchasing managers and other divisional and Central Office representatives—25 in all—into four teams and asked each team to engage in what Dr. Elliott termed "force field" analysis. That is, the teams were asked to identify all the positive and negative concerns working for and against the success of the new concept. Seventeen negative factors in all were identified. Then in subsequent meetings team representatives got together to classify the negative concerns as critical (listed by at least four teams), shared (listed by 2–3 teams), and other (noted by one team). The major advantages of the regional purchasing concept were seen as:

Cost savings
—product
—efficiency [in purchasing]
—inventory pooling
—standardization
· More specialized and knowledgeable buyers
· Reduced supplier operating cost
· Better service from suppliers

The critical concerns were identified as:

· Effect on people and organization
· Cost of implementation: hardware systems, coding, forms
· Impact on local suppliers
· Lack of understanding
· Lack of support from local plant managements
· Difficulty in getting acceptance for standardization
· Buyer loss of plant knowledge and rapport
· Possibility that benefits would not be greater than the cost

Each team's task was to develop a plan for regional purchasing that would minimize the concerns. In a next step two members of each of these teams came together to reconcile any differences among the three plans and to come up with one scheme. The key idea coming out of these meetings was that a regional non-product purchasing organization should report to GM Central Office Purchasing but would be influenced and guided by the desires of a council composed of local division general managers and/or plant managers, local financial managers, a regional manager for non-product purchasing and one member of the Central Office staff (presumably Mr. Beall).

This concept was then reviewed by the three teams to determine whether in their judgments the consensus plan would meet GM Central Office objectives, on the one hand, and would sufficiently minimize the negative concerns. The process in which Messrs. Beall and Elliott and the 11 representatives was engaged is diagrammed in Exhibit 1. The basic consensus concept is shown schematically in Exhibit 2.

Recalling the meetings, Mr. Beall noted that:

There really was a lot of apprehension in those meetings because the purchasing departments in the Flint area would lose large parts of their personnel to a RNPP–F organization. AC Spark Plug, for example, would have to transfer about 11 out of approximately 25 personnel.

Dr. Elliott commented afterward:

The discussion in those meetings reflected two rather prevalent myths. One is that control and influence are finite and when you give more to one group you have to take it away from others. Loss of control was an underlying concern of these meetings but it wasn't being discussed.

A second myth, which comes from growing up as a decentralized company, is that what's good for a division is good for GM. That's not necessarily so. Sometimes you have to sub-optimize in one part of a system to arrive at optimal solutions for the system as a whole.

What we were really looking for in those meetings though, were "win/win" solutions, not "win/lose."

Following this series of meetings a presentation was made by representatives of the group to Mr. Lindsay and he became aware of the fact that there had been opposition to the regional non-product purchasing concept. His response to the presentation, as recalled by Dr. Elliott, was:

Nice job. But I want you to know I'm flexible and if we don't all agree I'm willing to start over with a blank sheet of paper.

The status of RNPP–F was reviewed in a Procurement Policy Group meeting in late July. Mr. Beall made a brief presentation to this group at the start of the discussion and his comments are quoted below.

I should now like to turn to the discussion of regional purchasing. You will recall in our February meeting that we presented a plan that called for putting ourselves together in regional areas in a new way. These programs would be established in geographical areas where there is a high concentration of GM facilities. The plan captured the basic premise that by combining our volumes and our efforts, we could do a better job of purchasing for the Corporation in the non-product type of commodities. We would receive lower material prices and at the same time improve purchasing activity efficiency.

The regional approach to purchasing of our non-product materials was selected for several reasons:

1) Seeking an effective middle ground between decentralization and centralization.

2) Preserves local influence and control through a regional non-product purchasing policy council.
3) At the same time, provides for greater coordination and integration of local non-product purchasing.
4) Regional organization will operate as a service arm of the plant and as a results-oriented, coordinating arm of the Corporation.

We have made a start in Flint. As expected, it has not been easy. Any time we approach new ideas that require individuals to be realigned, it understandably needs to be done carefully. Our approach has been just that. We have completed the discussions with all of the plant management personnel in the Flint area and have had general support for the idea. Some areas have been stronger in their support for the idea than others. The general resistance encountered has been centered on the fear of losing control of the management of the plant and having shortages or other problems arise that would affect the plant operation.

We began working with the 11 Flint Area plant divisions purchasing managers in April. The purchasing managers were involved in all phases of the development of the regional purchasing concept. Their participation increased the probability of their acceptance of the concept.

The process used to develop the regional purchasing concept is shown [in Exhibit 1]. We aren't going into the process in detail but it focused on permitting the purchasing managers to develop the concept so it would eliminate or minimize concerns they had while at the same time still achieve corporate objectives.

During this process the 11 purchasing managers' points of view were reduced to two or three dominate concepts. One view was strong enough to emerge as a consensus concept of the regional purchasing program. The purchasing managers felt confident enough of the concept to rate it as having high probability of success in meeting the objectives and minimizing their concerns. We have been assisted throughout the process by a member of the Corporate Organization Research and Development Department.

Now our current position. We are trying to enlarge the circle of acceptance of the idea. Just as the local purchasing managers had trouble at the start understanding that the Corporation was serious about this program, some of the general managers, plant managers, and divisional purchasing management personnel are currently experiencing this same feeling.

We know that it will take a year or two to get the coding and data systems completed so that our buyers will have all the proper tools at their fingertips. It has been our hope that we could convince the operating management people in Flint of this basic idea sufficient to allow the start of the action as the longer range tools are being perfected. In this spirit, we have appointed Ron Decker as Manager of GM Regional Purchasing—Flint. Ron came right out of the regional purchasing group, as his former job was Purchasing Agent for Chevrolet Flint Manufacturing.

With the concept developed, we are working up an implementation plan which will result in a gradual transfer of responsibilities. This, of course, means transferring personnel to work in the regional purchasing office as the effort moves ahead. At this time, we are not attempting to put a time estimate on the completion of the activity, but rather let the progress determine the rate at which we go.

As you are well aware, the basic issue we are dealing with is change—change from decentralization to a more coordinated approach.

Apparently, people in the field are receiving either mixed signals or no signals at all about the Corporation's intent to coordinate its purchasing activity. As a result there is no shortage of difficulties in moving forward with the program.

In this report we should candidly say to you, the Procurement Policy Group, that it is necessary that corporate management communicate their support in order to portray the message that we are serious.

We plan to keep this policy group in close touch with our efforts in this area.

Discussion at the meeting ranged widely with some members of the Procurement Policy Group expressing concern that perhaps control of purchasing at the division level would be impaired. In general, however, there was substantial support expressed for the regional purchasing idea and a willingness on the part of Procurement Policy group members to talk to division general managers in their respective groups.

August Meeting of Key Managers. On August 19, a meeting was held in Flint which was attended by the following GM managers all of whom were vitally concerned about the Regional Purchasing Plan:

AC Division:	General Manager
	Director-Purchasing, Traffic,
	Production Control
Buick Division:	General Manager
	Director-Purchasing, Traffic,
	Production Control
Fisher Body Division:	Director of Purchases
	2 Plant Managers
GM Parts Division:	Director-Purchasing, Traffic,
	Production Control
Chevrolet Division:	General Manufacturing Manager
	Director-Purchasing, Traffic,
	Production Control
	Director of Purchases
	2 Plant Managers
	Assistant Divisional Comptroller
	1 Plant Purchasing Agent
	1 Plant Comptroller
GM Institute:	President

The meeting was addressed, first, by Mr. Lindsay as follows:

Without a doubt, much of General Motors' success over the years has resulted from its decentralized operations. There is naturally a reluctance to change the way in which we do things. Now, the Corporation is at a crossroads, and all of us must begin to question whether past practices will be adequate to return us to previous profit levels. We must seek and try new ways to create profits. As Roger Smith told us at the Executive Conference last February, ''We have run the gamut of routine measures. We must enter new areas and put our managerial skills to the real test and show that we can cast aside interdivisional rivalries and inter-staff friction and do only what is best for General Motors.''

Slide 1

**WE MUST ENTER NEW AREAS AND
PUT OUR MANAGERIAL SKILLS
TO THE REAL TEST**

As you know, the Procurement and Production Control Staff was formed last September and given the responsibility to coordinate all General Motors activities in the areas of purchasing, logistics and production control.

Slide 2

COORDINATION IS THE KEY

To me, the key word in this mandate is *coordination*. It doesn't mean that we are to *take over* the purchasing functions of the divisions, but to *coordinate* them—to maintain a close liaison with the divisions and the staffs so that there is more effective control in the purchase and use of basic manufacturing materials and in the most efficient use of transportation. GM is not taking full advantage of volume potential in making procurement and shipping decisions. There is an urgent need for coordination.

Again, coordination is the key to the activities of the Procurement and Production Control Staff. To make it work, we need strong divisional and staff inputs. We are all in this battle together, and each of us must know what the other is doing if we are going to make a unified effort effective.

Slide 3

PROBLEMS

Worldwide Shortage of Materials

Price Fluctuations

Self-Sufficiency is a Thing of the Past

Worldwide Flow of Commodities is a Precarious Pipeline

What's this battle all about? Let's look at some of the problems we're facing. There is mounting evidence of a worldwide shortage of many materials—steel, copper, lead, petroleum products, and natural gas—to name a few.

There are monumental price fluctuations in materials around the world. Not a little bit of this can be laid to the practice of the producing nations putting it to the consuming nations—following the example of the OPEC countries in forming cartels to control the prices of materials.

It is painfully obvious that self-sufficiency—as far as nations and their available resources and raw materials are concerned—is a thing of the past. The worldwide flow of commodities is a precarious pipeline, indeed, equipped with numerous shut-off valves, some unfortunately in the hands of political figures eager to demonstrate their power.

Slide 4

PROCUREMENT POLICY GROUP

T.H. LOCKHART, Chairman

D.P. LINDSAY	F.L. PALFREY	M.V. PARKER
P.E. DOUGLAS	J.M. MacMURRAY	A.A. TANNENBAUM
A.S. SCHIRMER		J.B. PARKER

T.S. BARNES, Legal Advisor
J.L. COWAN, Secretary

The warning signs have caused the Corporation so much concern that the Chairman late last year established the Procurement Policy Group to provide guidance in seeking more effective means of coordinating and performing the purchasing function in General Motors. This important Policy Group is headed by our Vice Chairman. Its members include Paul Douglas, Arthur Schirmer, Frank Palfrey, Joe MacMurray, Mike Parker, Al Tannenbaum, Jack Parker and myself. Jim Cowan, who as you know is our Executive in Charge of Purchasing Activities, serves as Secretary.

The Policy Group is diligently seeking solutions to problems of supply that may lie on the horizon. It is looking for ways to exert more effective control over key supplies for our immediate production requirements and to plan more intelligently for our long-range needs.

I'm sure it is no surprise to you that the purchasing function in General Motors is no dime store activity. In 1974, GM's total sales were $31.5 billion, and 51% of this went to our suppliers—40,000 of them—to purchase things vital to our business.

Slide 5

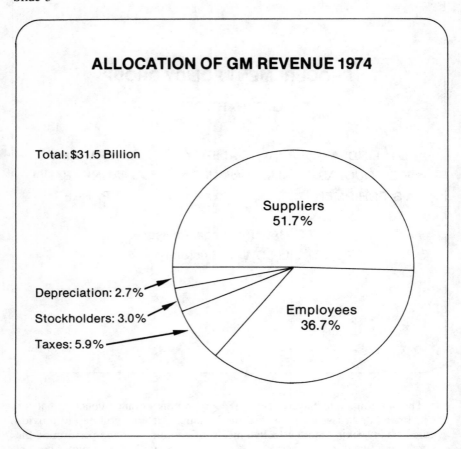

In this constant flow of funds there is an abundance of opportunities to cut costs. To find them is going to take some imagination, some digging, some decisions that might not be all that popular.

Slide 6

COST SAVINGS

Work Gloves—Over $1,000,000 Per Year

Car Price Stickers—72%

Steel and the other materials are, of course, big ticket items which can represent substantial savings. But even on seemingly insignificant cost items there are ample opportunities for savings. Most of you are familiar with the work glove example that we have discussed before, in which we expect to realize savings of over a million dollars a year by coordinating our sourcing. We are looking for additional opportunities to make better use of our purchasing dollars. One of these will go into effect when the 1976 products hit the showrooms in the next few weeks. It is the coordinated purchase of new car price stickers from which we will realize a 72% cost savings. Other coordinated non-product purchasing programs that we are considering include duplicating papers, xerographic toners, safety items such as goggles and hard hats, janitorial supplies, stationery supplies and mill supplies—to name only a few. With all of these things in mind, we have embarked on a pilot program of regional non-product procurement for the 11 plants in the Flint area.

There are several ways to approach the job of purchasing in Flint. As you are well aware, there are those in the Corporation who advocate centralization—so, we can enjoy the benefits which it readily permits, such as:

Slide 7

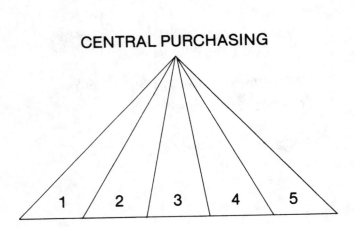

Others in the Corporation are concerned about preserving the advantages of local purchasing and the important needs it fulfills, such as:

Slide 8

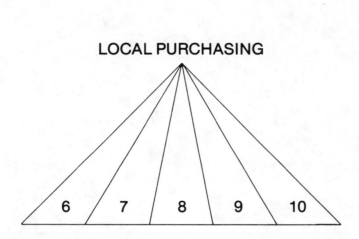

We believe the best of both worlds can be secured through a regional purchasing organization. The regional concept offers an effective middle ground between centralization and decentralization. For example, in the regional purchasing concept developed by Flint area purchasing agents, both supplier proximity and consolidation of requirements are provided through the regional organization. This organization will be guided and evaluated by a local policy council. Having divisional and local plant managers and financial managers involved will preserve local influence and control while providing for greater coordination and integration of local purchasing. The regional organization will operate as a service arm of the plants, and as a results-oriented, coordinating arm of the Corporation.

Slide 9

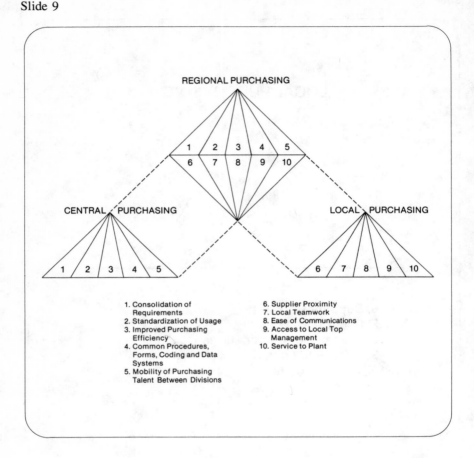

Annual expenditures in non-product purchasing by the Flint area plants are at a level offering important savings potential through a coordinated approach. A good indicator of this is the fact that for electrical and non-product steel supplies alone, these plants currently spend about $13,000,000 a year. While speaking of cost savings potential, I might add that some of our Flint area suppliers have said regional purchasing will reduce their costs in doing business with GM—because of reduced sales contacts and paperwork plus standardization of forms and procedures. In the long run, this will help them hold the line on their prices to us in these inflationary times. The potential cost savings and supplier advantages in the Flint area can eventually be multiplied many times since Flint is a pilot effort which will lead to other GM regional purchasing groups throughout the country.

Slide 10

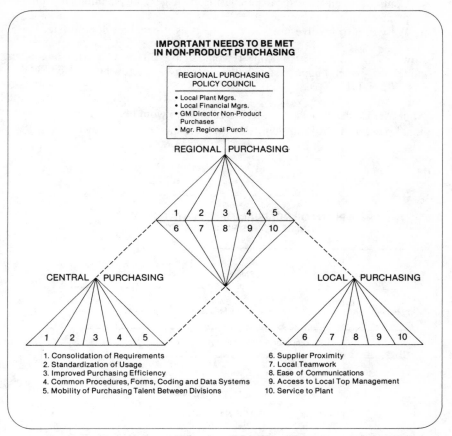

IMPORTANT NEEDS TO BE MET
IN NON-PRODUCT PURCHASING

REGIONAL PURCHASING
POLICY COUNCIL

- Local Plant Mgrs.
- Local Financial Mgrs.
- GM Director Non-Product Purchases
- Mgr. Regional Purch.

REGIONAL PURCHASING

CENTRAL PURCHASING

LOCAL PURCHASING

1. Consolidation of Requirements
2. Standardization of Usage
3. Improved Purchasing Efficiency
4. Common Procedures, Forms, Coding and Data Systems
5. Mobility of Purchasing Talent Between Divisions

6. Supplier Proximity
7. Local Teamwork
8. Ease of Communications
9. Access to Local Top Management
10. Service to Plant

Most of us here today have been participants in difficult innovations undertaken by GM in the past. These new actions have met with success because of our determination to make them succeed. Our top management group has said clearly that we are to move ahead with establishing a regional purchasing program in Flint. Each of you present today must also give a strong, clear and continuing signal to your organization. With your full support for this regional program, we can help this great Corporation gear its purchasing to the demanding and pressing challenges expected in the years ahead! Now, Ron Decker will present a method of implementing regional purchasing in Flint. Having listened very carefully to many of you in this room, I have asked that his approach to the job incorporate these guidelines:

1. Implement the Flint regional purchasing concept *gradually*.
2. Build in pilot phases early in this process.

3. Measure as you go.
4. Continue to involve local purchasing managers in planning the full implementation of this concept.
5. We will also involve users in the plants as it becomes appropriate.

Now, as we all listen to Ron, I would leave all of you with one other guideline—which I hope to state in the clearest way I know how—LET'S GET ON WITH THE JOB!!!

After Mr. Lindsay spoke, Mr. Ron Decker who would be the new manager of regional purchasing at Flint then addressed the meeting as follows:

Slide 11

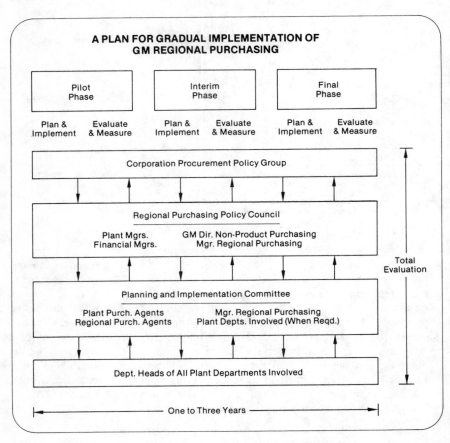

Don Lindsay has stressed the importance of *coordination* in our purchasing activities. In the plan for regional purchasing, I'd like to emphasize *flexibility*. The complexity of what we are about to do is such that we can't possibly have all the answers "up front." As we go forward, experience will dictate the planning improvements and changes necessary to achieve the best result for all concerned. These improvements and changes *will* be made. *Gradualism* is important, too. We will proceed on a gradual, considered basis. If a serious problem is encountered, the solution will be found before we continue. There is no timetable for implementing the plan other than the obvious one of moving ahead as expeditiously as possible. We must *measure and evaluate* our progress each step of the way. The plan provides for this evaluation to involve the

Slide 12

PILOT PHASE

1. Select location of regional purchasing.
2. Consolidate requirements and buy common items on blanket orders.
3. Begin work on common code.
4. Begin work on common data system.

division and plant managers, comptrollers, plant department heads and purchasing agents. In the committee and sub-committee meetings to be held during the Pilot Phase of our plan, a "yardstick" will be developed to measure results and savings.

1. First, we will select a location for regional purchasing—one of the area GM plants. Selection is to be made in September by the Planning and Implementation Committee subject to the approval of the Regional Purchasing Policy Council.
2. We will then transfer three experienced non-product buyers from the Divisions to Regional Purchasing. They will be replaced by the Divisions. On a systematic basis, current usages and prices will be gathered from all plants on common purchased items, using Chevrolet Flint Manufacturing computer lists as a base. The first three categories to be studied with approximate annual expenditures for each, are Electrical—$10,000,000, Non-Product Steel—$3,000,000 and Plumbing—$2,000,000. The consolidated requirements of all Flint Plants will be inquiried on a broad, competitive basis and regional blanket orders issued on Corporate forms for all plants to release against. Savings will be recorded and this process will continue until all common categories are covered. Since there are many common categories and the work will be necessarily largely on a manual basis, this effort will continue all through the Pilot and Interim Phases and on in to the Final Phase before it can be handled more efficiently through common code and data system. During this time, we expect to proceed and achieve all possible savings without the common code and data system.
3. A Code Coordinator, who will report to the Corporation, will be appointed in September. We will select a code and arrange for personnel to begin coding. A Corporate Systems Analyst has completed a detailed study of available codes within and outside the Corporation and will make his recommendation on code selection at the first meeting of the Regional Purchasing Policy Council. The methods used in establishing personnel to do the coding should be the same as has already been used by the Chevrolet Division. Each of their plants furnished one or two men for the time necessary to code their own items. This is fair since each plant will eventually enjoy the benefits of the common code.
4. Next, the type of data system required for regional purchasing must be determined. Corporation Data Systems personnel will then begin work to make it available. Currently a study of systems within and outside the Corporation is being made by a Corporate Systems Analyst. He will be in a position to recommend a data system to the Regional Purchasing Policy Council in September.

Slide 13

INTERIM PHASE

1. Transfer personnel to Regional Purchasing.
2. Consolidate buying and personnel.
3. Work on common code and data system continues.

1. On a gradual basis, a plant at a time, Purchasing Agents and non-product buying personnel will move to the regional purchasing location. When this physical move takes place, they will be transferred to the regional purchasing staff. At least one buyer will remain at each plant to handle all "rush" purchases plus other special items. He will be transferred to the regional purchasing staff at the same time as his co-workers. The fact he may still be working in proximity to divisional buying personnel will present no unique salaried personnel policy problems. Our plan calls for these transfers to be made on a gradual basis over whatever period of time is necessary to properly digest and evaluate each move. Prior to personnel transfers being made, individual and group meetings will be held with those involved to insure their complete understanding of the goals and opportunities of regional purchasing. Where the Purchasing Agent of a multi-plant division transfers, it will be necessary for his division to ar-

range for product buying personnel remaining at the plant to report either to another plant or the divisional office. While moves are being made, all personnel will continue doing the same work as at present. The costs will be charged to each plant on the basis of its percentage of total requisitions and buy cards processed. The savings developed will automatically be realized by each plant as they pay for items received.

2. As soon as possible after moves are complete, buying categories and personnel will be consolidated and the use of standardized forms and procedures will begin.
3. During this phase, purchasing, stores and receiving activity will continue on a manual basis since work on the common code and data system will not yet be complete.

Slide 14

FINAL PHASE

1. Complete work on common code and put into use.

2. Complete work on common data system and put into use.

3. As a result of having the code and data system, we will realize efficiencies in buying, stores and receiving activity plus the opportunity to more efficiently pursue usage standardization between plants and divisions.

I have tried to be complete and exact in this plan. Even so, some of your questions may be unanswered or you may want discussion. In a few minutes, we'll take the opportunity for this, but first I'd like to make a few comments. As I said earlier, this must be a very *flexible* plan, and we will certainly change and improve it in many ways before the job is done. There are a few aspects of the plan, however, which should not be changed because they are essential in achieving the objectives of GM regional purchasing.

Slide 15

OBJECTIVES OF G.M. REGIONAL PURCHASING

1. Substantial cost savings from standardization and consolidation of requirements.

2. Increased efficiency of purchasing operations.

3. Improved communications between plants and divisions through use of a common data system and code to identify and monitor materials.

4. Reduced supplier costs in doing business with G.M. in the Flint Area. In the long run, this will serve to reduce G.M. costs.

5. Improved coordination and greater mobility of purchasing personnel between plants and divisions.

6. Purchasing service equal to or better than in the past.

We will not attempt to include machinery, equipment or construction in regional purchasing until our actual experience indicates there are benefits to GM by so doing.

Questions have been raised about the possibility of having to do the coding job a second time after the metric system comes in. Regardless of the method used to indicate the specifications of a non-product item, the code number will remain the same. If it is necessary to carry more than one code number on an item for a time, the code being recommended for adoption has sufficient scope to permit this.

As we move ahead, we will make every effort to utilize the experience gained in the GMASA Program and, as Lou Kalush suggested at the last Plant City meeting, to benefit from the experience of GMPD who in recent years has been through a consolidation much like regional purchasing.

I want to assure each of you that my personal commitment, first and last, will be to maintain your plant operations.

Slide 16

ELEMENTS NECESSARY TO EFFECTIVELY ACHIEVE OBJECTIVES OF G.M. REGIONAL PURCHASING

1. Regional Purchasing Policy Council and subcommittees to include Plant Managers, Financial Managers, Purchasing Agents, Personnel Managers, Managers of involved Plant Departments, R.M. Beall, R.S. Decker.

2. Uniform code to identify common purchased items.

3. Common data system to facilitate handling information related to buying, receiving and inventory control.

4. Buying personnel reporting to Regional Purchasing for necessary objectivity.

The discussion which followed reflected a broad acceptance of the regional purchasing concept for non-product procurement. There were some questions, for example:

Chevrolet Assistant Divisional Comptroller: How many non-product dollars are being spent in Flint Plants and what will the savings be?

Chevrolet Plant Purchasing Agent: Will tools and dies be included in the plan? (Answer from Mr. Cowan: Not now, but the idea will be studied.)

And a few reservations:

Chevrolet Director of Purchases: Personnel: How can there be increased personnel mobility when there are no divisional purchasing positions left after everyone transfers to regional purchasing?

Chevrolet Plant Comptroller, Flint: Make sure there is computer time to run blanket order listings.

Chevrolet Plant Manager, Flint: Communications between the plant and the regional office could present problems, as could the fact that divisional and corporate personnel would be working side by side in the regional office.

Of those present, five mentioned that it was important to evaluate the plan carefully as it moved through the pilot stage and to measure results.

Exhibit 1
GENERAL MOTORS (2)

Process Used By Purchasing Managers In Developing The Flint—GM Regional Purchasing Concept

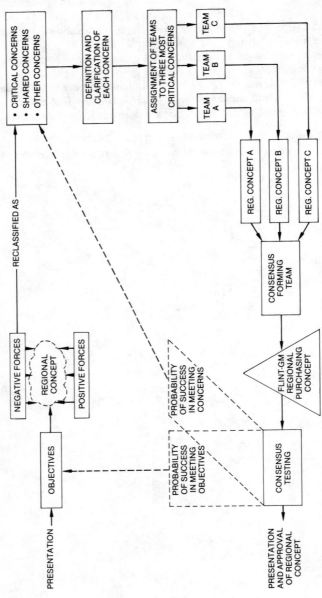

Exhibit 2
GENERAL MOTORS (2)

Regional Purchasing Concept

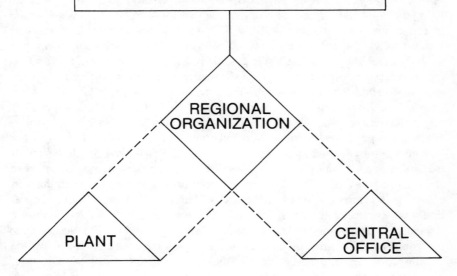

REGIONAL NON-PRODUCT PURCHASING COUNCIL

- Local Plant Managers
- Local Financial Managers
- Regional Manager, Non-Product Purchasing
- GM Director, Non-Product Purchasing

REGIONAL ORGANIZATION

PLANT

CENTRAL OFFICE

- Seeking an Effective Middle Ground Between Decentralization and Centralization.
- Preserves Local Influence and Control Through a Regional Non-Product Purchasing Policy Council.
- At the Same Time, Provides for Greater Coordination and Integration of Local Non-Product Purchasing.
- Regional Organization Will Operate as a Service Arm of the Plant and as a Result — Oriented, Coordinating Arm of the Corporation.

INTERNATIONAL BUSINESS MACHINES (1)

Negotiating Corporate Contracts

In the spring of 1975 Mr. Bob Pitt, manager of the Corporate Contract group at International Business Machines (IBM) and Mr. Harry MacDonald, a contract specialist, were completing negotiations on the corporate contract that IBM had arranged for the purchase of computer-room furniture. All IBM plants and offices in the United States would buy their furniture from the manufacturer with whom the contract was signed and at the prices specified in the agreement. The contract was one of the larger purchases organized by the Corporate Contract group.

Computer Room Equipment Buying Before 1970. Shortly after World War II, IBM purchased all its data-processing furniture from Allied Furniture, one of the largest companies in the business. At this time, the procurement function was much more centralized and all furniture purchases were organized by a buyer at the IBM Syracuse plant. This buyer placed all the business with Allied Furniture for three reasons. First, there was a wide variety of designs available at the time and using a single source assured some standardization. Second, Allied Furniture gave a 15% discount off list-price and, third, this vendor had ample supplies of raw materials at a time when there were general shortages. No commitment to any level of purchase was made to the supplier.

With the introduction in the late 1950's of the Lewis-Levi-Smith design all major computer-room furniture manufacturers began producing goods similar in style. During the 1960's IBM buyers arranged pricing agreements with the four major manufacturers, Allied Furniture, C.F. Barnett, the Metal Office Corporation, and Record Protection so that any IBM location could buy any item at a discount off the list-price. These discounts varied from 10% to 30% according to the company. The lines of all the manufacturers had been approved by the Interior Design team, which was part of the Real Estate & Construction Division, and by the Corporate Safety group, which was part of SPD located at South Bend. The pricing agreements were arranged primarily for the convenience of establishing the smaller computer rooms and for individual replacements at the plants. Whenever large quantitites were required buyers would arrange for the manufacturers to bid on each order. In accepting the national pricing discounts, IBM gave the manufacturers no commitment that any level of purchase would be reached. There was no pressure on buyers to purchase from a particular manufacturer. Similar discounts were offered to comparable furniture accounts.

Despite the similarity among brands strong preferences developed at IBM buying-locations based, apparently, on the service which some manufacturers

Names of personnel, all figures not publicly available, and locations are disguised.

provided. Accurate shipping statements, efficient handling of complaints about damaged equipment, repair service, and prompt delivery were the most important elements of vendor service. One of the four companies, Metal Office, performed particularly well and became the major supplier at many locations. Once Metal Office equipment had been chosen for a few major plants it also became the first choice for replacement. First, an exact match would be obtained and, second, the plant maintenance personnel became used to the brand. Mr. MacDonald commented:

> Metal Office had a good national accounts manager who really went after our business. He did a fantastic job. Once they had become accepted as the main source a really strong brand preference built up.

In 1969 the new manager of corporate contracts at IBM headquarters formed a small task force of buyers who were responsible for computer room equipment purchases at various locations, to investigate possible ways that IBM could buy equipment more efficiently and at a lower cost. One suggestion was that IBM buy all its equipment in bulk, warehouse it and release it to offices and plants as required. The cost of doublehandling and of money tied up in inventory however, made this proposal uneconomical. Eventually it was decided that a single corporate contract be established so that IBM plants and offices would be able to order equipment at prices established by the contract. This would lead to the greatest overall savings.

The Corporate Contract group had several problems when considering a national contract. How should existing brand preferences be taken into account? How much emphasis should be placed on the perceived or actual benefits of superior service? How would bids on a list of items be evaluated? How could they be compared with what IBM user-locations were currently paying? Mr. Pitt explained:

> There has to be a clear advantage in going to a corporate contract. Otherwise it is better to leave it to the divisions and stress the local service angle and the flexibility in competitive bidding. You wouldn't win the battles up the line or with the divisions if the savings were only marginal.

In an effort to quantify both service and any difference in quality the Corporate Contract group contacted 10 large IBM locations and asked them to rank each of the four suppliers on a scale of 1–10. The returns are shown in Exhibit 1.

The Interior Design team was then asked to evaluate each supplier's products on a variety of factors. Again a 1–10 scale was used. The results are shown in Exhibit 2. There was only a small difference among the scores.

The total ratings given by the locations were halved and added to the ratings given by the Interior Design Team. Metal Office was given a rating of 100 points and the others received the total number of points achieved by the combined location and Design Team rating. On the basis of this scoring system Record Protection received 85 points, C.F. Barnett and Allied Furniture received 91 points and Metal Office 100 points.

These ratings, it was decided by the Corporate Contract group, could justify giving Metal Office a 17.6% advantage over Record Protection and a 9.9% advantage over the other companies at the bidding stage. In other words, Metal Office could theoretically have been awarded the contract if its sealed bid was no more than 9.9% higher than its nearest competitor. Bob Pitt said: "As a rule we wouldn't have considered this approach in that we only ask qualified suppliers to quote and then make our award on the basis of lowest price. In this case, we didn't have specifications, unanimous agreement on product acceptability, or for that matter a program. This was a first-time proposition."

The next step was to determine the amount spent on computer-room equipment by IBM and the prices being paid for the main items. Records were not immediately available to show what the major equipment purchases were and, therefore, an estimate had to be made as to the items that represented the largest dollar expenditures. A survey of major offices and plants was then made. Exhibit 3 shows the total dollars IBM spent on equipment in 1968 and 1969 and the lower outlays projected for 1970. Exhibit 4 shows the equipment expenditures using the national pricing agreements compared with purchases made through competitive bidding in 1969. The regional offices surveyed had fewer opportunities to put their orders out for bids because they bought in smaller quantities. Exhibit 5 compares the prices paid for tape-reel cabinets in 1969 when bought on the pricing agreements and when purchased through RFQ procedures. A considerable difference between the two prices can be noted.

At the end of 1969 it was decided to ask the four companies to bid for all of IBM's purchases for a period of one year. The time was limited to a single year so that IBM could gain experience with the contract over a short period. It was suggested that the companies should be asked to bid on the six major pieces individually, and to indicate the discounts they would allow off the list-price for other items. Quotations would be solicited on total annual volumes of $750 thousand and $1.5 million. The six major pieces were separated from the others as it was believed that they accounted for a large proportion of total expenditure and the bids submitted would be compared on these items.

Record Protection submitted bids that were substantially lower than the other companies' quotes on every major item. Mr. MacDonald, who took charge of the contract for IBM in 1972, commented: "Record Protection was well below everybody else. Even if you took account of the previously-agreed weights they would still have won."

As shown in Exhibit 6, there was a difference of about 3–4% between the prices Record Protection quoted for the $750,000 and $1.5 million total expenditure levels.

The prices included a percentage to be paid to distributors for delivery service. If the equipment was to be set up and arranged inside an office, an additional 7–9% charge would be made.

IBM awarded a one-year contract to Record Protection and made a commitment that it would spend a minimum of $1.5 million in 1970. The buyers at each IBM location received notification of the contract and were informed that they had to buy from it.[1] Top management was also informed of the contract and the reasons why it had been arranged. The Corporate Contract group felt that it was important that everybody realize the savings available from making this purchase commitment.

The Corporate Contracts in Use. The first contract came into effect on January 1, 1970. During the year the contract specialist in charge of the contract received a few telephone calls with minor complaints about Record Protection's performance but, overall, it was felt to be very satisfactory. IBM, however, failed to reach its commitment to spend $1.5 million in 1970 due to the fact that shortly after the beginning of the year furniture purchases were sharply curtailed because of declining economic conditions. Although Record Protection could legally have demanded that IBM pay the difference between the $1.5 million and the $750,000 prices it did not do so. The contract was renewed on the same terms for 1971, but in 1972 it was agreed that IBM would pay the $750,000 commitment prices. Expenditures under the contract were as follows:

> 1970—$ 532,839
> 1971—$ 293,043
> 1972—$1,242,574

By the end of 1972 Mr. MacDonald, in consultation with Mr. Pitt, decided that it was time that the contract be put out for future competitive bids. In any case, the cost/price inflation of the previous three years made it necessary to negotiate a new contract.

When working on the plans for the next contract, Mr. MacDonald thought it might be advantageous to IBM to give vendors an opportunity to bid on a two-year agreement. He thought it would take a new supplier six months to become used to IBM's requirements and that it would have a better chance of performing satisfactorily if it was given a longer period to prove its capabilities. Although Record Protection was already used to IBM's requirements, it was thought that, even if it submitted the lowest bid, there could be financial advantages in signing a longer contract. He also decided that Record Protection's performance had been good enough that no special weighting would be given for service or quality on the premise that all four bidders could perform satisfactorily

1. The contract was coded "1" in the Corporate Contract Manual. This meant that it was mandatory for IBM locations to use the contract for all furniture items it covered.

on these counts. The list of individual items that the companies were asked to bid on was also changed slightly.

RFQs were sent out in October 1972.[2] The companies were asked to quote prices at varying commitment levels and to name penalties for failure to reach a commitment. The bids are summarized in Exhibit 7. As can be seen, Record Protection again submitted the lowest bids on every item.

All four companies would claim no penalty if the commitment was not met. All the bids contained increases in prices over those obtained for the 1970 contract. For example, in the case of the tape-reel cabinet Record Protection increased its price by 12%, Metal Office by 18%, Allied Furniture by 9% and C.F. Barnett by 5%.

Before requesting quotes Mr. MacDonald had asked for an analysis of cost elements in the manufacture of the tape-reel cabinet by the Industrial Engineering Department at IBM's Winana plant. Although unable to give an exact breakdown of costs, the department had estimated that, on the basis of Record Protection's 1970 quote, which was felt to be reasonable, and assuming a 19% increase in material, G&A and profit and a 12% increase in labor and burden, that a breakdown of the costs for a tape-reel cabinet should be something like:

	1970	1972
Material (20%)	$16.00	$ 19.00
Labor (30%)	24.00	27.00
Burden (30%)	24.00	27.00
G&A and Profit (20%)	16.00	19.00
Total F.O.B.	$80.00	$ 92.00
Freight	10.00	15.00
Total	$90.00	$107.00

Given these figures Mr. MacDonald decided to accept Record Protection's bid.

The next decision was whether to settle for a one- or a two-year contract. Mr. MacDonald and Mr. Pitt worked on the basis of the following assumptions:

· IBM would buy the same amount of equipment in 1974 as in 1973.
· List prices would go up more than 5% before January 1, 1974.
· The mix of furniture purchases would be 65% from the seven major items and 35% from the pieces bought at a discount from list prices.

At post-bid negotiations with Record Protection in December 1972 a two-year contract was concluded. Prices would remain fixed for 1973. For 1974 the prices of the seven major items under the contract could rise up to a maximum of 5% corresponding to any increase in Record Protection costs while list prices and discounts on other items as applied to IBM would remain firm. To support any

2. Each company was asked to bid on a one-year contract and to give its terms for a second year.

price increases claimed under these provisions, Record Protection would permit IBM to audit its manufacturing costs for two items, the tape-reel cabinet and the console. In February 1973 the vendor supplied the first cost breakdown to IBM. In November 1973 a second cost breakdown was provided and, on the basis of this information, a 5% increase was, in fact, applied in 1974.

In November 1973 it was also agreed to extend the contract to February 28, 1975. The extra two months were added for IBM's convenience. The IBM financial year ended on December 31 and the new starting date for the furniture contract would allow the Corporate Contract group to use finalized budgets in planning its requirements.

In 1974 demand for equipment increased dramatically and at the same time, many materials came into short supply resulting in an extension of Record Protection's lead times. In order to avoid future difficulties, Record Protection and IBM set up a stocking program on the supplier's premises based on order-flow patterns. The supplier proposed a stocking program so that IBM would be billed on shipment. A one-month supply of the major items would be kept and, in the event of contract termination, IBM would have 90 days to draw out the warehouse stock. This plan cut down delivery times and protected IBM against supply interruptions. For inventory planning purposes Record Protection gave Mr. MacDonald a breakdown of IBM's order-mix pattern in March 1974. This was the first time that he had such information.

Over the two-year period there was dramatic cost/price inflation. According to a *Purchasing World* magazine survey, computer-room equipment went up 9.7% in 1973 and 24.9% in 1973–4. During this time many corporate contracts in other areas were renegotiated as vendors said they were unable to supply goods or services at previously agreed-upon prices because of general inflation. Record Protection honored the contract and its chief executive officer explained to Mr. MacDonald that it was able to do so because the increase in demand for its products had resulted in increased internal operating efficiencies. IBM itself spent almost $2.6 million in 1973 and about $4.5 million on equipment in 1974.

Contract for 1975–76. In October 1974, RFQ's were sent out to the four companies. The requests had become far more complex due to the experience gained from the 1973–74 contract. First, the vendors were asked if they wanted to quote different prices for different parts of the country. Mr. MacDonald had calculated that IBM purchased 79% of its equipment in the East (Zone 1), 2% in the center of the U.S. (Zone 2) and 19% in the West (Zone 3). Second, bidders were asked to quote on both a one- and two-year contract. Third, they were asked what sort of stocking program they would propose. Fourth, they were requested to suggest any ideas they had to lower IBM's overall equipment costs. Fifth, it was suggested that they might want to quote two sets of prices. The first would be for individual orders of under $10,000 and the second for orders over $10,000. The figure was chosen because $10,000 was generally regarded as a full truckload.

When the bids were received, Record Protection specified the same prices across the country, Allied Furniture had two prices, one for Zone 1, and another for Zones 2 and 3, while the other two vendors had different prices for each zone. Record Protection and Allied Furniture would give a pricebreak on single orders of $10,000 or more while the others would not. Metal Office quoted different prices on annual commitments of $750,000 or $1.5 million. The others required a commitment of $750,000 but specified no penalty if the commitment was not met. Record Protection and Allied Furniture would carry stock for IBM at no charge, Metal Office would charge for stocking and C.F. Barnett had no facilities to store that amount of inventory.

The quotes received are shown in Exhibit 8. They are already weighted to reflect IBM's buying patterns across the three zones. No clear, overall winner was apparent.

From the information obtained from Record Protection Mr. MacDonald knew that the unit mix of the seven major items was the following:

Tape-Reel Cabinets	36%
Consoles	14
Tables	8
Operator's chairs	12
Side Chairs	14
A Disc files	10
B Disc files	6

Mr. MacDonald contacted a few buying locations to determine the proportion of orders which were over $10,000. He estimated that this was about 50% of the total dollar amount. Using these weights it was calculated that the increase over the 1974 closing prices would be 22.5% if Record Protection was used, 25.5% for Allied Furniture and 30.7% for Metal Office (using Metal Office's $2 million commitment figure).

In January 1975, as Mr. Pitt and Mr. MacDonald were considering what to do, they were informed by Mr. John Bradshaw, corporate director of procurement, that, because of the recession, IBM would be severely limiting the purchase of equipment during the immediate future. The significance of this statement was that the planned expenditure would be far less than those which Mr. MacDonald was forecasting based on a recent survey he had made of user-locations. He would need to be cautious, therefore, in making any commitments.

Mr. Pitt and Mr. MacDonald considered the choices that they could take at this stage. Four strategies seemed possible:

(1) *Buy the lowest-priced item from each vendor.* This course of action would lead to a net increase of 19% over 1974 prices and had several disadvantages. It would make the contracts very complicated from the point of view of the plant buyers. In fact, buyers at various locations who were

telephoned by Mr. MacDonald said the amount of extra time involved would be prohibitive with present purchasing staffs. It would mean making commitments of $3 million, which IBM could not do. However, it would be impossible to coordinate deliveries. Finally, there would be a loss in the number of orders over $10,000.

(2) *Split the business between Record Protection and Allied Furniture.* The saving was only 1% compared with giving all the business to Record Protection and it would be more difficult to assemble single orders of over $10,000.

(3) *Give Metal Office the file orders[3] and Record Protection the rest.* This would save a total of 20% and the plant buyers saw little extra work involved. Disc files were often ordered separately in any case.

(4) *Negotiate with Record Protection.* Mr. Pitt thought that Record Protection had built in a large inflation-contingency factor and that there might be ways of eliminating this factor from its bid. He also wanted to investigate other possible contracting arrangements.

From data previously obtained from Record Protection and from cost-trend statistics IBM cost engineers calculated that the vendor had included an inflation factor of around 10%. The estimates are in Exhibit 9. Without this inflation factor it was reckoned that the price of the cabinet should be about $113 and the price of the console should be $118.

Exhibit 1
INTERNATIONAL BUSINESS MACHINES (1)

Survey of Locations' Ratings of Equipment Suppliers

Location	Record Protection	C.F. Barnett	Allied Furniture	Metal Office
1	8	6	6	10
2	1	9	9	10
3	6	6	6	10
4	6	6	10	10
5	1	9	9	10
6	9	9	8	10
7	7	9	1	10
8	9	7	8	10
9	9	6	6	10
10	10	9	7	8
	66	76	70	98

3. IBM already spent about $560,000 annually with Metal Office on certain unique items such as card files and tables and this could be included in the $750,000 commitment.

Exhibit 2
INTERNATIONAL BUSINESS MACHINES (1)

Ranking of Equipment Manufacturers By Interior Design Team

Factor	Record Protection	C.F. Barnett	Allied Furniture	Metal Office
Styling Detail	8	9	10	9
Finish	9	9	9	9
Hardware	8	8	9	9
Drawer Mechanisms	9	9	9	9
Structural Stability	9	9	10	9
Misc. Items	9	9	9	9
	52	53	56	54

Exhibit 3
INTERNATIONAL BUSINESS MACHINES (1)

Total Amount Spent on Computer-Room Furniture

1968	$6,170,250
1969	$5,658,225
1970 (Projected)	$4,356,825 (23% reduction)

Exhibit 4
INTERNATIONAL BUSINESS MACHINES (1)

Comparison Of Amounts Spent On Furniture Using Pricing Agreements And Competitive Bidding At Locations Surveyed (1969)

	RFQ Purchases	Pricing-Agreement Purchases
Plants	44%	56%
Regional Offices	26%	74%
Total	34%	66%

Exhibit 5
INTERNATIONAL BUSINESS MACHINES (1)

Prices Paid for Tape-Reel Cabinets in 1969*

Vendor	Pricing Agreement	Average RFQ Price	Average Plant Price	Average Regional Office Price
Metal Office	$114.00	$ 96.00	$104.59	$108.71
Allied Furniture	132.00	91.61	102.61	118.61
C.F. Barnett	110.07	100.70	104.58	103.76
Record Protection	106.25	96.59	100.58	103.56

*Not including inside delivery and set-up charges.

Exhibit 6
INTERNATIONAL BUSINESS MACHINES (1)

Record Protection's Price Quotations (November 1969)

	$750,000 Annual Commitment	$1.5 Million Annual Commitment
Tape-Reel Cabinet	$94.74	$92.24
Console	96.53	94.05
Operator's Chair	44.94	42.89
Table	41.99	40.89
A Disc File	68.30	66.41
B Disc File	33.68	32.79

Exhibit 7
INTERNATIONAL BUSINESS MACHINES (1)

November 1972 Price Quotations for a Two-Year Contract

	C.F. Barnett	Allied Furniture	Metal Office	Record Protection
Tape Reel Cabinet	$136	$115	$140	$108
Console	176	162	191	126
Operator's Chair	66	74	66	51
Side Chair	41	40	37	30
Table	82	71	82	47
A Disc File	74	62	63	51
B Disc File	90	86	90	75
Required Commitment	$1.5 million	$1.5 million	$750,000 each year	$750,000 each year
Extension	1 year No Extension	2 years 6 months at same prices; then renegotiation	No Extension	One year at 5% increase

Exhibit 8
INTERNATIONAL BUSINESS MACHINES (1)

1975 Prices Weighted by Zone

	Record Protection Orders of		Metal Office Commitments of		Allied Furniture Orders of		C.F. Barnett All orders
	$0–10,000	$10,000+	$750 Thousand	$1.5 million	$0–10,000	$10,000+	
Tape-Reel Cabinet	138.24	135.74	138.84	136.63	138.18	131.37	159.00
Console	164.45	162.95	191.53	187.78	202.69	195.13	247.50
Table	62.82	59.67	77.38	76.34	63.72	59.30	92.25
Operators Chair	67.41	63.75	67.65	65.48	62.50	59.99	75.88
Side Chair	39.68	38.06	42.74	40.50	41.04	40.13	45.47
A Disc File	102.54	95.75	90.35	86.39	104.18	100.61	109.35
B Disc File	56.48	55.58	47.43	45.93	58.89	57.09	62.41
Other Catalogue Items	Average 55% discount off list-price		48% off list-price		40% off list-price		50% off list-price

Exhibit 9
INTERNATIONAL BUSINESS MACHINES (1)

IBM Internal Estimates Of Costs For Tape-Reel Cabinet And Console

	IBM Cost Estimates 1/1/75		IBM Cost Projections for 1/1/76 (made 1/1/75)	
	Tape Reel Cabinet	Console	Tape Reel Cabinet	Console
Steel	$ 23.07	$ 23.82	$ 23.92	$24.74
Paint	2.26	2.06	2.58	2.25
Hardware	16.43	12.23	17.85	13.50
Package	3.86	3.95	4.29	3.83
Labor	10.59	12.90	11.25	13.88
Manufacturing Burden	25.63	30.84	28.23	33.75
Commercial Burden	13.50	15.27	17.21	16.50
Cost	$ 95.34	$101.07	$105.33	$108.45
Profit and Inflation	32.04	28.98	22.04	21.60
Price	$127.38	$130.05	$127.37	$130.05

INTERNATIONAL BUSINESS MACHINES (2)

Negotiations with a Single-Source Supplier

This is the most difficult problem I've seen. I've been in purchasing for 28 years and I've been through some tough ones but this is the toughest.

With these words Mr. Paul Secor, Manager of Procurement of the Systems Product Division (SPD) Components Procurement Group, summed up his feelings about IBM's relations with a supplier of small integrator units, a type of integrated circuit. This vendor had supplied a family of units to IBM and when Mr. Secor indicated that IBM would take over the manufacture of one of the units itself, the vendor had announced price increases on the other two members of the family that would make up in total for the loss of revenue on the third. This case traces the history of IBM's procurement of these components and describes the discussions that took place within IBM when the decision to make rather than buy was made.

Initial Purchases and the Build-Up of Volume. In 1970 the SPD Components Procurement Group was informed by the IBM System Communication Division (SCD) of the need for integrator units for a coordinator display unit, the D27, that was due to be announced in 1972. There were three items involved. The first was a bit register (BR1) that would be produced in high volume. The second part was a less complex bit register (BR2) that would be produced in a volume of about one-fifth of that of the BR1. The third was an erase memory (EM) with a total production required of just over one-half of that of the BR2. A bit register held information for a short time as it was shifted through the unit. In the case of the BR1, the information was moved 480 times through each unit and this allowed the message to be delayed 80 microseconds. Its task was to slow up the information so that it arrived at the display unit in large quantities and could be arranged and put on the screen to be read. The EM defined a bit pattern. Every time it received a certain bit of information it produced a corresponding instruction or announcement. The unit, therefore, had to be languaged, programmed and tailored to each system model and to the customer's usage. There would be about 150 EM part numbers. The parts would be placed on the cards at the IBM Syracuse facility and the coordinator display unit would be finally assembled at the IBM Mishawaka plant.

At the time that the Components Procurement Group first learned of the requirement for the items it was also given the forecast requirements for each item over the first three years of the life of the product and the maximum failure rate allowed for the memory units. It was expected that, in the case of the BR1, one million would be required in 1972, 2.5 million in 1973 and two million in 1974. Acceptable quality levels (AQLs) were set at a maximum failure rate of

Names of personnel, all figures not publicly available and locations are disguised.

1.75% of the units after 100,000 hours of usage for the first batch declining to .75% by the end of 1974. These AQLs were significantly tighter than those normally expected of similar commercially-available parts. In fact, commercially-available components were generally sold with only a 30-day guarantee.

Requests for information (RFIs) were sent to Connecticut Electronics, Semiconductors Inc., Princeton Instruments, and International Systems, all of which manufactured similar products. The RFIs contained general information for planning purposes on the specifications of the units and the approximate gross volumes required over the lifetime of the D27.

IBM engineers started working with Connecticut Electronics and International Systems, the two companies that expressed interest. The Product Assurance Group, a department located at South Bend, devised a program to approve suppliers of these items. This group was independent of SPD Component Procurement and worked with IBM divisions as well as outside suppliers to make sure that items that went into IBM products were of acceptable quality. The approval process for an integrated-circuit supplier could take 10–14 months and cost between $90,000 and $150,000. Once this group had approved a supplier it was the Procurement Group's responsibility to test incoming items to make sure that they met the AQLs. It was regarded as very serious if SPD Component Procurement failed to provide products on schedule at the AQLs to which it had committed.

The two suppliers were very different. Connecticut Electronics was a technically-advanced company with large resources. Its sales in 1970 were $300 million and by 1974 they had grown to $800 million. International Systems was a small aggressive company with sales of $20 million in 1970, which grew to $75 million in 1974. After about six months, however, work with Connecticut Electronics was discontinued. Its samples had failed IBM's testing procedures and there had been long delays.

During the testing period Connecticut Electronics management had been asked to forecast prices for items over the next five years. Using these forecasts and their own judgment based on prior experience, buyers from the Components Procurement Group prepared estimates of the total price, including the cost of purchasing, that the IBM Syracuse, N.Y. facility would incur for the units. The unit price on the BR1 was $9 at the start of the program, dropping to $2.75 by mid-1975. In making such estimates it was made clear that they were contingent on Components Procurement's being able to obtain more than one supplier and on no tightening of AQLs.

In 1971, 40,000 units were bought from International Systems. By this stage there was a working prototype of the D27 and the units had performed satisfactorily. By the year-end the SPD Components Procurement Group had made performance and price commitments and had sent out a Request for Quote (RFQ) to International Systems asking the company to quote on the first-half 1972 requirements. Despite the fact that this vendor was the sole source for the family,

Mr. Al Chester, purchasing manager for integrated circuits and semiconductors thought that IBM had a possible negotiating position:

> International Systems had never done business with us before and if they wanted to become a regular supplier it was in their interest to quote a reasonable price. They knew we had the capability to manufacture the devices ourselves and we could always try to bring in new suppliers. Finally, and this is most important, IBM is a good customer. We pay our bills on time. A small, rapidly growing semiconductor firm often has cash-flow problems, and IBM makes an excellent customer.

The quotes were received and accepted, and the prices paid for the BR1 and volume delivered in 1972 are shown in Exhibit 1. After that a steady decline in prices was negotiated, although one price increase was sustained in 1973 when AQLs were tightened. The prices for the third quarter were reached only after a long negotiation between Mr. Secor and the chief executive officer of International Systems. Any price higher than the $4.75 eventually agreed upon for the BR1 would have meant that the Components Procurement Group would have failed to meet its committed price for that period, even allowing for the contingency factor for the tightened AQLs.

Quality Problems. In mid-1974 the AQLs were again tightened because failure-rate reports from the field indicated that the parts were not meeting performance commitments. No price increase was requested by International Systems at this time since the units had been meeting the tighter specifications before they were implemented. At the end of the fourth quarter, however, quality began to fall off and IBM rejected some lots of the BR1 after testing. Further lots failed the testing procedure at the vendor's plant. In all, some 277,000 units were rejected between December 1974 and March 1975.

The vendor argued that the rejections were based on unfortunate statistical results. Tests were carried out on 500 units from each 20,000 lot and a failure rate of five units was acceptable. While the failure rate in mid-1974 had been running at the level of 1–2, it started edging up until the rejection level was reached. International Systems management suggested that testing another 500 units could well lead to acceptance of a rejected lot. IBM buyers argued that the consistency of the failure pattern made this seem unlikely. Mr. Jack Gregory, SPD Director of Procurement explained: "We looked at other indices at the International Systems line which is dedicated to IBM, such as the yield rates, and they all pointed in the same direction. The pattern suggested a process that was under control, moved out of control and then, with some effort, was brought back under control again."

IBM buyers speculated that, with declining overall sales, the supplier might have rotated labor on the line that was dedicated to IBM products. There was no other specific cause to which the problems could be traced. Some questions of the cleanliness of the air on the line and general housekeeping problems were raised. Mr. Chester talked about the manufacturing process.

Making this sort of thing is black magic. A perfectly good line can suddenly start turning out a bad product and nobody knows why. This isn't a new technology but such things can happen. The wafers are made in Maine and shipped elsewhere for assembly. The units are tested back in Maine. The problems arose with the wafers.

Another possibility was that they were having cash-flow problems. When the problems started they might have sped up the line to be sure that they could ship us enough acceptable product so we would continue payments. I don't know if that's true.

When a lot was rejected, IBM debited its International Systems payables account since payments were normally made regularly as units were delivered.

By March 1975 the quality problems had been resolved and all seemed to be going well. In August of the year before IBM had signed a letter of intent to buy 1.0 million BR1s, and a proportional number of BR2s and EMs for the last quarter of 1974 and the whole of 1975. This was not a commitment, but an indication of the quantities expected and on which prices would be based. If actual volumes were lower, prices would be adjusted for the shortfall. Exact quantities for delivery would be ordered one quarter in advance. With the solution of the quality problems this volume could be met with no difficulty. Furthermore it was felt that IBM's demand for the units had peaked and would now gradually decline. Although further discussion had been held with Connecticut Electronics and Princeton Instruments in an effort to bring on a second source, they had led nowhere. Samples submitted by these suppliers had proven unsatisfactory and, in any case, IBM buyers were satisfied with the prices and performance of International Systems. The possibility of finding another source became less as time passed since more advanced units were being produced by other manufacturers.

The Proposal to Make the BR1. In the business turndown of 1972 one of IBM's plants had made some prototypes of the BR1. This plant, which was part of the Systems Division and manufactured integrated circuits, had been short of work at this time. In order to keep its resources utilized, the plant management had looked for products used by IBM which the facility was able to manufacture. After the Product Assurance Group had qualified the plant as a supplier of the unit, however, the facility's manufacturing volume had picked up and it was decided not to manufacture the BR1. At no time did the IBM plant management consider making the BR2 or the EM.

In December 1974, management of the plant that had made the BR1 prototype informed the SPD Components Procurement Group that because of the general decline in its manufacturing volume, it was reconsidering the possibility of manufacturing the BR1. Mr. Chester supplied the facility with details of the prices paid for the unit, the revisions in the AQLs that had occurred in 1972, a summary of IBM's obligations to International Systems to take the 1.0 million units and the required delivery schedule. In January 1975 the IBM plant prepared estimates for the BR1 based on incremental costs that were slightly below what was being paid to International Systems and announced that it was about to start manufacture. The costs and the notice to make the BR1 were sent to SPD Components Procurement and the D27 program manager. Mr. Chester explained the costing:

> There's no way purchase cost can match in-house costs when they consider out-of-pocket expenses. Of course, when it comes to full costing, it is usually less expensive to buy. In determining whether to make or buy when we're trying to maintain full resource utilization we always use incremental costs; but the buying plant, or in this case the D27 program manager, has to pay actual costs. Transfer costs between plants at IBM are always made on an actual basis.

Because IBM attempted to maintain full resource utilization, the decision to manufacture would normally have been accepted automatically. In this case, however, Mr. Gregory decided to appeal the decision and, because the plant was not a part of SPD, a meeting was arranged with the corporate vice-president of manufacturing in March 1975. Mr. Gregory, the D27 program manager and the plant manager were also present.

The views of the four participants could be summarized as follows:

(1) Mr. Gregory was concerned about overall prices and quality. Because International Systems maintained a line dedicated to IBM the overall costs for all three units had not been considered. The overheads of the line would have to be borne by the BR2 and the EM. The line would have to be kept open to make sure that the quality of the two lower-volume units was maintained.

   Another consideration was that the SPD Components Procurement Group needed to spread its procurement burden over as large a volume as possible. The International Systems contract, of about $9 million a year, represented approximately 5% of the group's dollars spent. Normally the group's procurement burden was between 10% and 15% but, because of the turndown, was running higher at this stage.

(2) The D27 program manager needed reliability, sure delivery and low cost. This was a cost-significant part and his costs were going up. He was concerned about delivery performance but, most important, he was concerned about whether the IBM-manufactured BR1 would exactly replicate the performance of the International System's BR1.

(3) The IBM plant manager needed the work to maintain full resource utilization.

(4) It was the responsibility of the vice president of manufacturing to carry out IBM's practice of full resource utilization even during a business decline. This implied that if, in the short run, internal incremental costs were lower

than the full costs paid to outside vendors, and IBM resources would otherwise be idle, the work should be brought in-house.

Given the pressures of the full utilization practice, the decision on the IBM plant was ratified for the time being. Therefore, the chief executive officer of International Systems was informed in February 1975 that an IBM evaluation team was considering the possibility of IBM's making the BR1. In March, Mr. Chester notified the supplier that the decision had been made to withdraw the BR1. IBM proposed to take the 500,000 units ordered for the first quarter and to spread out the delivery of the 300,000 units that would have been ordered in the second quarter and a further 200,000 units through November. This would allow the vendor's line to be phased down gradually as the IBM line built up and would make sure that IBM would be receiving supplies from two sources during the changeover. At all times the buyers were conscious of the fact that they wanted to keep the supplier's line running as long as possible. If there was an increase in business or if the IBM plant had technical difficulties with the BR1, the decision to manufacture could be reversed.

When Mr. Chester formally told the supplier of IBM's decision, he was surprised to learn that, not only had International Systems management assumed that there would be no decline in demand for the units in the second quarter of 1975 but the company had also started production for future quarters. The vendor had 540,000 BR1s in production for the second quarter of 1975 and a further 540,000 in production for later supply. Given the decreased demand for the unit, International Systems had, in fact, started work on BR1s that would totally fulfill IBM's requirements through the first quarter of 1976.

The vendor had two explanations for the increased starts. First, the quality problems of the second half of 1974 had lowered the yields obtained and in order to make sure that the delivery schedule was maintained, it had been decided to increase production starts. Second, there seemed to be little risk involved. The supplier knew it was the sole source.

Given this information, Mr. Chester asked International Systems for two quotes:

(a) a quote on the 500,000 extra BR1s already started, 200,000 BR2s and 100,000 EMs.

(b) A quote on 200,000 BR2s and 100,000 EM's.

When the vendor refused to supply a quote on (a), Mr. Chester was not surprised. The quote received on (b) is shown in Exhibit 2. The increases in cost compared with the previous prices were dramatic.

The increased prices were explained by the International Systems negotiators, as the result of transferring the overhead of the complete line to the two lower-volume items. It was denied that the costs of the overrun were being included.

Mr. Chester was wondering what to do. He considered asking International Systems to bid on the total lifetime expected requirements of the BR2 and the EM for delivery when manufactured. This would enable the IBM dedicated line to be kept open until all requirements had been met. There were, however, several problems with this approach. It would be difficult to estimate total requirements accurately and since these parts were no longer manufactured by other companies it would be difficult and expensive to find other sources. The supplier's representative made it clear that the vendor would not want to bid on this basis. Finally, he assumed that the IBM plant would continue making the BR1 until the end of the program.

Exhibit 1
INTERNATIONAL BUSINESS MACHINES (2)

Prices And Volumes of BR1

	Volume (in thousands)	Unit Price
1972		
1st Half	250	$7.00
2nd Half	500	5.00
1973		
1st Quarter	400	4.75
2nd Quarter	360	4.00
3rd Quarter	600	4.75
4th Quarter	650	4.00
1974		
1st Quarter	400	3.75
2nd Quarter	500	3.75
3rd Quarter	425	3.75
4th Quarter	500	3.25
1975		
1st Quarter	500	3.25
2nd Quarter	350	2.10

Exhibit 2
INTERNATIONAL BUSINESS MACHINES (2)

New Quote Received In April 1975

Current Prices			New Quotations	
Unit Price	Volume		Unit Price	Volume
BR2 $2.50	400,000		$15.00	200,000
EM $7.00	200,000		$21.00	100,000

RAYTHEON COMPANY (1)

Negotiating Corporate-Wide Agreements—1971

In early February 1971, Mr. J. D. Bradley, a company-wide purchasing specialist in Raytheon's corporate purchasing organization was considering how many electronic components distributors (ECDs) he should appoint to the Approved Electronics Distributor List (AEDL), and which distributors should be appointed to it. The AEDL would specify the distributors from which the purchasers at Raytheon's plants and laboratories could purchase electronics components.

In December 1970, Mr. Bradley had sent requests for quotations (RFQs) to the 40 distributors with whom Raytheon had done business in that year. Many of the vendors had submitted proposals by the end of January. By early February, Mr. Bradley had eliminated 28 of the distributors from further consideration, and had successfully completed contract negotiations with six. The remaining six ECDs were the focus of his consideration.

One criterion that was important to Mr. Bradley in selecting distributors for the AEDL was the level of rebate that each would offer based on total annual-volume of purchases from the distributor by Raytheon. While vendors on the list had given Raytheon rebates totalling $30,000 in 1970, Mr. Bradley set his target at $100,000 for 1971.

Corporate Purchase Agreements. In 1959, Raytheon's corporate-purchasing staff began to use corporate-wide agreements (CWAs) as a part of its cost-savings program. By 1963, over 100 such agreements were in force, and in August 1970, more than 300 were being used, covering more than $100 million annual purchases. These CWAs were in the form of contracts that set the price at which the vendor would supply all Raytheon plants and laboratories with specific items named in that agreement. Raytheon was not bound, however, to purchase those items from the contracted vendor. Exhibit 1 gives excerpts from an address on contract buying from one of Mr. Bradley's predecessors, a corporate-purchasing specialist, to a meeting of Raytheon vendors in early 1969.

The corporate-purchasing specialists set the CWAs with the vendors, under which the buyers at Raytheon's plants and laboratories made purchases. These buyers were called "line buyers" because they reported to the manager of the plant or lab at which they were located.

In soliciting quotations for CWAs, the corporate-purchasing staff first met with the purchasing agents in the various Raytheon plants and compiled annual-usage rates for the items under consideration. Having calculated annual volumes

The names of all personnel, all companies except Raytheon, and all quantitative data not publicly available have been disguised.

of purchases and a value for the average size of order for the items under consideration, the purchasing specialist would invite quotations from suppliers on the company's Qualified Vendor List, a listing that was compiled and kept current by the corporate staff in cooperation with the line buyers. Upon receipt of the quotations, and after negotiations with the quoting vendors, CWAs were written. These agreements were then circulated to the various plants for use by the line buyers.

CWAs were thought to be most effective in achieving cost economies when the usage patterns for standard items were fractionalized among a number of departments which were relatively concentrated in a given geographic area. Such agreements were especially useful, too, for small orders. In Raytheon there were approximately 50,000 orders a year of which 40,000 were for less than $100. In the case of orders under $100, competition was not required. While quotations from at least two sources was specified for larger orders, company auditors did not concern themselves with checking orders under $1,000.

Types of CWAs. CWAs could be classified by the pricing arrangement, or by whether they were mandatory or optional. *Mandatory agreements* were those that required the buyer to purchase items from the vendor with whom the agreement was made, unless the quality of materials or the speed of delivery required could not be obtained from that vendor. These agreements were awarded on a competitive basis, usually to the low bidder. Occasionally consideration such as service and delivery dictated that a vendor other than the low bidder be selected.

Optional agreements were written when the purchasing specialist felt that there had been insufficient competition in the competitive bidding. The line buyer was required to justify by competition or cost-price analysis each procurement of the items covered by the optional agreement, but all other things being equal, the vendor with whom the agreement was made was favored over others.

The different pricing agreements were *cost-plus* (a percentage over cost), *discount* (a percentage off list-price for each item), and *plateau* (percentage rebate based on the total dollar volume of purchases from the vendor). If a plateau-discount arrangement was negotiated, the vendor would agree to pay back to Raytheon a certain sum (or a certain per cent of purchases) if Raytheon purchased more than an agreed-upon plateau amount from the vendor. For example, a 1% rebate might be given in the first $100,000 of annual sales to Raytheon and 3% on all sales over $100,000.[1]

Over 90% of Raytheon's CWAs were with manufacturers. These agreements were for specific product lines. For example, Raytheon might have four CWAs

---

1. Mr. Bradley estimated that the average cost savings that accrued to Raytheon from the use of CWAs was around 15%. This amount varied from savings of 1–2% on bulk commodities, to about 35% on semiconductor purchases. Occasionally negotiations for CWAs had resulted in price decreases of 75% in semiconductors.

with General Electric, one for light bulbs, one for electric motors, one for resistors, and one for electronic tubes. Most agreements specified a minimum-order size. Usually manufacturers would not fill orders under $100. For smaller orders, line buyers could purchase from the manufacturers at prices other than those specified on the CWA, or purchase from local distributors.

Raytheon had CWAs with a few local distributors. A few of these were for specific products, such as semiconductor devices or electric wire and cable, but usually they were for all product lines the distributor carried. For example, Raytheon had CWAs with a local hardware distributor and a steel warehouse.

Manufacturers rarely involved their distributors in contract agreements they made with their customers. One large semiconductor manufacturer, however, authorized its distributors to sell its devices to Raytheon at CWA prices, and reimbursed its distributors for the difference in profits.

Problems in Administering Corporate-Wide Agreements. "The major problem with CWAs," said Mr. Bradley, "is getting people—both vendors and purchasers—to abide by them. Corporate people just don't make edicts and have them obeyed 100%."

There were over 200 line buyers at Raytheon making use of CWAs to a greater or lesser extent. While these buyers were obligated to use the agreements, they might not always do so—ostensibly for reasons of quality, delivery or availability. The practice of buying items covered by CWAs from vendors not on the AEDL was known as "sharpshooting the agreement." "There is a very fine line," Mr. Bradley commented, "between legitimate digression from a CWA and sharpshooting it. A CWA is very hard to police."

Since CWAs were written with the average size of order in mind, the price on a CWA was sometimes higher for a plant that ordered larger quantities of the item in question than the price that plant could negotiate on its own. Thus a high-volume user of certain items might have to pay higher prices than it would normally pay in order to give Raytheon purchasing power to lower substantially the prices paid by lower volume users. The buyers, however, had responsibility to their plant managers, and often to program managers, who had the responsibility for the profitability of their operations. The high-volume line buyer was thus often under pressure to sharpshoot or deal outside the CWA.

Vendors, too, sometimes would sharpshoot a CWA. The prices that were negotiated on such an agreement were quickly known throughout the successful bidder's industry. A supplier who had been unsuccessful in his bid would sometimes "cherry-pick," or offer prices lower than those on the CWA for certain high-volume items to the line buyers. Both line buyers and vendors would sharpshoot a CWA, as well, if market prices subsequently fell well below the prices that had been negotiated in the agreement. In practice, however, most contracts had renegotiation or cancellation clauses. Such provisions were relatively easy to negotiate when market prices were soft. Mr. Bradley commented:

If a CWA is subject to sharpshooting, it probably deserves to be and I won't force it down the line buyers' throats. When I find deviations, though, I talk quietly with the line buyer—but not his boss.

Electronic Component Distributors. Over 40 distributors of electronic components had warehouses and sales offices in the Greater Boston area. More than 20 of these ECDs had each supplied Raytheon with over $25,000 in goods in 1969. Many of these vendors were on Raytheon's Approved Electronic Distributor List.

Of the over $60 million in electronics components that Raytheon purchased annually, less than 12% was purchased from ECDs. Exhibit 2 shows Raytheon purchases of different electronic components from all sources and from distributors in 1969. Program planning often enabled Raytheon to know its requirements six months to a year in advance of the date of requirements, so goods could be ordered directly from the manufacturer (direct purchases). Direct purchases generally had a minimum order size of at least $100 (as noted earlier) and required a lead time of two to four weeks. Raytheon thus purchased from ECDs when the order size was small and when rapid delivery was required.

The Product Line of ECDs.[2] Although the ECDs in the Greater Boston area differed from one another in breadth of product line (number of component types) and in depth of each component type (number of brands of each component and unit volume of inventory of each component), several of their common characteristics are worthy of note. Most of the ECDs carried more than one brand of each component type. Manufacturers awarded franchises on a selective basis by component type to one or more ECDs in each market area and in general, an ECD did not carry more than one component type of a multicomponent manufacturer. In addition, many ECDs sacrificed general product-line breadth for particular depth in one component type. Exceptions to this generalization were the larger ECDs which had great product-line breadth.

The various component types were priced differently. For example, capacitors, whose prices were determined almost exclusively by market demand, usually carried a 50% margin. Wire, on the other hand, had a markup of less than 15%. Because the different manufacturers of a given product line generally followed similar pricing strategies, so did the different ECDs of that product line.

It may be noted that for some component types, Raytheon required several brands. Differences in brands, real and perceived, caused Raytheon engineers to specify particular brands for certain component types.

---

2. For purposes of discussion the case proceeds under the following definitions: *Component* or *component type:* one of the 14 items delineated in Exhibit 2. *Brand:* each manufacturer of a component is assumed to brand the component. *Product line:* the range of component types held by an ECD.

Raytheon Purchases from ECDs. Exhibit 3 shows the dollar volume of purchases from ECDs by Raytheon's plants and laboratories in 1967, 1968, and 1969. In general, the plants that performed many short production runs, and the engineering-development laboratories purchased more from ECDs than the one-or-two-product plants. At Raytheon's laboratories where design and development projects were conducted, material requirements were often discovered as the job progressed. The ECDs were thus very important to design and development engineers. Most of the plants and laboratories that bought from ECDs purchased essentially the same mix of component types.

The average order that Raytheon placed with an ECD was about $30, although they ranged from $5 to $1,000. Generally an order was for two or more component types. Occasionally, a line buyer would have as many as 400 requisitions for components from ECDs on his desk at one time.

Raytheon's orders from ECDs could be classified by their urgency; *routine orders, rush orders,* and *panic orders.*

About one-third of the orders that Raytheon placed with ECDs were *routine orders*. Many of these were orders for components that were used in short production runs. These orders were placed as much as three weeks ahead of the required delivery date. Other routine orders were for standard parts that were kept on hand at the laboratories.

Around half of Raytheon's orders were *rush orders*. Rush orders were typically required within the next day or two. In design work, on-time delivery of components was critical. Time lags in design and development work often broke the engineer's train of thought and led to delays in entire projects.

The remaining orders were *panic orders*. These were "unreasonable requirements" for components within the next four hours. Many rush orders that were not expedited became panic orders.

Key Variables in ECD Competition. As was earlier pointed out, one of the most important determinants of an ECD's success was the breadth and depth of its product line and of component types within the product line. Thus, the manufacturers whom an ECD represented, and the stock inventory it maintained were probably the major factors influencing an ECD's sales volume.

All the ECDs in the Boston area maintained just one location for stocking industrial goods. Although the different distributors' locations were widely dispersed over the Boston area, they provided uniformly satisfactory delivery by maintaining fleets of delivery trucks.

The typical ECD sales representative had little or no product knowledge. Many of them had entertainment budgets, and although Raytheon line buyers were forbidden to accept gifts from vendors, many line buyers occasionally availed themselves of a free "business luncheon" with an ECD sales representative. The sales representative usually called only on the purchaser, and rarely saw the engineers who used the components. If an engineer required information, he/she went to the manufacturer.

Often when a line buyer was overwhelmed with orders for components, he/she would telephone one of the ECD sales representatives and invite him/her to sift through the orders. The representative could take any low dollar orders under $25 that he wanted.

Raytheon's line buyers were required, however, to justify each order for over $100 of components by competing bids from distributors on the AEDL. This practice promoted strong price competition. Although some manufacturers discouraged ECDs from discounting their brands, distributors sometimes offered special prices on these brands. All distributors offered cash terms.

The Approved Electronic Distributor List. After serving for three years as a line buyer in Raytheon's Aerospace Division, Mr. Bradley was given responsibility for corporate-wide agreements with ECDs in November 1969. He quickly ascertained that Raytheon was not exercising its full purchasing power in its dealings with ECDs. In 1969, 12 ECDs had been on the AEDL. Although most of the vendors on the AEDL offered special price concessions on certain component types, only four of them had offered rebates to Raytheon and only three vendors had paid rebates. Rebates, which were remitted in the form of either a credit to Raytheon's account or a check at the end of the year, amounted to about $30,000 in 1969. These rebates were distributed among the plants and laboratories on the basis of their purchases from the ECDs.

When Mr. Bradley reviewed the agreements with electronic components distributors, he decided to attempt to secure rebate agreements from every distributor with whom Raytheon did business, in addition to the special price concessions already in existence. Mr. Bradley thus solicited proposals from possible vendors, with a view to creating a new AEDL.

On December 19, 1969, Mr. Bradley sent RFQs to about 40 ECDs. Exhibit 4 shows the cover letter and the RFQ. Included in these 40 distributors were all the vendors with whom Raytheon's plants and laboratories in New England had done business in 1969.

The Proposals. By late January, Mr. Bradley had received proposals from almost 20 distributors. Several of these proposals were from ECDs who had supplied Raytheon with less than $20,000 in components in 1969, and several of Raytheon's largest vendors had not responded to the RFQ.

To help him in evaluating these proposals, Mr. Bradley collected certain information from his line buyers. Exhibit 5 shows the vendors with whom Raytheon did over $50,000 business in 1969. Exhibit 6 is a rating of distributors by buying supervisors for electronic components at each plant, based on the ECD's potential usefulness to the plant at which the buyer was located.

A limiting factor on Mr. Bradley's ability to appraise the ECDs was the short time in which he felt he should make a decision. He had decided that the AEDL agreements should be finalized by the middle of February at the latest. Thus, he felt that a line-by-line appraisal of each vendor would be impractical. Not only would it require a great deal of time, but it would probably not influence his decision greatly.

At the outset, Mr. Bradley was able to reject 28 of the 40 ECDs on the basis of the low dollar volume they had done with Raytheon in previous years, and the low ratings they received from Raytheon's line buyers. Of the remaining 12, he considered six as virtually certain members of the AEDL. These vendors were:

> Watson Electronics Corp.
> Goring Radio Supply, Inc.
> New England Audio, Inc.
> Mira Components, Inc.
> Blackstone Electronics, Inc.
> East Coast Electric Supply, Inc.

Two of these vendors had not submitted proposals to Mr. Bradley, and only three of the six had proposed satisfactory rebate schedules. These three ECDs—New England Audio, Blackstone and East Coast—had given Raytheon rebates in 1969. As Mr. Bradley set out his negotiating plan for the three other ECDs, he was aware of the difficulties he faced as he attempted to win further price concessions from them. Not only did each of them have long-standing relations with buyers at certain plant locations, but they each were authorized distributors for certain brands of component types whose products Raytheon had used for many years.

Nonetheless, Mr. Bradley felt that his inexperience in dealing with ECDs could be used to his advantage. Although he felt sure that the three ECDs considered themselves vital to Raytheon, he was confident that he could convince each of them that he was unaware of their importance. If he could succeed in convincing them that he might make an irrational decision (not include them on the AEDL), he felt that he could persuade them to agree to attractive rebate schedules.

Negotiations with Watson, Goring and Mira. The negotiations with the three vendors that Mr. Bradley felt were virtually certain members of the AEDL had mixed results, but were generally successful. A brief description of each of the three negotiations follows:

1. *Watson Electronics Corp.* Watson was a large Boston-based distributor with sales of over $30 million and 15 branches through the eastern U.S. From 1967 to

1969, Raytheon had entered into consignment stores arrangements with Watson. Watson maintained stores at those Raytheon plants that used large amounts of standard components. By the end of 1969, Watson was selling components from six consignment stores at an annual rate of over $2 million. These sales were made on an audited cost-plus arrangement, and were at the lowest prices Raytheon felt it could obtain. Watson staffed four of the consignment stores, and used a perpetual inventory system at the other two.[3]

Watson was generally considered to be the largest and best distributor in the Massachusetts market. It had a large and competent sales force and large inventories of most of the major manufacturers of semiconductors, resistors, connectors, tubes and capacitors. Watson's product lines could satisfy most of Raytheon's requirements.

Mr. Bradley was disturbed when Watson did not submit a proposal to him. Instead, Mr. Watson, President of Watson Electronics, sent a letter to Mr. Bradley, acknowledging the RFQ and offering the following discount schedule:

Sales Volume ($000)	Rebate
0–200	0%
200–300	1
300–up	2

Mr. Bradley had not expected a rebate on the $2 million in components that were purchased from the six consignment stores, located at Raytheon plants and laboratories. He felt, however, that Watson's sales to Raytheon over the $2 million should include a rebate in keeping with other rebate schedules. He thus set out to convince Mr. Watson and his sales manager, Mr. Harrison, that an inexperienced purchasing specialist on Raytheon's corporate staff wielded enough power to hurt Watson's sales.

A meeting was arranged in early February between Watson's Messrs. Watson and Harrison, and Raytheon's Messrs. Beal and Bradley. Mr. Beal was Raytheon's manager of corporate purchasing. While he agreed to accompany Mr. Bradley at the negotiation meeting with Watson, he was concerned that Raytheon had no bargaining power with Watson and did not want to endanger Raytheon's long-standing relationships with this vendor.

The meeting lasted over two hours, during which Mr. Bradley candidly discussed Raytheon's purchases from vendors with Watson. He showed Messrs. Watson and Harrison Raytheon's total purchases and its distribution of business with the various vendors. Mr. Watson reciprocated, and showed Mr. Bradley

3. For its 25% margin over cost, Watson relieved Raytheon of its inventory holding costs and obsolescence risks. Other advantages to Raytheon were increased convenience from decreased materials handling and reduced requisition processing (the users of the components could draw them directly from the consignment stores).

Watson's data on sales and margins. Mr. Bradley's final remarks were as follows:

> We both know that you'd like to increase your sales to Raytheon, and I have no objections at all. But it's my job to do as well for Raytheon as I can, and you can't increase your sales without me on your side. You could force me to put you on the AEDL, but I'd make sure that all the line buyers knew that you were the least preferred guy on the list. I know you'd like to increase your sales to us, but I don't know how badly you want to. Make me a believer.

Mr. Harrison eventually suggested the schedule shown in Exhibit 8, and all parties agreed to it.

2. Goring Radio Supply. Goring was a Boston-based company with both consumer audio equipment and industrial component sales. Sales for the company in 1969 had been over $10 million, with over half of this amount being industrial sales. Goring stocked a broad line of all-electronic components, including Raytheon products.

Goring had been one of Raytheon's vendors for over 25 years, and the owner of the company had long-standing relationships with many important people in the community, in the industry, and Raytheon's top management. Mr. Story, Goring's recently hired general manager, was highly respected by Raytheon's line buyers. His organization was efficient and his salesmen had more product knowledge than most competitors' representatives.

In early February, Mr. Bradley contacted Mr. Story to inquire if Goring was planning on submitting a proposal. Mr. Story stated that he knew of no proposals being submitted and said that Goring had not received an RFQ. When Mr. Bradley suggested that only those ECDs that submitted proposals would be considered as candidates for the AEDL, Mr. Story said that he would check with Mr. Goring, and would submit a proposal as soon as possible. Two days later, a Goring sales representative submitted a one-page proposal to Raytheon. Mr. Bradley was disappointed with the rebate schedule which Mr. Story proposed:

Volume ($000)	% Rebate
0–100	0%
100–300	2
300–up	3

When Mr. Bradley met with Messrs. Goring and Story, he began by telling them about the wonderful reputation Goring had at Raytheon headquarters, and how sorry he was that Goring could not afford to offer a better rebate schedule. In competition with the other major ECDs, Mr. Bradley said, the Goring proposal was not good enough for the AEDL. After an hour of discussion, Mr. Story told Mr. Bradley that he and Mr. Goring would like to spend a few moments together.

In ten minutes, Mr. Goring called Mr. Bradley back to the room and suggested the rebate schedule shown in Exhibit 8. This schedule formed the basis for Goring's appointment to AEDL.

3. *Mira Components.* Mira, a national firm with sales over $40 million and 22 branches, had purchased Berensen Electronics, a local distributor with two other branches in the East and sales of $4 million, in November 1969. Berensen was a well-known semiconductor distributor, and was one of the two local distributors for Spencer Electronics, an important manufacturer of semiconductor components. Berensen's sales to Raytheon in 1969 had been around $75,000, of which over $40,000 had been semiconductor sales and $20,000 in resistor and potentiometer sales.

Mira had branches throughout the country and was particularly strong in California where Raytheon had several plants. On the East Coast, Mira's major strengths were in connectors, wire and cable. One of Mira's subsidiaries, Lincoln Industries, Inc., a distributor of wire and cable, had supplied one of Raytheon's plants with over $30,000 worth of these components in 1969. Mira had maintained a small office in Boston prior to its acquisition of Berensen and as of February 1970, the two operations had not been consolidated.

The Mira representative submitted a separate proposal to Raytheon in which he proposed an 0.5% rebate for all purchases over $500,000. Berensen offered a relatively satisfactory discount schedule, although at the probable level of business Raytheon would do with Berensen, the rebate would be only 1%.

Surprised by their lack of coordination, Mr. Bradley contacted the local managers of the two ECDs and asked them separately to meet with him at the same time. As Mr. Bradley suspected, the two managers were flabbergasted to meet each other in Mr. Bradley's office. When Mr. Bradley presented them with the two widely divergent proposals, and threatened to exclude them both from the AEDL, the Mira manager suggested that the Berensen rebate schedule (Exhibit 8) be effective for Mira's and Berensen's combined sales. Mr. Bradley agreed.

Exhibit 7 is a summary of the proposals from the six key distributors and Exhibit 8 shows the rebate schedules that were negotiated with these firms.

Current Status of the AEDL. With six of the largest local ECDs on the list, Mr. Bradley felt that most of the brands of component types that Raytheon required were available under the existing agreements. Because most of these large ECDs carried connectors, controls, filters, lights, lamps, switches, resistors, potentiometers, tubes, wire and cable, government requirements for competition in procurement were met for these component types. None of the special price agreements that were effective in 1969 had been changed.

Possible Further Members of the AEDL. There were six other distributors that Mr. Bradley was still considering for appointment to the AEDL. Five of them had submitted proposals to Mr. Bradley, but several of the proposed rebate schedules were much weaker than he had expected.

The six vendors under consideration were:

1. Gordon Electronics, Inc.
2. Knowlton Electronics, Inc.
3. Atlantic Distributors Corp.
4. Abbot Electronic Equipment, Inc.
5. Right Electronics, Inc.
6. Robertson Electronics, Inc.

A summary of the vendors' proposals, is shown in Exhibit 9. Exhibit 10 shows proposed rebate schedules.

Gordon Electronics, Inc. Gordon's relationship with newly acquired Wilkins, Inc. was very similar to the Mira-Berensen relationship. A significant difference was that both Gordon and Wilkins had their headquarters in the Boston area. Nonetheless, like Mira and Berensen, the two ECDs had submitted separate proposals.

Both proposals mentioned that under the new consolidation a central ordering and stocking facility would be set up in Boston, and that the companies would be narrowing their product lines, to specialize in connectors, relays, and semiconductors.

Wilkins' sales representatives had relationships of long standing with the buyers at several Raytheon's plants. Gordon's management had a reputation for being both knowledgeable and reliable.

Knowlton Electronics, Inc. Knowlton's sales of $300,000 to Raytheon in 1969 belied its small size (total sales under $4 million). Raytheon bought two types of capacitors from Knowlton on a CWA, but Knowlton's diversified product line helped the company avoid dependency on just capacitors. Resistors and potentiometers were its second highest selling products. Knowlton had a large sales force that devoted a good deal of its time to its accounts. Knowlton had never given Raytheon a rebate in over 15 years of doing business.

Altantic Distributors Corp. Atlantic, situated in Boston, had annual sales of around $5 million. Over 80% of these sales were in capacitors, with the bulk of its other sales in semiconductors. Atlantic carried every important brand of capacitor, and shipped air freight to anywhere in the U.S. Mr. Bradley felt that Atlantic was one of the strongest capacitor vendors in the country. Atlantic had submitted a comprehensive and elaborate proposal to Raytheon.

Abbot Electronic Equipment, Inc. Abbot was a Boston distributor with sales under $2 million. Abbot's sales were almost entirely in wire. Although almost all distributors carried wire, Abbot's large inventories and extensive facilities for making, stripping and rolling wire made the company the best wire house in Boston. Abbot also carried two lines of semiconductors. The company maintained small inventories of these devices and discounted them heavily. Raytheon had a CWA with Abbot for certain brands of wire and cable.

Abbot's facilities were small, and the company was run almost single-handedly. The manager dealt with Raytheon's buyers, administered the CWA and often processed orders himself.

Right Electronics. Right was the Boston subsidiary of National Electronics, a large, decentralized company with sales of almost $30 million. Right had not responded to Mr. Bradley's RFQ. The company carried a broad line of components and was one of the two distributors of Spencer Electronics components in Massachusetts. The company also had special dealerships for certain lines of switches, resistors, and transformers. Right had never discounted any of its exclusive lines except for Spencer and two other brands of components for which Raytheon had agreements with their manufacturers.

Right was building a new warehouse and sales office beside Raytheon's Lowell Plant. When Mr. Bradley phoned Right's manager about the company's failure to submit a proposal, he was told that Right had not received an RFQ.

Robertson Electronics, Inc. Robertson, like Right, was a member of a large, decentralized company. Distributor sales around the country for the parent company were almost $50 million. Robertson had a broad product line, but had particular strength in relays, switches, and connectors.

Robertson's proposal had been submitted over two weeks late, and was incomplete and disorganized. Robertson was the only ECD still under consideration about which Mr. Bradley had heard complaints from his line buyers.

Summing up his own views toward negotiating plateau rebate schedules with distributors, Mr. Bradley commented:

My wife loves trading stamps. I hate them because I assume that I would otherwise see a more than compensating reduction in price. But as long as I must shop at a trading stamp store, I might as well pick up the stamps. We really believe that plateau savings are "gravy." And plateau savings are part of the total cost savings on which my performance is measured.

Exhibit 1
RAYTHEON COMPANY (1)

Excerpts From An Address To Raytheon's Major Vendors

Contract buying (or systems buying) is here to stay so it is vital for us all to adjust our modus operandi to make it work for the good of all. It would be short-sighted to ignore its benefits or fight against it. Competition in the market place—whether commercial or government-oriented business—has caused Raytheon to find ways to improve its position. The government has put the responsibility of a true cost reduction program squarely in the laps of industry if they wish to participate in government business. The resulting savings from our company-wide contracts are a part of the periodic cost-saving reports presented to DOD.

Let us define contract buying as we view it from our office: it is the concentration of buying power usually committed at least annually to one or more suppliers for particular services or products at a predetermined price. It may also be an incentive or discount schedule due to the potential volume that we represent in the market.

It might be interesting to examine some of the advantages and disadvantages to both buyer and seller—first, the buyer.

1. Reduction in cost of materials and services with the use of total buying power speaks for itself.
2. Standardization of products and nomenclature.
3. The reduction of paper work, the bane of all our existence will be realized—in other words—administrative costs will be lowered. With the increasing use of electronic data processing the day is not too far off when all purchase orders and invoicing as we know it now, will be eliminated with our contract suppliers. This change provides opportunity for the buyer to upgrade himself not only by contributing to improve systems buying, but he will be able to concentrate and do a better job on the more sophisticated items. The clerical aspects as they are known now and being just an ''order placer'' will be a thing of the past.

Now the seller:

1. Advertising, sales, and methods of doing business are changed by contract buying. Costs in these areas are reduced and improved planning will result.
2. A better understanding of the buyer's needs are developed and in the R&D efforts the seller is certainly in an excellent position.
3. Increased volume is assured, therefore, he may develop economies even within his own operations which can be passed on.
4. Administrative costs are reduced as the normal bid and buy aspects are eliminated or substantially reduced. EDP certainly will play an important role.
5. Exposure within our company via our agreements is a definite advantage to a contract supplier. We issue about 300 sets of agreements—distributed to engineering, reliability, specifications and, of course, most importantly— your departments. If the product and economics are given to our engineering-oriented departments, it is our experience that they will use them in their design efforts.

One disadvantage of contract buying is that competition is restricted for a period of time. However, each vendor company is working on new developments and products all the time. Marketing is dedicated to bring these to the attention of potential customers.

It is feared that the unsuccessful bidders will no longer service the company. This has proven not to be the case. It appears that they work even harder to remain on the bid base for the next round of RFQs. They are prepared to help if the contract supplier falls down on commitments.

Finally, many feel that the companies using contract buying may be paying a higher price than those using the old bid and buy basis. We find that in the overall picture this is not the case. Agreed that in some given situations one may beat contract prices, but contract buying is not set up with the idea of using contract prices as leverage. Before any contractual ties are made on a commitment type of agreement, our office received proposals based on our estimated total company requirements. After an award is made to a qualified supplier, we issue pricing schedules throughout the company, and it is not long before the world knows what the prices are. Some unsuccessful bidders even have copies of the releases. This could set the stage for an auction—after the award and commitment has been made. We must not let this happen. We must protect the image and integrity of our company and ourselves.

We have tried to cover changing market conditions in our agreements and specifically state that our supplier must give us the lowest and most favorable prices. However, if a problem arises, it is important to let our office know. We will evaluate the market conditions and our supplier's proposals and make adjustments if required.

If the volume of one of our operations exceeds the needs of the rest of the company, it would be very unlikely that the others could buy as well. If, however, the total is combined under our agreement, then all will benefit. The smalls would ride the coat-tails of the bigs. This office is not in competition with any plant; we are the vehicle to bring the company's needs together for cost reductions.

Exhibit 2
RAYTHEON COMPANY (1)

Annual Purchases Of Electronic Components

	1969 Volume ($000)	Purchases From Distributors ($000)
1. Capacitors*	$ 4,853	$ 857
2. Connectors*	4,079	843

	1969 Volume ($000)	Purchases From Distributors ($000)
3. Controls	367	51
4. Filters	248	51
5. Indicator Lights	27	3
6. Lamps	117	12
7. Potentiometers	253	46
8. Relays*	2,271	286
9. Resistors*	3,334	168
10. Semiconductors*	20,089	3,271
11. Switches*	1,365	144
12. Transformers*	9,206	477
13. Tubes*	17,788	565
14. Wire and Cable*	2,051	329

*CWAs with one or more manufacturers for each of these components.

Exhibit 3
RAYTHEON COMPANY (1)

Total Purchases From Electronic Distributors By Location ($000s omitted)

Plant Location	1967	1968	1969
A	144	100	135
B	43	82	139
C	177	262	268
D	300	240	372
E	22	18	
F	1,516	1,151	514
G	32	34	45
H	636	973	786
I	175	261	535
J	1,319	1,272	1,599
K	375	360	519
L	58	56	118
M	424	736	728
N	652	573	540
O	106	96	281
P	25	14	12
Q	24	36	28
	6,028	6,264	6,619

Exhibit 4
RAYTHEON COMPANY (1)

Cover Letter Sent With RFQ To Distributors Of Electronics Components

December 19, 1969

Gentlemen:

Raytheon Company advises by this letter that it is surveying Electronic Distributors with the purpose of selecting and announcing to the plants and laboratories a new list of approved sources.

The purposes in limiting the list of suppliers is to concentrate volume potential within a small group of selected distributors, thereby realizing the best possible discount schedule and service while preserving optimum competition. A further reason is to conserve the time of Raytheon employees by limiting distributor contacts to a necessary few approved suppliers.

If you are interested in becoming an approved Raytheon distributor, you are invited to respond to this request for proposal. In your proposal, please give specific answers in concise form to the questions and avoid lengthy answers if possible. Refer to the question you are answering by number.
The proposal submission deadline is close of business January 19, 1970.

Yours truly,

RAYTHEON COMPANY
Corporate Purchasing
J. D. Bradley
Purchasing Specialist

Information Required

1. What pricing arrangement do you propose? Raytheon cannot guarantee a minimum level of business since a multiple of sources will exist.
2. Please present a matrix (not an essay) which describes your size characteristics. The vertical axis should list the locations. The horizontal axis should include the following (approximations):

    a. Square feet
    b. Value of inventory, if any (at cost)
    c. The number of inventory turns you experience in one year
    d. Number of employees

3. In addition to or as a substitute for discounts or cost-plus type contract features, you may wish to propose a plateau-type contract. If such is the case, Raytheon desires to adjudge the proposed plateaus on an equivalent basis. Accordingly, if you are quoting a plateau agreement, choose plateau points in even $100,000 increments. Up to $100,000, choose plateaus in even $10,000 increments. This is not to imply that you should provide a break at each $10,000 or $100,000 level.

4. Please present a matrix which describes your major lines. The vertical axis should list the lines. The horizontal axis should include the following (approximations):
    a. Commodity
    b. Authorized franchised distributor for Massachusetts (Yes—No)
    c. Distributor for Massachusetts (Yes—No)
    d. Approximate combined value of inventory at all locations at cost

    You should list lines in the following order:
      1. Capacitors
      2. Connectors
      3. Controls
      4. Filters
      5. Indicator Lights
      6. Lamps
      7. Potentiometers
      8. Relays
      9. Resistors
    10. Semiconductors
    11. Switches
    12. Transformers, coils and chokes
    13. Tubes
    14. Wires and cable

5. Financial and Management Data
    a. Chief Corporate Officer and location
    b. Chief Electronic Distributor Division Officer and location
    c. Net sales of Electronic Distributor sales 1968, 1969 (exclude other commodities or services)
    d. Ownership (privately held or publicly held)
    e. Cash terms
    f. F.O.B. point

g. Can you and are you willing to maintain accurate records of Raytheon purchases by Raytheon location, releasing these statistics to Raytheon Corporate as required, but not more frequently than quarterly? (Yes—No)

h. List special in-house service capabilities, if any, such as marking, testing, assembly of connectors, parametric selection, etc.

i. Describe expediting and follow-up system (in less than 50 words if possible)

j. Describe extent of computer usage in carrying on your day-to-day business (in less than 50 words if possible)

k. Raytheon sales 1969; by location, if practical

Exhibit 5
RAYTHEON COMPANY (1)

Volume Of Vendor Sales To Raytheon

Vendor	Sales to Raytheon in 1969 ($000)
Watson*	1,900
Blackstone*	700
East Coast*	700
Goring*	500
Knowlton*	380
Abbot	200
New England Audio*	180
Robertson*	180
Wilkins*	270
Gordon*	110
Right Electronics*	85
Atlantic Distributors	75
Mira*	100
Berensen	60

*On the 1969 AEDL.

Exhibit 6
RAYTHEON COMPANY (1)

Distributor Ratings By Purchasing Managers By Plant Location

	A	B	C	D	E	F	G	H	I	J	K	L	M	N	Total
1. Watson	3	1	1	2	2	2	1	1	2	1	2	1	7	9	34
2. Goring	2	2	2	3	1	8	2	2	8	2	10	5	2	5	54
3. East Coast	3	3	8	4		2	6	3	5	7	5	8	3	3	79
4. New England Audio	4	3	7	8	3	3	8	5	3	9	7				93
5. Blackstone		3	3	9	10			10	1	3			1	1	95
6. Knowlton	5	3	5	7	6	10		8	7	4			6	2	96
7. Robertson	1		4	6	5		7		4	8		3	4		97
8. Gordon-Wilkins	6	3					3	7	9	10	3		9	10	115
9. Abbot	8				8	6	4		10	6	9			7	124
10. Mira-Berensen	8	3					5		6			7	10		128
11. Right Electronics				5		7						10		4	128
12. Atlantic Distributors		6													149

Ratings 1 through 10 (unrated vendors rated 11) on the basis of potential value to each location. 1 indicates most valuable, 2 second most, etc. These ratings were solicited by Mr. Bradley in January 1970. At each location, the distributor buying supervisor rated the vendors.

Exhibit 7
RAYTHEON COMPANY (1)

Summary of Proposals

Distributor	Sales Volume Last Year ($000,000)	Distributor Locations	Total Square Footage (000)	Value of Inventory ($000,000)	Annual Inventory Turnover	Number of Employees	Computer Usage
New England Audio	6	Los Angeles and East Coast	51	1.6	3.5	82	Yes
Watson*	30	Eastern U.S.	?	6.0	4.0	525	Yes
Goring*	10	Boston; New York	?	2.0	4.0	190	No
Blackstone	6	East Coast	41	1.5	4.0	87	Yes
East Coast	25	East Coast	87	5.5	4.5	480	Yes
Mira	40	National	265	10.0	4.0	866	Yes
Berensen**	4	Boston	30	.8	5.0	75	No

*No response to RFQ; Mr. Bradley's estimates.
**Berensen was acquired by Mira in late 1969.

Exhibit 8
RAYTHEON COMPANY (1)

Negotiated Rebate Schedules
(Percentages Of Dollar Volume)

Plateaus ($000's)	Blackstone*	Goring	East Coast	New England Audio	Watson	Mira-Berensen
0–100	1	1	1	2	0	1
100–200	1.25	2	4	3	0	2
200–300	1.625	3	4	5	0	3
300–400	2	3	7	5	0	4
400–500	2	3	7	7	0	5
500–600	2	3	7	7	0	6
600–800	2	3	10	7	0	6
800–2,000	2	3	10	9	0	6
2,000–2,500	2	3	10	9	1.5	6
2,500–3,500	2	3	10	9	3	6
3,500–4,000	2	3	10	9	4	6
4,000–Up	2	3	10	9	5	6

*Blackstone supplied Raytheon with semiconductors at a considerable discount.

Exhibit 9
RAYTHEON COMPANY (1)

Summary Of Proposals

Distributor	Sales Volume Last Year ($000,000)	Distributor Locations	Square Footage (000)	Value of Inventory ($000,000)	Annual Inventory Turnover	Number of Employees	Computer Usage
Wilkins*	26	15, Nat'l	151	8.8	3.0	627	Yes
Gordon*	30	National	165	10.8	3.4	435	Yes
Knowlton	3.2	Waltham	10	0.75	5.0	52	No
Atlantic Distributors	3.5	Medford	28	2.2	4.0	70	No
Abbot	1.5	Boston	9.5	0.4	4.0	26	No
Right		No Response to RFQ					
Robertson	N/A	National	15.0	1.0	4.0	N/A	Yes

*Wilkins was acquired by Gordon in late 1969.

Exhibit 10
RAYTHEON COMPANY (1)

Distributor Rebate Proposals

Plateaus ($000's)	Wilkins	Gordon	Knowlton	Atlantic	Abbot	Robertson	Right
0–10	1%	2%	0%	0%	0%	1%	
10–50	1	2	0	0.5	0	1	N
50–100	1	2	0	1	0	1.5	O
100–200	2	3	0	2	0.5	2	
200–300	3	4	0	2	1	2	P
300–400	4	5	0.5	2	1.25	3	R
400–500	5	6	0.75	2	1.5	3	O
500–600	8	7	1	2	2	3	P
600–700	8	8	1.25	2	2	3	O
700–800	8	8	1.5	2	2	3	S
800–900	8	8	1.75	2	2	3	A
900–1,000	8	8	2	2	2	3	L
1,000–Up	8	8	3	2	2	3	

RAYTHEON COMPANY (2)

Centralized Purchasing of Electronic Components—1976

In March 1976 Mr. Bob Odegaard, a senior purchasing specialist at Raytheon's corporate purchasing office, was considering the responses he had received from electronic components distributors (ECD's) in reply to his request for quotations. His purpose was to prepare the Approved Electronics Distributor List (AEDL) for 1976–77.

Raytheon buyers were required to use the AEDL, and by 1975, 90% of the dollar value of all electronic components purchased from distributors were supplied by vendors on this list (up from 86% the year before). Between April 1, 1975 and March 31, 1976, on purchases of about $6 million (down from $7.5 million in 1974) Raytheon had obtained rebates of $400,000. Mr. Odegaard talked about the system.

> Five years ago we were concentrating firmly on achieving the largest possible rebates. Since then we've thought much more about what we want from our distributors. Rebates are still important but what we need more are service, competitive pricing and quality.
>
> One of the uses of the distributor network is to provide a means of holding inventory. A lot of the items we buy from them are also purchased directly from the manufacturer if we have a large order. But often, in this sort of business, orders aren't large and, then, we go to the distributor. And we have to pay him a realistic markup for the service he's giving us.
>
> Since we are a large supplier to the government and use a lot of parts peculiar to the government business, we must encourage the distributors to stock, understand, and invest in parts peculiar to the government marketplace.
>
> This is a key issue because the nature of the distributor business is efficient movement of inventory; and the government marketplace is small in comparison with the industrial marketplace.
>
> To put it another way, the distributor has just so much money to invest in inventory and we must encourage him to service the government area.
>
> We also want good quality goods. We often encourage distributors to become specialists so they can really understand one small part of the business. He'll cover that area better and will also improve his stocking job.
>
> I'm sure I'm still measured on the rebates. But that's not the most important item. We don't want to ''pay for our rebates'' by having a distributor quote higher prices to us so he can cover his costs. We use our buying power to obtain rebates but, even more important, is the service these small firms can give us.

Since 1970 there had been considerable turnover among the firms on the AEDL. Goring Radio Supply, for example, had gone out of business on the death

The names of all personnel, all companies except Raytheon, and all quantitative data not publicly available have been disguised.

of its owner and Right Electronics had been disbanded when its parent company had decided to move out of the distribution business.

Arranging the Contracts. In January 1976 Mr. Odegaard sent all Raytheon buyers who used the AEDL a short questionnaire, shown as Exhibit 1. It ranks the buyers' perceptions of the distributors' performances. A similar questionnaire checked the quality of the goods they supplied. The results were tabulated and compared with those obtained from previous years' surveys. These tables are shown in Exhibit 2.

In February 1976 Mr. Odegaard sent RFQs to all distributors which had been on the AEDL for the year commencing April 1, 1975. The RFQ shown in Exhibit 3. asked for a large amount of information, only one part of which dealt with proposed rebates. The suppliers included two distributors which serviced the West Coast and which had been on the list the year before. Three new companies were also included as a result of recommendations from plant buyers, or from previous experience. Arch was a minority distributor that had been doing a certain amount of business with a Raytheon plant. Walen was an old Boston distributor from which Raytheon had purchased specialty items for several years. It was regularly asked to participate in the AEDL scheme but always refused. Barth had been on the AEDL for several years but had been taken off in 1973. Before then it had had sales to Raytheon of over $300,000 each year but in 1973, a year in which purchases from other distributors had increased significantly, its sales to Raytheon had plummeted. Mr. Odegaard believed that, in the strong economic climate of that year Barth had found it easier to sell to other companies.

As the quotes came in Mr. Odegaard prepared the performance charts shown in Exhibit 4. He did not include the rebate figures for each firm because he did not feel that they were among the most important data to be used in deciding whether a distributor should be kept on the list. In fact, the rebates offered varied but the ranges were at 1.5%–3% for total purchases from a single distributor of $0–$300,000 and 2.5%–6% for purchases of over $300,000.

Preparation of the Final List. After the quotes had been received Mr. Odegaard debated about which distributors to retain on the AEDL. He commented:

> We want to keep the list reasonably small. There's no point in having distributors on it who offer nothing that the others already have. We have a finite amount of business, and the more the shares of the business are divided, the less important a place on the list becomes. Removing those who do not perform enables us to keep management control.

Warshaw and Cox, who were minor suppliers on the West Coast, would be reappointed. Of the remaining 14 which had bid (Walen, as usual, had not bid), Mr. Odegaard was concerned about the position of five vendors.

Barth had offered nothing new and seemed to have no greater interest than shown in 1973 to provide good service. Mr. Odegaard could see no reason to add this supplier to the list, especially since it had not performed well in the past.

Abbot was a small area firm that specialized in wire. It had received low performance and quality rankings from the plant buyers, but Mr. Odegaard thought that it had done a good job as a wire supplier over the past few years. He was anxious to encourage small businesses.

Murfree was a local minority supplier that had not been in business long. Mr. Odegaard believed its performance was likely to improve.

Robertson and Knowlton were the third and fourth largest electronic distributors in the country with sales of $70 million and $65 million in 1975 respectively. They each had stocking locations in each major area of the United States and each had a district stocking location in New England. Mr. Odegaard said that their relatively poor performance and, in particular, their decline from 1974 to 1975 was due to local management changes. He suspected that district managers had built up too much inventory at the beginning of 1974. When the economic recession struck, they had been dismissed, and their replacements were neither as good salesmen nor as good supply managers as their predecessors.

Knowlton had nothing unique to offer Raytheon. It had, at one time, been the best supplier of [Brand X] components but Boardman now performed better. It was also one of the distributors used by Ulein[1] for tantalum capacitors but Atlantic did a good job as the other distributor specified in the contract.

Robertson supplied [Brand Y] components but these could also be purchased from Watson.

As Mr. Odegaard considered dropping Robertson, the president and owner of this distributor asked to see him. The president proposed what he called a "get-well-program" in an effort to improve service to Raytheon. Mr. Odegaard was not impressed by the program in that it seemed vague and lacked concrete proposals.

Mr. Odegaard commented:

The most important point I always bear in mind is that my negotiations with the distributors accurately reflect the judgment of the 60 buyers who use the distributors' services. Full weight of the buyers' judgment as indicated on the rating sheets must be reflected in the suppliers selected. We've reached a situation where 90% of the dollars paid to distributors go to firms on the AEDL and I think that's a great success. But we have to continue providing good service to the buyers by making the right distributor selections.

The five vendors discussed above fall into two different groups. Barth, Robertson and Knowlton are large companies and we expect a lot from them. If they don't provide it, they leave the list. But we want to keep a mix of national and local distributors, and we don't expect the same degree of sophistication from a small, local supplier. Next year is going to be very important.

1. Ulein was a manufacturer of tantalum capacitors and sold to Raytheon both direct and through two distributors, Knowlton and Atlantic.

The component manufacturers are becoming busier, and they just won't be interested in small orders. The distribution industry is going to grow and our relations with it are very important.

Exhibit 1
RAYTHEON COMPANY (2)

Plant Buyers' Questionnaire

I. You are requested to rate the approved distributors' service to you during 1975. Rate both the adequacy of their service and their relative performance so that appropriate corrective action can be taken. Only rate the distributors that you use.

Distributor	Service to you. Check one block for each distributor.			Performance Rank (Best is #1, 2nd is #2, etc.	Remarks
	Adequate	Inadequate	Don't Use		
_____	_____	_____	_____	_____	_____
_____	_____	_____	_____	_____	_____

II. *Proposed Additions to the Approved List*
   Are there any distributors who you feel should be added to the Approved Distributor List? Include the reason for the addition.

Distributor Name	Reason for adding to the Approved Distributor Program
_____	_____
_____	_____

Location _____ Buyer _____ Date _____

Exhibit 2
RAYTHEON COMPANY (2)

1975 Buyers' Performance Ratings

	Adequate	Inadequate	Don't Use
New England Audio	28	1	30
Knowlton	44	3	7
Cox	17	1	33
Atlantic	35	2	21
Montgomery	41	1	12
Mira	47	4	5
Watson	61	1	1
Boardman	47	—	10
Robertson	37	2	15
Abbot	21	1	31
Murfree	28	2	24
Gordon	38	2	13

Exhibit 2 (cont)
RAYTHEON COMPANY (2)

1975 Buyers' Ratings Of Service Approved Distributors
(N.B. Lowest Score Is Best) Ratings From 60 Buyers

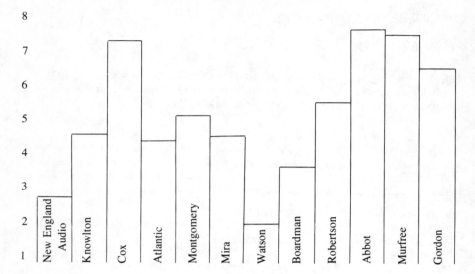

Exhibit 2 (cont)
RAYTHEON COMPANY (2)

Summary Of Approved Distributors' Quality And Performance Ratings
1971–1975

Distributor	1975		1974		1973	1972	1971
	Perf	Qual	Perf	Qual			
Watson	1	1	1	2	1	1	1
Montgomery	7	2	9	3	8	6	4
Mira	5	4	2	7	3	7	8
Boardman	3	8	3	8	7	5	5
Knowlton	6	5	5	8	4	3	3
New England Audio	2	3	8	6	5	8	6
Atlantic	4	7	7	4	6	9	9
Robertson	8	12	6	1	9	10	12
Abbot	12	9	10	9			
Murfree	11	11	—	—			
Gordon	9	6					
Cox	10	10					

Exhibit 3
RAYTHEON COMPANY (2)

RFQ—1976

February 13, 1976

Subject: Request for Quotation—Mandatory
Companywide Agreement for Distributor
Purchases

Gentlemen:

Your company is requested to submit a proposal for the supply of electronic components and material for the twelve month period commencing April 1, 1976.

While the total volume of our distributor purchases was less in 1975 than in prior years, we are pleased to note that the percentage of business that was awarded to the approved distributor list increased to 90%. This was due in large measure to the improved service and performance levels achieved by some of the participating distributors. We will continue to make service, along with quality and competitive performance, the key criteria for selecting the distributors in the agreement in 1976.

We sense a turn upward in the general level of business activity in 1976. Continued emphasis on service and innovative ideas will be required from all of us to keep pace. Accordingly, we have simplified the traditional questions asked in the proposal request. However, we're serious about soliciting your new ideas and thinking on how to improve our business relationship in the coming year. See Part VI New Ideas in the Proposal Instructions for details.

Your proposal will be evaluated along with others and final decisions made in March to select this year's participating suppliers. We reserve the right to reject any and all proposals.

Enclosed is a copy of our Terms and Conditions dated November 1974. Include any exceptions with your proposal.

Submit your quotation on or before the close of business on Friday, March 5, 1976. If there are any questions, please contact the undersigned.

Very truly yours,

RAYTHEON COMPANY
Purchasing Operations

R. E. Odegaard
Sr. Procurement Specialist

REO:b
Encl.

PROPOSAL INSTRUCTIONS

I. PERFORMANCE PLAN FOR RAYTHEON

A. *Account Penetration and Service*

a) List by location your planned sales to Raytheon. Describe the operation of the outside sales and operating staff. Include the frequency of visits to each location.

B. *Delivery Performance*

a) With lead times lengthening in 1976, tell us how your organization will keep the Raytheon plants appraised of open order status and how often you will update the information.

C. *Special Product Service Features*

a) Do you have any special service programs or relationships with manufacturers such as "on-line" stock availability checks, or "Hot Line" communication arrangements that you would offer to Raytheon?

D. *Inventory Stocking*

a) What lines are stocked in depth locally that are used by Raytheon?

E. *Actual vs. Planned Performance*

a) How will you report actual sales performance with the locations during the year?

F. *Special Capabilities*

a) List special local in-house service capabilities such as marking, testing, programming, engraving, connector assembly, etc. which you have available.

G. *Quality Control*

a) Name the individual specifically responsible for quality control and inspection of material for Raytheon.

II. LINE COVERAGE

Supply a matrix which describes your major lines. The vertical axis should list the manufacturers. The horizontal axis should include the following:

a) Commodity

b) Authorized franchised distributor for New England (Yes–No).

c) Approximate combined value of inventory at all locations at cost.

You should list commodities in the following order:

1. Diodes
2. Transistors
3. Integrated Circuits
4. Capacitors
5. Connectors
6. Filters

     7. Potentiometers
     8. Wire and Cable
     9. Lamps
   10. Relays
   11. Switches
   12. Transformers, coils and chokes
   13. Resistors

III. *FINANCIAL AND MANAGEMENT DATA*

Supply the following information as part of your proposal.

     1. Financial results for the calendar year 1975.
     2. Include ownership details and number of employees, cash terms of sale and F.O.B. point.

IV. *PRICE PROPOSAL*

A minimum level of business cannot be guaranteed because a multiple number of sources will exist. You may elect to propose any arrangement or combinations of discount, cost, earned credit, or plateau agreements. No earned credit exclusions will be permitted except for those subsidiary agreements specifically negotiated beforehand with Corporate Procurement. If you are quoting a plateau agreement, choose plateau points in even $100,000 increments. This is not to imply that you should provide a break at each $100,000 level.

V. *NEW IDEAS*

Please surface three or four specific ideas on how we can improve our business relationship. Consider such things as:

    · Simplified paperwork approaches
    · Computer terminal applications
    · Special stocking plans you would implement
    · Ways to make sales calls more effective
    · Better coordination with your inside sales organization

Exhibit 4
RAYTHEON COMPANY (2)

Percentage Of Business Awarded To Approved Distributors

Distributor	1975	1974	1973
Watson	28%	30%	31%
Montgomery	6	5	5
Mira	13	14	11
Boardman	9	5	4
Knowlton	10	12	11
New England			
Audio	5	8	4
Atlantic	6	6	8
Robertson	5	6	6
Abbot	3	1	1
Murfree	1		
Gordon	11		
Cox	3		
Merritt	—	11	11

Exhibit 4 (cont)
RAYTHEON COMPANY (2)

1975 Analysis Of Approved Distributors

Name	Jan—Dec 1975 Purchases ($000)	% Of Total Dollars	Dollar Rank	Performance Rank	Quality Rank	Remarks
Watson	1,512	28%	1	1	1	Outstanding job by any standards.
Montgomery	319	6	6	7	2	Stronger this year.
Mira	737	13	2	5	4	Maintained share of Raytheon market but performance slipped.
Boardman	489	9	5	3	8	Doubled share of Raytheon market. Strong.
Knowlton	540	10	4	6	5	Slipped badly.
New England Audio	275	5	8	2	3	Lost market share but stronger ratings.
Atlantic	340	6	6	4	7	
Robertson	260	5	8	8	12	Performance and market share slipped badly.
Abbot	141	3	10	12	9	No change.
Murfree	47	1	12	11	11	About as expected.
Gordon	569	11	3	9	6	Steady.
Cox	143	3	10	10	10	Change in Cox policies hurts.
Warshaw	27	0	13			
	5,399	100%				

HEINZ USA (1)

Procurement of Ketchup Bottles

With its headquarters in Pittsburgh, Pennsylvania, and with sales of $1.4 billion in 1975, the H.J. Heinz Company ranked as the 11th largest multinational processed-food manufacturing company in the United States. In that year the company owned 24 affiliates in 16 countries.

In February 1973 Mr. Alexander Carr, formerly vice president of manufacturing and development, was named president of Heinz USA. Mr. Carr made an analysis of Heinz USA's position and came to the conclusion that the company faced problems in several areas. One of the areas where it was felt that significant improvements could be made was purchasing. Heinz goods contained a large proportion of purchased ingredients and packaging. Improved performance in this area could make a significant contribution to improved profitability. An item of particular importance to Heinz USA was ketchup bottles, the sourcing of which is the subject of this and the two subsequent cases.

After describing the procurement organization at Heinz USA this case describes the sourcing of glass bottles for ketchup. A second case in the series considers some of the problems of introducing design modifications in ketchup bottles. The third case takes up a proposal that Heinz USA build facilities for making ketchup bottles rather than buy them from outside vendors. It considers the origin of the proposal, the results of a make-vs.-buy study and the final disposition of the idea. Altogether the three-case series treats strategy and decision-making processes in an important area to the company and one in which managers in different functions and at different levels of the organization had a vital interest.

The Heinz Procurement Organization. Mr. J.M. Adams, vice president of manufacturing and development, who was brought in from outside Heinz in 1973, had charge of the following functions: manufacturing, technical development, procurement, and physical distribution.

Procurement had five major departments. The first, *Food Materials* bought all food products (sugar, meat, poultry, vegetables, fruits, etc.) used to make Heinz products. Although most of the purchasing was done out of Pittsburgh headquarters, buyers at Heinz plants located in certain primary producing areas might be given responsibility for buying particular crops. For example, the factory purchasing-agent in one Heinz plant in the heart of a prime apple-growing area, was in charge of buying apples for Heinz.

The second, *Containers,* bought all glass containers, paper and cardboard boxes, and the tinplate that was made into cans on Heinz's can-making lines, located in Pittsburgh. A senior purchasing-manager for *Machinery and Operating Supplies* handled the procurement of all production equipment and transportation vehicles as well as office equipment, such as desks and typewriters, and office supplies. Local plant buyers ordered these items from approved vendor lists.

There was also a senior procurement-manager for the *Western Region.* He was responsible for buying certain ingredients, such as apricots, plums and pears which were grown primarily west of the Rockies. He handled all equipment, supply and packaging items for his area, as well. His buying activities had to be closely coordinated with headquarters purchasing on common items such as sugar and office supplies. On equipment, he was limited in his authority to contracts for under $20,000.

The *Procurement Development* (PD) function had been a recent addition to the procurement organization. It had grown out of a recommendation made by outside consultants. PD made in-depth analyses of the basic industries on which Heinz relied for its supplies. Information developed by PD was sometimes shared with suppliers for the purpose of getting them to plan, to modernize their production processes and possibly to reduce their prices.

The buying process for ingredients began with forecasts from marketing. A yearly budget was prepared in October and November for the fiscal year beginning the next May 1. The forecasts were prepared for each item, size, and market area by month for the coming year and sent to *Manufacturing Analysis* where they were broken down so that production runs for each item could be planned and the amounts of each raw material required could be calculated and delivery schedules planned. In this planning process Heinz managers worked against two constraints. The first was the urgent targets that had been set for increasing inventory turnover. (In 1973 inventory turnover had doubled to contribute substantially to improve earnings performance.) The second had to do with shipping performance on customer orders. Heinz guaranteed its customers that 97% of all cases ordered would be shipped in three days, a level of performance that was equaled by only two other food companies in the United States.

Purchasing received the annual buying-requirements for each item from Manufacturing Analysis. Some ingredients had to be ordered a year in advance while packaging and supply items required 30–120 day lead-times. However, major packaging suppliers were normally given much longer notice of approximate requirements to allow them to plan their production. Because the forecasts were constantly revised to reflect changing requirements, Procurement spent a certain amount of time trying to rearrange orders at the last minute.

Another consideration which strongly affected buying patterns in periods of short supply was escalating prices. If a buyer had reason to believe that items for which he was responsible might move up in price, he could recommend forward buying.

Purchasing Ketchup Bottles. Of total Heinz glass container purchases of $37 million in 1974, ketchup bottles amounted to over $15 million or approximately 2% of total glass industry food-container shipments. Heinz packed about 45% of its ketchup in bottles, the rest being sold in bulk to food-service outlets and other large users. It relied extensively on the three largest glass producers who together accounted for 45% of total glass-container industry capacity. Allegheny Glass met 38% of Heinz's ketchup bottle requirements, Shearson Container 28% and Green River Glass 30%. A smaller producer, Medford Corporation, supplied 4%. It may be noted that for Heinz's total glass-container needs (baby food, ketchup, vinegar, pickles and sauces) the split of business in 1974 was somewhat different: 30% to Allegheny, 44% to Green River, 22% to Shearson, about 2% Medford and 2% to other small manufacturers. Allegheny's share had declined steadily from 51% in 1958 while Green River's and Shearson's had increased from 28% and 14% respectively.

The proportions of bottle requirements for each of Heinz's five ketchup plants that each vendor supplied varied considerably. At one plant Shearson supplied 100% of the bottles and at another only 10%. Medford supplied ketchup bottles to only one location but it was a major supplier of vinegar bottles at two others. The sourcing pattern was, of course, strongly influenced by the proximity of suppliers' plants to Heinz producing locations. The amount of Heinz business (for all glass containers) supplied from any one supplier's plant ranged from 1% to 20% of the plant's capacity. Their flexibility in shifting the capacity allocated to Heinz production was limited. For one reason glass suppliers made large investments in molds to produce containers uniquely designed for Heinz. The average cost of a set of molds to make 12–16 14-ounce bottles in one cycle was about $10,000. The average life for such a set was 600,000 dozen bottles. Suppliers invested in molds with the understanding that Heinz would purchase enough glass to allow for amortization of the molds over a two-year period.[1]

According to Mr. Ken Robards, the Heinz glass buyer, different suppliers played different roles in his sourcing pattern. Major shares went to Allegheny and Green River because Heinz's heavy seasonal needs meant having to rely on suppliers who could meet these peaks. Profit margins on ketchup bottles were lower than on other glass containers and the small companies didn't want to invest in molds to make enough glass for short periods. A company like Green River, Mr. Robards indicated, also gave Heinz superior service, good quality and technical assistance. A company like Medford, however, was "in the picture" to insure competitive pricing by the majors and to "keep them honest." Medford was qualified to serve as a larger supplier at two Heinz plants but Mr. Robards

1. Mold amortization represented about one percent of bottle manufacturing costs.

saw no particular advantage in that for Heinz in terms of price, quality or service. Green River was Heinz's largest supplier and had been increasing its share of business simply because it had outperformed the others, and now Heinz was their largest customer. According to Mr. Robards, Green River was willing to work on new designs and was most responsive to requests for prototypes for testing. As one example: the 32-ounce ketchup bottle was very hard to make and Heinz had had significant breakage problems with it. Green River redesigned the bottle and reduced breakage in one plant by 70%.

Container quality was of primary concern to Mr. Robards. When defective glass appeared on the line or when breakages occurred, there were major operating problems. With lines moving at about 600–1000 bottles per minute the costs of a stoppage in terms of labor and materials mounted rapidly. The cost of a bottle shattering in the line, closing the line, discarding all other open or suspect bottles and cleaning up, was considerable. Also of importance was delivery, quality and reliability.

In monitoring supplier performance, Mr. Robards relied heavily on weekly summaries from Manufacturing of glass performance by plant, by production line, by type of bottle. The summaries contained information on late deliveries, the level of defects (such as blisters in the glass; inaccurate bottle capacity; faulty in-bound containerization) in incoming shipments based on sampling inspections and the number of breaks per million dozen on the filling lines. Suppliers were informed of deficiencies immediately, and once a year each was given a summary report showing his performance on quality against that of his competitors, who were unnamed in the report.

As for prices paid, the general levels tended to be influenced by the published list-prices and terms for glass food containers of Allegheny Glass. Nevertheless, given Heinz's position as a large buyer and the fact that it used unique designs, Mr. Robards spent a lot of his time in negotiating on price with his suppliers. Illustrative of his different strategies are the following:

(1) *Trade-offs on delivery scheduling.* At one time, Allegheny had proposed a 40¢-a-gross price decrease on a price of $8-a-gross if Heinz would take its production on a steady year-round basis. (This is known as the "dedicated line" concept.) In fact problems had arisen and Heinz had been unable to take the agreed amounts on schedule. However, to regain its share of Heinz business Shearson had met the Allegheny reduced price but on the usual seasonal delivery basis and thus Allegheny was unable to raise the price to its former level when the "dedicated line" idea was abandoned.

(2) *Quantity discounts.* Two years before Mr. Robards had tried to get lower prices by asking suppliers to bid on a different basis than before. He encouraged individual suppliers to attempt to achieve a large proportion of Heinz's ketchup-

bottle business by quoting lower prices in return for larger orders on which the supplier might realize the benefits of lower manufacturing and/or distribution costs. They were asked to submit bids on three bases:

(1) To provide all of the glass used for ketchup at any one plant.
(2) To provide all of Heinz's requirements for any one size bottle at any or all of Heinz's plants.
(3) To provide 60% of total bottle requirements for Heinz ketchup.

The suppliers, in general, did not respond. Green River representatives said they couldn't handle this volume. Shearson managers indicated that they thought it unwise to be so heavily dependent on one customer. Allegheny gave no reply. It was Mr. Robards' guess that such responses came out of a consideration for the heavy mold-investments required, the relatively low level of profit in ketchup bottles, and a concern that they would have to deprive other customers especially during seasonal peaks.

Shearson, though, did negotiate lower prices for ketchup glass for one Heinz plant on the condition that it would be guaranteed 75% of the plant's ketchup-bottle business. Shearson had a glass-manufacturing plant across the street from this Heinz facility. The other supplier to the same plant, Allegheny, had immediately met the new low price despite the fact that it would have to deliver from 43 miles away.

(3) *New competition.* Heinz's strategy with respect to new suppliers changed during 1974 because of a decline in overall demand for glass containers. Plant capacity was available because several traditional users of glass bottles were decreasing, or at least, not increasing their usage. In particular, the packaging of beer was changing with an increasingly large proportion being sold in cans. As for soft drinks, a rapid increase in the price of sugar had led to increased soft-drink prices and lower sales. Several manufacturers with spare plant capacity had approached Heinz suggesting that they would like to become suppliers of ketchup bottles. Before 1974 Mr. Robards would have been unlikely to have accepted any of these proposals. He would have been concerned that if business picked up in their traditional markets they would go back to them. Under 1974 conditions, however, he thought he should seriously consider taking on new suppliers. Nevertheless, he was concerned that any new supplier might be subject to counterattack from one of the larger glass suppliers in its traditional market and would, thus, be of use to Heinz for only a short period. He explained that Heinz had to be careful in using a smaller glass company. It was important to understand its total market position with regard to both its customers and its competitors. According to Mr. Robards:

If a company gets hurt in its major traditional market while it's supplying us, they may not be able to remain a reliable high-quality supplier to Heinz.

On receiving approaches from other companies Mr. Robards had attempted to obtain quotes and had then used them when negotiating with the three major vendors after he had satisfied himself that a new potential supplier had the capability for producing a quality container at the quoted price. In 1973, he had, in fact, accepted one bid from a smaller company which had made some 14-ounce bottles at a lower price than he had been paying before. This lower price was eventually met by the traditional suppliers. The new company had not developed into a major supplier because it had been unable to maintain quality. Nevertheless, it had since submitted bids on other bottle sizes and Mr. Robards expected to accept one of its bids in the near future.

Thus new market conditions had led to a change in Mr. Robards' strategy. The small glass companies were looking for new customers and were prepared to reduce their commitments to their existing, declining market segments.

(4) *Shifting purchases*. In early 1975, Mr. Robards reallocated some preliminary orders in an effort to make Allegheny change its payment terms. In late 1974 Allegheny had announced a change in the dates when payment would be required for ketchup bottles. Rather than accepting one-third of the annual amount in each of September, October and November, it announced a schedule which was financially much less favorable to buyers. The new schedule was also adopted by other manufacturers and represented a considerable change from prior practice.

Because of the high interest-rates that had prevailed in the second half of 1974, the change had not come as a surprise to Mr. Robards. Nevertheless, he came back with a compromise counter-proposal. Eventually Mr. Robards negotiated compromises with Green River and Shearson on payment terms but not with Allegheny. He believed, however, that Allegheny might eventually reconsider after it had seen some orders originally destined for it go to other vendors.

(5) *Other possible strategies*. Although Mr. Robards felt that his strategies to date had kept prices down, he believed that more could be done in the future. Two ideas in particular were:

(1) Manufacture own glass.
(2) Change the design of the bottles. Removing the panels so that the bottles were round rather than octagonal and lowering the height and weight of the bottles could lead to considerable savings.

A New Strategic Approach. In the spring of 1975, Mr. Adams shifted the assignment of those reporting to him and Mr. Bob Conners became director of procurement. He had had prior experience in general administration but not in purchasing. Recognizing the importance of glass-bottle purchases, Mr. Conners expressed his ideas as follows:

Probably there are some suppliers out there who are generically right for us and we have to find out who that is or could be. And we're not going to do it by accepting the low short-term bid all the time because that keeps sourcing relations in turmoil. My aim is to identify the right suppliers by asking our vendors to convince us, not by low price, but by *something more*. We're open to new kinds of relations with vendors. That could mean long-range commitments to justify new supplier investments. It could mean changing our buying and using behavior. We are willing to have our ordering and usage behavior constrained to achieve savings in the supplier's plant, in which we may share.

I've visited all our major glass suppliers with this message and I get "We understand. We'll think about it and be back to you." In two instances, they've come back with modest price cuts and I've said, "You really haven't heard me; we're looking for a new vendor/supplier relation. And you have to understand you can't keep prices going up across-the-board. If you want price increases, I'm going to ask: 'Based on what elements of your costs?' "

One large supplier, however, had offered a significant price-reduction if Heinz would agree to a two-year contract, minimum runs of two weeks, a specified steady ordering-pattern and a must-take provision with penalty clauses. On these conditions the supplier would set up dedicated lines for Heinz production.

The offer seemed timely because a study made during the prior summer by a Harvard Business School student had shown that steady ordering-patterns on Heinz's part could indeed result in vendor-cost reductions. The single most troublesome and costly factor for vendors was sudden "11th-hour" shifts on the part of Heinz factories in orders placed on the glass suppliers. Heinz manufacturing-efficiency measures had never taken into account the hidden costs of erratic ordering.

Evaluation of Purchasing. Asked how he was evaluated, Mr. Robards stated that one measure was Heinz's cost of bottles compared with what competitors paid. He believed that he performed well on this count, from information occasionally supplied to him by vendors' salesmen. A second measure was the number of complaints he received from the plants about glass supplier quality and service.

More formal measures were based on the amount Mr. Robards saved in purchasing costs each year by:

(1) Negotiating prices below forecasted price-levels.
(2) Bottle redesigns which result in cost reductions.
(3) Negotiated savings in inbound freight.
(4) Getting suppliers to postpone scheduled price-increases.

In addition, Mr. Robards typically made commitments to his superior to achieve certain nonquantifiable objectives such as bringing in new suppliers.

Mr. Robards' immediate superior, when asked how the glass purchasing function was appraised, stated:

The most important thing is to keep the plants operating.

Mr. Adams appraised the purchasing function on three criteria:

The first is *sourcing* and here we do very well. When almost everybody else was running out, we did not lose half a shift. Years of painstaking relation-building paid off. The second is *price negotiation,* and here we have room for improvement. We have been training our people in the art of negotiation, but we still have some way to go. I want us to be opportunistic and entrepreneurial in the purchasing area. The attitude has always been "We must have top quality goods." Well, I agree with that; we must retain our reputation. I want to change the attitude, though, in the buying process so that we measure quality by what comes out—our product—and not just by what goes in. If we can maintain the same quality product but use other ingredients, then we should. The third criterion on which I judge procurement is by the amount and quality of the *research* they produce. If you are to be a major buyer in any field, you must have a deep economic understanding of that field.

HEINZ USA (2)

A Packaging-Redesign Proposal

At one point during the summer of 1972 a sharp increase in the breakage rate on ketchup bottles delivered by Green River Glass to one of Heinz's ketchup plants became a matter of considerable concern to the Heinz glass buyer, plant engineers and Green River technical-service personnel. The problem was diagnosed as resulting from the fact that the wall in the lower, panelled section of the bottle had thin spots in one truckload of glass and the flaw had gone undetected either at the Green River plant or during Heinz in-coming inspection.

In the early fall of 1972, Mr. Warren Mannheim, senior manager, packaging procurement, Mr. Ken Robards, Heinz glass-buyer and Mr. Joe Colley, manager of Heinz's packaging development unit in the Technical Development[1] group of the Manufacturing & Development Division (see Exhibit 1) were on a routine visit to Green River's headquarters offices and were shown two ketchup bottles. One was the container currently in use; the other was a modified design with the difference between the two being discernible only on close inspection. The existing bottle-design, the one long associated with Heinz ketchup, was octagonal in shape in the bottom half with scallops on top where the flat side-panels met the rounded, tapered top-portion of the bottle. The new design, by contrast, was round but the scalloped configuration was retained at the point where the bottle began tapering down in circumference. Green River managers indicated that the new design had several advantages. It would require less glass and, at the same time, would be stronger than the present bottle. It would permit a smoother flow of molten glass into the mold to result in consistent, high-quality production, and reduce breakage in glass-manufacturing, glass-shipment and glass-filling operations. Further, inspection procedures could be automated and made considerably more precise and accurate.

The claimed advantages were sufficiently convincing that Messrs. Mannheim, Colley and Robards agreed to study the proposal carefully. Further study by teams of technicians and managers at Heinz did, in fact, substantiate the alleged benefits. As of the fall 1975, however, no change had been made, and this was a matter of particular concern and frustration to Mr. Robards, the glass buyer. Since the glass bottle represented a significant percentage of the variable cost of producing a bottle of ketchup and since Heinz USA purchased and filled in

---

1. The Technical Development group had responsibility for determining all product and package specifications, designing all manufacturing processes and continually monitoring product quality.

This case study was prepared to provide the basis for understanding some aspects of procurement decision-making. Statements made herein are not necessarily factual. Locations, names and titles of persons, names of companies other than Heinz USA and certain other data have been disguised. In addition, all quantitative information in this case was prepared by the case writer for illustrative and discussion purposes only and has been disguised, as well.

excess of 200 million ketchup bottles annually, any savings that could accrue from a bottle redesign could be quite important.

Heinz USA supplied ketchup for retail sale in four sizes, 14-ounce, 20-ounce, 26-ounce and 32-ounce. Ketchup sales were made through retail grocery outlets to consumers and to institutional buyers.

The Bottle Design Committee. Shortly after the meeting at Green River, Mr. Colley formed a Bottle-Design Committee to study the round-bottle proposal. Roger Chrisman, assistant manager for packaging testing, was named project coordinator and given a committee that included Warren Mannheim, manager of packaging procurement, as well as representatives from Heinz manufacturing and engineering functions.

The committee made little progress and in September 1973 it was reconstituted and given a more broadly defined mission. Now it was to concern itself with "optimum ketchup-packaging" which included both the bottle and the cartons used for the in-bound empty bottles and out-bound shipments. Chrisman remained as coordinator. Mr. Bill Zawecki, supervisor, glass-bottle design, was added as was a representative from Package Planning in the Marketing group and one from Engineering Services. Robards replaced Mannheim.

The new committee then solicited proposals for bottle redesign from each of Heinz's three major glass suppliers. Green River representatives were informed of this request and registered no objection, knowing that if Heinz did in fact go to a new design, it would still have to use multiple sources.

Of Heinz's three major glass-bottle suppliers, Shearson Container submitted one proposal, Green River offered a further redesign, and Allegheny Glass did not respond. The committee then had three proposals before it as follows (See Exhibit 2):

Design I. The original Green River proposal (round bottle with scallops)

Design II. A second Green River submission the same as Design I except that in the 14-ounce size the bottle would be a half-inch shorter than the current 14-ounce bottle. (7⅞ in. vs. 8⅜ in.)

Design III. A Shearson design with a round body, scallops, a somewhat shorter neck with rounded bottom edge; 7⅞ in. high over-all in the 14-ounce size. A major difference, from a manufacturing point of view, between Designs II and III was the more rounded bottom edge of the latter design. According to Mr. Robards, the sharper the bottom edge the farther molten glass had to travel in the forming process and the greater the risk of inadequate glass distribution at the bottom of the mold.

Estimates of annual cost-savings from the glass suppliers were offset by incremental Heinz plant investments to convert the filling lines to round bottles as follows:

	Line-Conversion Investment	Annual Savings in Glass Purchases
Design I	$ 37,500	$161,320
Design II	$215,000	$436,868
Design III	$215,000	$725,635

In addition savings would accrue on the production line of an estimated $1 million, according to Mr. Adrian Monceau, manager of process planning, by being able to increase the line speed at the point where the bottles were labelled. While the filling machinery operated at the rate of 360-bottles-a-minute, the labelers ran at about 120-a-minute because each bottle had to be positioned for centering the label on a panel. It required three labelling machines to keep each filling line operating at optimum speed. If a round bottle was used a labelling machine could move at about 180 to 210-bottles-per-minute. One labelling station per line could be eliminated, then, and labor for this operation could be reduced from approximately $3 million to $2 million annually. Mr. Monceau anticipated that additional savings would result from having fewer breakages and line stoppages, although he didn't believe that this element of savings could be readily quantified.

The production-line cost-savings were not included, however, in estimates of savings from a bottle redesign as the proposal was screened by members of the Marketing organization. Mr. Chrisman indicated that manufacturing savings were not readily quantifiable without making some tenuous assumptions about labelling-efficiency, lower-breakage and line-stoppage factors. To get reliable data would require 2–4 weeks of actual production experience. That, in turn, would mean that the Marketing Division would have to accept this output and place it on retail shelves.

Reactions in Marketing. Within the Marketing Department, reactions were mixed. Mr. Ray Scott, manager of retail marketing, welcomed the idea and said that he was "fed up" with receiving proposals about product changes that would have only a marginal effect on ketchup costs. He was interested in three major cost-elements: tomatoes, sugar and glass.

But Mr. Tom Pinchuk, the ketchup product-manager, had doubts:

> My initial reaction was "you've gotta be kidding." You don't fool around with that sort of thing. If you lose even 1% of sales it wouldn't be worth it.

Both Messrs. Scott and Pinchuk, however, immediately rejected Designs II and III. These would have made the Heinz 14 oz. bottle shorter than the bottles of both the two major competitors and they believed that an unfavorable size impression would harm sales. In addition, during the changeover, in the period when both the traditional and the round bottle would be on the shelves, a shorter new bottle might confuse consumers and lead them to believe either that there was less ketchup than in the traditional bottle or that some change had been made in the contents. For these reasons the managers in Marketing decided not to test any proposal except the original Green River one.

The test involved mailing bottles of ketchup to 1000 Heinz ketchup users. Half received old bottles and half received the redesigned bottle. The bottles were accompanied by questionnaires which asked about both the bottle and the contents. Of those who received a redesigned bottle 3% noticed it was different than the traditional one. One third of this small sample said they preferred it, one third said they preferred the old bottle while one third had no opinion. Reactions to the ketchup itself were very similar in the two groups. The cost of the research was $15,000 not including charges for the time of Heinz personnel or overhead allocations.

After the study had been completed Mr. Scott decided not to go ahead with the project.

> We thought there would be savings of around $1 million but when we chased it down the only savings that anybody would quantify was the $160,000 that was confirmed by the Financial Analysis people. We had been led to believe earlier that the savings would be far greater, but when I had them costed out by the financial people, that was what came back. Now I'm not going to make a major change in a product like this for that sort of money.
>
> I've learned my lesson. We're not going to test anything until we have the savings in black and white. I want them thoroughly investigated by Financial Analysis.

Mr. Pinchuk pointed out that the Marketing Division wanted to make savings but was not prepared to take unnecessary risks.

> We've already had a change with the bottle caps. For 70 years every cap had "Heinz" in red letters printed on it but when Manufacturing Development said we could save $70,000 a year if we took the "Heinz" off we did so. We did it in a spirit of cooperation. It's not going to hurt us. There's a big difference between that and a round bottle. We'll save the battles for the ones we care about.

Nevertheless, Messrs. Robards and Chrisman, in particular, believed that the round bottle design did, in fact, have enough in its favor so that they continued to press the matter. Robards felt reasonably sure that the savings in glass purchases had been underestimated by the vendors when asked for preliminary savings figures. He believed, too, that in addition to production-line cost-savings there would be some savings in both in-bound and out-bound freight because of lighter bottle-weight. He was especially conscious of the fact that the round bottle would be easier for glass suppliers to make, that they could better serve Heinz needs and there would be fewer complaints on the part of Heinz manufacturing personnel about defective glass.

Mr. Chrisman thought there were a lot of advantages and no real marketing risks, and indicated that $160,000 "is a lot of money to me." He recognized, however, that Marketing personnel felt that the risk was substantial relative to the savings. They were concerned that if the consumer perceived a difference in the bottle design she might infer that the ketchup recipe had been changed as well.

While Mr. Chrisman agreed that making the bottle a half-inch shorter was a major change, he was not persuaded that it would reduce sales. He noted that the Heinz 26-ounce size was the same height as the products of major competitors, that the 14-ounce Heinz bottle was a quarter-inch taller, and the 20-ounce size a half-inch shorter. Mr. Chrisman explained:

> Bottle size, I tell Marketing, doesn't sell ketchup. Ketchup sells ketchup. I talked to Scott and Pinchuk about this and they agreed that maybe the height impression wasn't as important as we might have thought. I believe the consumer is becoming much more cost conscious about price/weight factors as opposed to container shape.

Mr. Chrisman, however, thought that the main reason for considering the round bottle was not the purchasing cost-savings but the manufacturing cost-reductions that would result from fewer line stoppages. He indicated that ketchup had to be processed at a constant temperature to preserve its consistency and quality and that it was difficult to hold the temperature constant when the line was stopped.

In the meantime, Mr. Chrisman was conducting his own informal surveys. Frequently as visitors came into his office he would invite their attention to the traditional panelled-bottle and a round bottle standing side-by-side and ask whether there was any difference between the two. The results confirmed his conviction that the change in shape was not noticeable on sight and was recognized only when the visitor handled the bottles. He was particularly elated when Mr. Robards' predecessor, who had purchased glass bottles at Heinz for 15 years, hadn't noticed the difference.

In the meantime, Mr. Zawecki, another member of the Bottle Design task force, sought some support from Heinz plant personnel. It happened that Mr. Pinchuk had scheduled a visit to the plant at which the breakage problem had occurred. The manager of this plant had become enthusiastic about going to a round bottle, following his experience in running the 1000 bottles that Marketing had used in its consumer study. He was primed to talk to Pinchuk about the round bottle when the latter was at his plant. On returning from this visit, Mr. Pinchuk called Mr. Robards to request more samples to test, but these tests were not subsequently carried out.

The 32-Ounce-Bottle Proposal. In the summer of 1974, Robards submitted another proposal, this time suggesting particularly that the 32-ounce-bottle design be changed from panelled to round with scallops. About half the savings in glass purchases was attributable to this size alone. Further, there had been more line breakage problems on this size than on any of the other three. In addition, Marketing representatives might have less concern about consumer reaction to a design change in this size. It was jug-shaped and not so directly a member of the 14-, 20-, and 26-ounce "family." The proposal was that the bottle be round, that a glass bead near the top for gripping be reduced in thickness, and that the shoulder be more rounded (Exhibit 3). These changes would significantly facilitate the molding of the bottle and would result in higher yields in the manufacturing process, more consistent quality and reduced breakage on the filling lines. In addition there would be a saving of 2½ ounces of glass per bottle. According to Robards:

> I thought it would be easier to get one size through than the whole line of sizes. On the other hand, if we did get this one approved, we'd be achieving half the purchasing savings of the four sizes put together. Then there might not be much of a motivation to change the other three.

A meeting held with Scott and Pinchuk from Marketing and Chrisman, Robards and Zawecki of the Bottle Design task force in August, however, was not encouraging. It was reported in that meeting that, while Marketing would be willing to consider changing the shoulder, it would like to subject the proposed change to consumer testing. In addition, it was reported that Marketing was reviewing the data on the round bottle concept and had not yet reached a decision.

In the late fall, 1974, Mr. Robards sent a memo to Mr. Scott's superior[2] in which he referred to his proposal to redesign the 32-ounce container and asked that it be reviewed once again. In support of this request he noted that:

1. A ton of glass required approximately $21.00 worth of energy (gas, oil, power) to produce and that if each bottle could be reduced in weight by 2½ ounces it would result in savings of 7.5 million pounds of glass and conserve $77,000 worth of precious energy each year.
2. Heinz plants were continuing to experience breakage with the current container. A round version of this container would provide Heinz with:
   - A stronger container because glass distribution could be controlled to a greater extent in a round container.
   - A higher quality container as electronic inspection equipment used to determine thin spots on the body of a container could not be used on a panelled design but could be used on a round container.

2. Vice President, Retail Sales.

3. Labeling would be easier as a round container would not have to be oriented prior to applying the label.
4. Using the projected F.Y. 1975 pack (4 million dozen @ $.0712) total glass savings would have been $284,800.
5. A substantial savings in outgoing freight would also have been realized as each case of product would have been reduced by 1 lb. 14 ounces in weight.
6. The redesigned container would not require any capital investment to obtain the savings.
7. Since the 32-ounce ketchup bottle was not a member of the design family (14, 20 and 26 ounce) it would make sense to gain experience in this package, in the round versus panel design, to determine if all ketchup containers could eventually be converted to round versions for all the same above reasons.

When in the summer of 1975 a new director of procurement was appointed, Robards also sent a memorandum to him presenting the advantages of the round-bottle concept for all sizes and urging that Marketing test at least 100,000 dozen of a round 14-ounce container in a limited market area. By this time estimated purchasing cost-savings had risen with the general escalation of glass prices. Purchasing savings were now reckoned to be $340,293 for Design I and $825,337 for Design III. Design II had been dropped from consideration. It was not greatly different in appearance from Design III and the latter offered a significantly increased cost-savings potential. By this time, too, Marketing representatives had agreed to test a 32-ounce round bottle.

Finally in the fall of 1975, Allegheny Glass submitted two designs for consideration. One was the same height as the bottle presently being used; there was a straight taper from the neck to the point of maximum diameter and a rounded corner at the base. The second was similar but ⅝ inch shorter. Both were round and had scallops. Although these were the first design submissions from Allegheny, a year earlier this supplier's representatives had indicated that if Heinz should adopt a new bottle design which resulted in manufacturing cost-savings that Allegheny would lower its prices to Heinz accordingly.

Exhibit 1
HEINZ USA (2)

Manufacturing & Development Division
Partial Organization Chart 1972

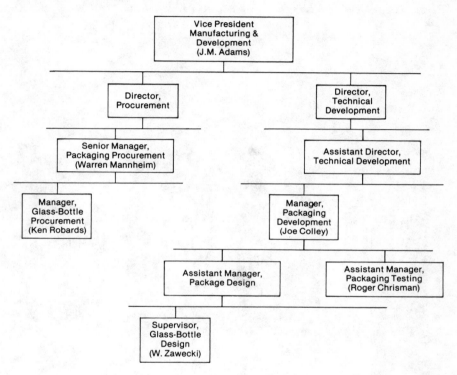

Exhibit 2
HEINZ USA (2)

Existing And Proposed Designs For The 14-Ounce Bottle—1973
(Front And Rear Views) *Left to right: existing design, original Green
River design, second Green River proposal, Shearson design.*

Exhibit 3
HEINZ USA (2)

Existing And Proposed Designs For The 32-Ounce Bottle—1974
(Front And Rear View) *Left: existing design; Right: proposed redesign*

HEINZ USA (3)

A Proposal to Manufacture Glass Bottles

I thought I had more clout then I really did. When Mr. Hill made me manager of CEP, it was for a period of two years, and it was clear that I was on the inside track. I reported to him and I thought I could get this through. In fact, there seems to have been other people in the company with more clout than I had.

With these words, Mr. Allen Barger, by then vice president of marketing for a small company, summed up his experience when he proposed that Heinz should manufacture some of its glass containers.

Mr. Barger had worked with Heinz for 11 years. Starting as a salesman, he had become a senior sales manager. In 1972 he was selected to head up the newly instituted Cost Effectiveness Program (CEP), a program which operated through a series of ad hoc committees assigned to examine specific proposals for reducing costs in Heinz operations.

When Mr. Barger had been made manager of CEP it seemed clear to him that this was an opportunity to move quickly up the Heinz management structure. Although Mr. Barger officially reported to the controller's office, unofficially he would keep in close contact with the president and keep him informed of the progress of CEP proposals.

Among the ideas that CEP examined in the period when Mr. Barger was its manager was the proposal that Heinz should manufacture some of its own glass, but no committee was formed to investigate it. Instead Mr. Barger decided to investigate the idea himself and spent over one year working on the project.

Heinz's Purchases of Glass. Heinz USA had at one time owned and operated its own glass-making facility which it sold to one of its major suppliers in the late '40's. According to Mr. Mannheim, manager, packaging procurement:

As I remember, the reason for selling it was because we weren't maintaining the plant adequately and the quality of the glass coming out of it was atrocious. We sold the plant to Shearson Glass so they could supply us from this facility. Then, the first five carloads of glass they shipped to us from there we rejected because of poor quality!

In the early '70's interest at Heinz in owning and operating a ketchup bottle-making plant was rekindled. A combination of factors seemed to make this a feasible project to consider. First, McDermott, Heinz major competitor, made most of its own glass bottles, apparently successfully. Forrest Foods, another food-processing company, also operated its own bottle plant, supplying most of its needs from this facility and taking peak-load requirements from outside suppliers. On the face of it, it seemed that significant cost-savings could be available to Heinz from self-manufacture. Freight costs on inbound glass-shipments, a large cost factor, might be avoided, Barger thought, and there would be potential savings in making long runs of high-volume items.

Since the cost of bottles represented a major part of the finished-product cost and since Heinz purchases of ketchup bottles represented a large percentage of its total glass purchases, any cost savings in ketchup bottles could significantly reduce overall glass costs. The potential for cost reduction was further substantiated when a study by the Heinz Procurement Control group estimated that for one high-volume ketchup bottle for which Heinz paid $7.41[1]-a-gross, the direct material costs to the manufacturer were probably $1.46-a-gross. Whatever the exact cost-savings potential, it was known that some glass-bottle manufacturers whose total output was less than Heinz consumption were operating relatively profitably. Finally, it was relevant that Heinz did, in fact, make its own tin cans. It operated several can-making lines in a plant which supplied a significant portion of its needs. A study had shown that by making cans instead of buying from outside vendors, Heinz was saving between 20% and 60% (depending on the can specification).

The Proposal. In 1972 Mr. Barger started working on the proposal. During the year he spent on the project he consulted a large number of people. These included all major glass-suppliers to Heinz as well as other glass companies. Although suppliers did little to refute the figures produced by Mr. Barger, they did not seem to him to be particularly concerned by the possibility that Heinz might manufacture for itself.

As the study went on, he became increasingly interested in the possibility that Heinz move into glass-making. His own figures had indicated a discounted cash-flow ROI of 27% on an investment of $12 million and a pay-back in a little less than four years. He calculated the investment as follows:

	Millions
Building	$ 3.5
Machinery	7.1
Start-up Expenses	2.5
Working Capital	1.5
	$14.6

This investment would be sufficient to construct a plant with 85,000 tons annual-capacity. The glass plant would be located next to a large Heinz process-

1. Up from $4.61-a-gross 10 years earlier.

ing plant. If some production were shifted out of two other plants, this plant could absorb the output of the proposed bottle-making facility. The glass would be used for ketchup, barbecue sauce, vinegar, and chili sauce.

Mr. Barger's study based potential savings on what it was costing Heinz in May 1974 to buy ketchup bottles, $153.50-per-ton including inbound freight but not packaging. By comparison, his data indicated that Heinz production costs would, according to the most pessimistic forecast, decline from $105-a-ton in the first two years, to $95.00-a-ton. A more optimistic forecast (see Exhibit 1) showed greater savings. He also prepared proforma operating estimates (Exhibit 2) based on the pessimistic forecast of Exhibit 1.

At the start of the study raw materials and energy had been in ample supply but, by May 1974, both natural gas and soda ash, a vital raw-material for glass, were posing problems. Few technological developments had occurred in glass manufacturing during the previous 20 years but the energy crisis of 1974 had led some industry observers to the conclusion that more efficient processes would have to be adopted. A new technique, known as pelletizing, which produced glass of a more even quality and with less energy expenditure than with existing technology seemed particularly attractive.

Joint-Venture Proposal. One major objection that would be raised by top management, Mr. Barger assumed, was Heinz's lack of experience in glass manufacturing. Another possible objection was the size of the investment required, given Heinz USA's recent profit record. Thus, when Rutland Corporation, a glass manufacturer, suggested a joint venture he was interested.

Rutland Corporation had $240 million in sales. It had operated primarily as a maker of beverage bottles and other packaging products but was looking for other markets. Rutland's management had not seemed anxious to become involved in such a highly seasonal business as supplying bottles for ketchup and other tomato products. In 1974, however, the company management had contacted Heinz both with the idea of a joint venture and with proposals to sell directly to Heinz.

In the proposed joint-venture Heinz would provide $7 million out of a total capital structure of $12 million. It would pay $139.50 per ton for the glass as well as a management fee to Rutland of $450,000 a year. Mr. Barger estimated annual savings, based on the $14-per-ton savings as compared to the price paid to outside suppliers, at approximately $160,000 a year (see Exhibit 3). He also constructed an estimated Profit and Loss Statement (Exhibit 4).

Mr. Barger believed there would be a lot of advantages from a joint venture. Having the glass manufacturing know-how of an established company and access to R & D facilities would reduce the risk to Heinz. The management and supervisory personnel of the new plant could be partly recruited from the partner's existing staff. In addition, the procurement of raw materials might be easier for an established glass manufacturer than for Heinz entering the business *de novo*.

In May 1974 Mr. Barger prepared a formal report for the president that detailed his progress to date. It suggested that further action should consist of formal talks with Rutland and with other possible joint-venture partners. Such talks never took place.

Other Functions Involved. Mr. Ken Robards, who was responsible for glass buying, had been consulted during the study but was still somewhat puzzled about how it was done:

> An employee turned in a suggestion through the usual channels. First it went to the Procurement Control group and then to CEP. Allen Barger picked it up. Normally he delegated studies to somebody familiar with the problem. In this case Allen Barger ran the study himself. I'm not sure why he personally undertook this job.

Although the proposal to manufacture glass, either alone or in a joint venture, was never formally turned down it was recognized that the idea was "dead." Many reasons were given why no further progress was made. For example, Robards explained:

> In general I was not in favor of it. There were too many unanswered questions. It didn't go far enough. Some of the figures couldn't be true. The glass industry isn't a 12% after-tax industry. It's a 3–4% industry. He didn't look at backup suppliers or the fact that we would have to provide our own storage facilities. We'd have to move ketchup production out of two plants and consolidate it so that our glass plant could operate economically.
>
> This could complicate our price negotiations with suppliers. We would have our own glass plant making the high volume items and we would probably have to pay vendors higher prices for what we didn't make.

Mr. J. M. Adams, vice president, Manufacturing & Development, had also been opposed to the project. The May 1974 report had been presented about a year and a half after Mr. Adams had been appointed to his position. He explained:

> To begin with it looked attractive but after a bit of digging I began to feel uneasy. The figures were extremely thin and conservative on the cost side. There was nothing about fuel costs or the costs of storage. The glass industry is in the banking business. They send us the glass and charge us months later. There's nothing in the report about the cost-of-money for glass inventory.
>
> When I came in, two of my immediate goals were to achieve cost savings and to cut the capital investment program. Now somebody was proposing an expenditure of $15 million or something.
>
> There were really four main reasons why we could not do it at the time:
>
> (1) Capital was just too short. We were just not going to have it available.
> (2) Backward integration did not seem to be an attractive policy to follow. We ought to be looking for new market opportunities. In fact, we found more interesting things to do with available capital.

(3) I saw the possibility of setting up a new corporate venture and then running into a soda-ash shortage. I didn't give a damn how much I was going to save when I heard that.

(4) When I heard that there was a possibility that glass technology might be changing and we might have been entering with the wrong technology, there was no way I was going ahead with it.

I haven't given up the idea completely, though. Someday I'm going to go back and have the study redone.

Other Heinz managers had opinions too. Mr. Milt Rommel, general manager, production control, had arrived at Heinz with Mr. Adams. He explained his views:

We'd be vulnerable to crippling strikes which could shut down a whole factory. The glass-making unions are fairly militant and the glass companies have a hard time. I suppose in the case of a strike we could take the molds and get somebody else to make the glass for us, but I doubt if they would rescue us often.

There's a big difference between our making cans and making bottles. The capital investment is much lower—like about $1–2 million for each of three can lines and you don't have to run them continuously to make them pay.

But you know there's another consideration: a glass plant would have to work from Day One. Management wouldn't expect a long de-bugging phase and anybody who authorized the project would have to be sure it started up well.

Mr. Mannheim had this comment:

I just can't see self manufacture. The high cost of labor; the union problems; continuous operations; having to store glass. Can making is not so difficult and so complex. In glass making you're taking a lot of ingredients and mixing and forming them. So many things can go wrong. In can making you just buy tinplate and feed it through.

Exhibit 1
HEINZ USA (3)

Estimates Of Cost Of Glass If Manufactured By Heinz

	Optimistic Estimate		Pessimistic Estimate	
Years	Cost of Glass (excluding transportation and packaging)	Savings over current bought price ($153.50)	Cost of Glass (excluding transportation and packaging)	Savings over current bought price ($153.50)
1–2	$96.00	$57.50	$105.00	$48.50
3–5	90.00	63.50	100.00	53.50
6–10	87.00	66.50	95.00	58.50

Exhibit 2
HEINZ USA (3)

Proforma Operating Estimates For Glass-Manufacturing Facility
(In Thousands)

	Years 1–2	Years 3–5	Years 6–10
$48.50 × 85,000 tons	$4,123		
$53.50 × 90,000 tons		$4,815	
$58.50 × 90,000 tons			$5,265
N.O.P.B.T.	$4,123	$4,815	$5,265
Provision for taxes @ 50%	($2,062)	($2,408)	($2,633)
N.O.P.A.T.	$2,061	$2,407	$2,632
Depreciation			
Buildings @ 3.5%	$ 115	$ 115	$ 115
Machinery @ 7.0%	575	575	575
Start-up expense @ 20%	330	330	—
	$1,020	$1,020	$ 690

Exhibit 3
HEINZ USA (3)

Estimated Annual-Savings Available From The Joint Venture
(In Thousands)

	Years 1–2	Years 3–10
$14 × 85,000 tons	$1,190	
$14 × 90,000 tons		$1,260
Taxes @ 50%	595	630
	$ 595	$ 630

Exhibit 4
HEINZ USA (3)

Estimated Profit-and-Loss Statement—Heinz Share Of Heinz-Rutland
Joint Venture (In Thousands)

Net Sales	*Years 1–2*	*Years 3–5*	*Years 6–10*
$139.50 × 85,000 tons	$11,857		
$139.50 × 90,000 tons		$12,555	$12,555
Operating Costs			
$105.70 × 85,000 tons	$ 8,985		
$ 99.50 × 90,000 tons		$8,955	
$ 95.60 × 90,000 tons			$8,604
	$ 2,602	$ 3,600	$ 3,951
Operating Income			
Fee to Rutland	(450)	(450)	(450)
Interest expense			
(7.5% on $7 MM)	(525)	(525)	(525)
N.P.B.T.	$1,627	$ 2,625	$ 2,976
Provision for taxes @ 50%	(814)	(1,313)	(1,488)
N.P.A.T.	$ 813	$ 1,312	$ 1,488
Heinz portion @ 50%	$ 407	$ 656	$ 774

AMSDEER CORPORATION[1] (1)

Purchasing Reactors for the Central and Western Plants

On November 1, 1973, Mr. Tom Steele, Senior Purchasing Agent, in Amsdeer's Corporate Purchasing Department, received a Request for Quotations (RFQ) from the Engineering Department of the Commercial Chemicals Division for a reactor for the Central plant. The RFQ specified a reactor for making paint resins, having 6,000 gallons capacity x-wall construction, stainless steel, with an inside agitator. Shortly thereafter, RFQ's for two more units were received by Mr. Steele from Commercial Chemicals Engineering, a second unit for Central, and one for the Western plant. Bids were received on all three units from vendors and orders were placed during January 1974 for delivery late in the year. In January 1975, three more units were ordered. At that time, Mr. Steele reviewed the history of these procurements and expressed concern about two matters. First, the reactors on order were costing Amsdeer Corporation significantly more than the amounts for which the original awards had been made due to subsequent engineering changes in the specifications. Second, all six awards had been made to one vendor, the same one that had traditionally supplied all Commercial Chemicals Division reactors. Mr. Steele believed that among the other bidders there were some who were as well qualified as the winning bidder, and in retrospect it might have cost Amsdeer less to do business with them.

Reactor Design. A reactor is a large vessel for chemical processing. In Amsdeer's Commercial Chemicals Division, reactors are used for making alkyd resins for paint manufacture and certain special resins for sale to outside customers. Raw materials (such as pigment ingredients, solvents and catalytic agents) are "cooked" in the reactors at temperatures in excess of 500°F in various cycles spanning up to eight hours in length. Reactors have inner and outer steel shells between which hot oil is forced to heat the chemical mixture, and water to cool it. A typical resin line might contain four reactors, each costing between $65 and $80 thousand, and a complex of valves and piping and related process equipment amounting to over $6 million. Reactors have nozzles through which raw materials are inserted and resins drawn off. Each also has a manway on the top which may be opened for visual inspection while the reactor is in operation and through which maintenance workers may gain access to the interior space during downtime.

A so-called "conventional" reactor has a smooth stainless steel outer shell three-eighths of an inch to one and a quarter inches in thickness. By comparison, "dimpled construction" provides for an outer shell approximately one-eighth inch in thickness made stiff by a pattern of ridges stamped into the stainless steel sheet from which the outer surface is made. In recent years, dimpled construction had gained considerably in popularity as stainless steel construction prices

1. All names, locations, and quantitative data have been disguised.

skyrocketed and as this material was in short supply. In fact, some reactor manufacturers no longer offered the conventional design.

A third concept in reactor design was based on using "half-pipe coil" instead of an outer jacket. Stainless steel strip, perhaps six inches wide, was formed into a half-round which was then wrapped in tight coils around the outside surface of the inner jacket and welded in place. The half-pipe coil formed the channel through which heating and cooling liquids could be passed. This design had been used in Europe and South America for at least 15 years; it had only recently been introduced into the United States. A factor inhibiting its adoption had been the high cost of welding the half-pipe to the inner jacket. In 1959, however, an automated process had been developed in Germany for forming stainless steel strip into half-round, wrapping it around the vessel and welding it in place. The use of the new fabricating process considerably reduced the manufacturing cost of making reactors of this design.

The Equipment Procurement Process. Mr. Steele in Corporate Purchasing worked with the Engineering Departments in the Commercial Chemicals and Bulk Solids Divisions to buy plant equipment. The equipment procurement process began in the division with the development of a proposal to make a capital investment in either new units of equipment, or a new production line, or an entire new plant. Such proposals were generated through informal discussions at the division level among plant managers, engineers, controllers and the division president, usually in response to a need for new capacity. Engineering personnel were given the task of preparing project budgets and, depending on the size and complexity of the project, might contract for the services of consulting engineers to assist in making cost estimates. Because of inherent uncertainties in the estimating process, contingency factors and allowances for cost escalation were invariably built into capital expenditure proposals.

Depending on the amount involved such proposals could be approved at the level of the division president or might move up to Amsdeer's Board of Directors for acceptance. Once approved, the proposal became an authorization under which division personnel could expend up to the approved amount.

At that point, Engineering personnel developed detailed specifications on key pieces of equipment (such as reactors) and on new production lines or plants overall—again, usually with the help of consulting engineers. Requests for Quotations (RFQs) to be sent to vendors were drawn up and lists of suppliers who were considered qualified to bid were prepared. The RFQs and bid lists were submitted to Corporate Purchasing personnel, Mr. Steele in the case of equipment; Mr. Devon for construction. Each would normally make a cursory review of drawings and specifications to make sure they were clear. Then RFQs, together with statements of contract terms and conditions, were mailed to suppliers on the bid lists submitted by Engineering personnel as well as to other qualified vendors that Messrs. Steele or Devon respectively wished to add to the lists. Bids were received by the Corporate Purchasing representatives, analyzed and passed on to division personnel with written comments and a recommendation. Comments might concern vendors' performance records with Amsdeer on quality and delivery, vendors' shop capacity and how work might be allocated to avoid delays in delivery. If cost escalation or progress payments were stipulated in bids, these conditions would warrant comment. The final selections were made by division personnel, usually in the engineering departments. Once a winning bidder had been chosen, the Corporate Purchasing representative usually conducted further negotiations to bring down the original bid price if possible. To a significant extent, the performance of a Mr. Steele or a Mr. Devon was measured by what he could save Amsdeer by negotiating reductions from original winning bids.

Once an award had been made and any price reductions negotiated, the vendor prepared fabrication and/or construction drawings. These were reviewed in the Engineering Department of the buying division and some changes in specification (and in price) might be made at that point before final approval drawings were prepared. Price negotiations on these changes and any subsequent design modifications were carried on by Corporate Purchasing representatives.

The procurement of reactors for the Amsdeer Central and Western Plants serves as one illustration of the equipment purchasing process. The information immediately below was provided by Mr. Steele. There follows, then, an interview with Mr. Roger Weston, director of engineering in the Commercial Chemicals Division.

Interview with Mr. Steele. Mr. Tom Steele had been in his job as Senior Purchasing Agent in Corporate Purchasing since its inception in January 1973. Prior to that time he had spent 20 years in various engineering and manufacturing jobs in Amsdeer's Sheet Plastics Division.

Referring to his file on recent procurement actions on reactors, Mr. Steele recalled that the first of the three reactors ordered in January 1974 (RFQ #578) for the Central plant was intended for use in a new line and was planned to be identical to one already in operation. It would have a capacity of 6,000 gallons and would operate regularly at temperatures up to 500°F and inside pressures of 50 pounds per square inch (p.s.i.). It would be used to make alkyd resins, a basic material in Amsdeer paints.

Quotations were solicited from 13 bidders, six of whom were named by Commercial Chemicals ands seven by Mr. Steele. The only vendor to respond to RFQ #578, however, was Smith Corporation, the firm that had supplied almost all Commercial Chemicals Division reactors in the past. Smith's bid was $50,350, with delivery promised for 47 weeks. A second solicitation produced three more bids, one for $63,749 from Western Welding Company which had been a large Amsdeer supplier, one for $76,135 from IPC Engineers and a third for $40,790 with delivery in 52 weeks. This last bid was submitted by the Flat Iron Company, an equipment manufacturer who Mr. Steele regarded as experienced, highly qualified and very reputable. Flat Iron's low bid was explained in large part by the fact that this supplier had specified a "dimpled" outside jacket as opposed to a conventional jacket on which the other three bids were based.

The order was awarded to Smith on January 22, 1974, for $50,350.

On May 17, Commercial Chemicals Engineering changed the specification for the cover for the manway (an opening through which a person could pass) from manual to automatic. The automatic feature provided for a pneumatic opening device that could be activated by pressing a button. The cost of this change was negotiated with the contractor at $1,250. (Mr. Steele thought that if the automatic manway had been specified originally, it would have added no more than $250 to the bid price.) On August 5, Smith representatives notified Mr. Steele that they could not buy the manway from the supplier that Commercial Chemicals Engineering had originally specified and that the only alternative source would charge an additional $2,100. Mr. Steele checked with Commercial Chemicals Engineering to make sure that an automatic manway was really necessary, given the fact that it would increase the price of the reactor by $3,350. He was assured that it was a necessary feature. Further changes, some of which were cost saving and some of which added cost, balanced out at an increase of $360 for a final price of $54,060. Delivery would be made in January 1975, or 52 weeks from the time of the original award to Smith.

Commenting on the addition of the automatic manway, Mr. Steele stated:

> The alternative source had just taken over this product from the other supplier and I'm sure that their tooling costs were included in the bid, but we had no choice. Probably Commercial Chemicals Engineering wanted to standardize on automatic manways for ease of use. But you can sure open and close a manually-operated manway a lot of times before you've spent $3,000!

The second reactor (RFQ #579) which was also intended to be identical to another unit already in use at Central (and for which drawings were available) was ordered from Smith on January 22, 1974, without soliciting bids from other vendors. It was a 5,000 gallon unit with a conventional jacket and would operate at 500°F and 80 p.s.i. The price, $60,700, reflected the fact that it had more and larger nozzles than the first unit, for putting in raw materials and drawing off resins. Mr. Steele commented: "This job should have been bid. In retrospect it was a bad decision not to go through bids."

On examining fabrication drawings supplied shortly thereafter by Smith, Commercial Chemicals Engineers recognized that the unit currently in use and serving as a prototype of the one on order had been modified since it was installed and that the original drawings were out of date. To make the reactor on order identical to the one in use would add $2,402 to the original bid of $60,700. On April 2, Commercial Chemicals Engineering specified that this unit, too, should have an automatic manway, a change that added another $3,082. In August, when Smith notified Mr. Steele that the alternative manway supplier would have to be used, the price was increased by $2,190. On November 25, changes in nozzle specifications added $1,598 to the price to bring the total to $69,972 and on December 26 changes in bolthole sizes added $160. Inspection visit changes on January 14, 1975 added another $843. (These were on-site changes ordered by Commercial Chemicals.)

The third reactor, this one to be bought for the Western plant, had a 6,000 gallon capacity and would be the largest in use in the paint industry. It was to be used to make a new Amsdeer product. It would operate at 600°F and 75 p.s.i. Seven bidders were asked to quote on this unit (RFQ #580) and the following bids were received:

	Type of Jacket	Unit Price	Delivery
Flat Iron Company	Dimpled	$ 70,002	44 weeks
Smith Corporation	Conventional	86,266	58 weeks
	Conventional	126,266	44 weeks
IPC Engineers	Dimpled	117,300	24 weeks
Western Boiler Company	Conventional	50,000	48 weeks
		Plus Labor & Material	

On January 31, the order was given to Smith, although Mr. Steele expressed concern that Smith might then have difficulty meeting delivery schedules on all three units. Mr. Steele was able, however, to negotiate a 44-week delivery at $85,040 on the 6,000 gallon unit. On March 29, Smith representatives informed Mr. Steele that the company could not, in fact, meet the 44-week delivery condition because stainless for a conventional jacket was not available. If Commercial Chemicals Engineering was willing to accept 58-week delivery the unit could be constructed as specified. Alternatively, if Commercial Chemicals Engineering would accept a dimpled jacket, Smith could meet the original delivery time and would also reduce the price by $9,704.

The Commercial Chemicals Manager of Planning and Process Design (in the Engineering Department) agreed to accept the design change, and the price was therefore reduced to $75,336. On May 7, Commercial Chemicals Engineering changed the specifications on some oil-cooled baffles inside the reactor and the price was increased by $6,064. At the same time it increased the size of the bottom opening, adding $218. On August 3 an automatic manway cover was specified: $2,190. On August 14 a nozzle specification was changed; $739. On

September 6 a pneumatic switch bracket and guard assembly was added; $205. As of November 1, 1974, the price for this third unit stood at $84,752 and the work was proceeding on schedule. In contrast to the first two units, however, the contract on this one had specified that the final price would be adjusted to reflect any escalation in material costs up to 10% of the contract price or $5,000, whichever was lower.

In late November Mr. Steele received RFQs from Commercial Chemicals Engineering for three more reactors as follows:

2 units for the Mainline plant with 4,500 gallon capacity each; half-pipe coil design

1 unit for the Western plant with 3,600 gallon capacity; half-pipe coil design

The bid list received from Commercial Chemicals Engineering included five companies and with some difficulty Mr. Steele added six names to bring the total to 11. Flat Iron was not included on the bid list. After the RFQs were mailed out, Mr. Steele received calls from two companies on the list each wanting to know if Smith would be bidding. They said it cost them $1,000–$1,500 to prepare a bid and they didn't want to spend that money unnecessarily. Mr. Steele commented: "I couldn't divulge that information but they could certainly make a good guess at the answer to that question!"

Of the 11 companies invited to bid, seven did not respond. The other four, all named to the bid list by Commercial Chemicals Engineering, submitted bids as follows:

| | *Western* | | *Mainline* | |
	Unit Price	*Delivery*	*Unit Price*	*Delivery*
Fisk & Sons	$ 65,450	72 weeks	$ 67,130	72 weeks
Brown	68,980	62 weeks	73,895	62 weeks
Smith	72,998	84 weeks	85,142	84 weeks
Thomas	102,600	94 weeks	114,300	94 weeks

The lowest bidder, Fisk & Sons, was a family-owned shop, relatively small, but had a reputation with Commercial Chemicals Engineering for high-quality work. Fisk & Sons supplied Amsdeer with stainless steel vessels (not reactors) costing about $250,000 in 1974. Brown was a small, new company that had done extensive work for three large, well-known chemical companies and seemed anxious to add Amsdeer to its list of customers. Thomas was by far the largest of the companies on the list. A very reputable, well-established vendor, it had done a lot of work in the past for both the Metals and Sheet Plastic Divisions, and its work was of excellent quality.

Mr. Steele recommended that Fisk be awarded orders for the three units and noted in his comment that in the past it had been "extremely difficult to get qualified bidders because they are not given consideration even if they are competitive." However, Mr. Steele was directed by Commercial Chemicals Engineering to place the orders with Smith—which he did on January 10, 1975. He then requested a statement from Commercial Chemicals Engineering for his files explaining and supporting this award, in case in some future audit of his work he was asked why the three reactors had not been ordered from the low bidder.

Like the other three bidders, Smith had stipulated escalation on labor and materials. After the award was made, Mr. Steele was able to negotiate a change in this condition. Smith representatives agreed to provide in the contract for an "adjustment" in prices to take account of changes in material costs alone, adjustments to be based on the Bureau of Labor Statistics Metal and Metal Products Stainless Steel Plate Index. Pleased that he had been able to negotiate this change, Mr. Steele, speaking of Smith, said: "They're really nice people to deal with. I can tell them exactly what I think and they're always willing to negotiate."

Interview With Mr. Weston. Mr. Roger Weston had served as Manager of Engineering in the Commercial Chemicals Division since 1967, having held a comparable position prior to that time in the Fiber Division of Ajax Chemical Company. At Commercial Chemicals he managed a division that included six planning and process design engineers (four for resin manufacturing facilities and two for all non-resin plants—mostly paints and coatings) and eight project engineers. As their titles suggest, the former determined what production processes would be used and designed manufacturing facilities. The latter were involved in plant and equipment purchases (they prepared the RFQs and made up bid lists) and in installation. Mr. Weston evaluated the performance of the two types of engineers in different ways. Planning and process design engineers were judged by the quality and cost performance of the facilities they planned and on the effectiveness of their work with other Commercial Chemicals groups, especially Manufacturing and the Planning and Development Departments. (The latter was responsible for assembling strategic plans from all Commercial Chemicals functional departments and preparing overall business plans.)

Mr. Weston judged project engineers largely in terms of their records in meeting cost and schedule targets but also in terms of their ability to avoid procurement, installation, and start-up problems and to handle those which did arise. In the past year, the work of project engineers had become exceedingly complex and difficult, primarily because of equipment and construction materials shortages. Project engineers spent a lot of time in expediting, in locating materials and components for Amsdeer suppliers and often in arranging for on-site assembling of equipment that previously would have been completed and shipped to the job.

Mr. Weston, himself, reported to the Commercial Chemicals vice president of manufacturing but he also had direct and frequent access to the Commercial Chemicals president:

How does my superior appraise my work? Mainly, by how well the plants and equipment perform, on whether new facilities come on-stream within schedule and budget commitments and on the extent of start-up and de-bugging problems.

Asked about the procurement process for plant and equipment as it was before and after the formation of Corporate Purchasing, Mr. Weston noted that from his vantage point there really had been little change.

Before the Corporate Purchasing Department was started, we worked with one man in Commercial Chemicals Purchasing. He was assigned to plant and equipment procurement. We took the requisitions to him, told him what companies to get bids from (he wasn't very knowledgeable about equipment). He handled the paper work, and we made the decisions.

Tom Steele has much more engineering knowledge and can contribute more. But basically, we still prepare the specifications and make the decisions on whom to buy from.

Although Mr. Steele relayed bids to Commercial Chemicals Engineering with his comments and recommendations, the recommendations were accepted usually in instances where the equipment was of standard design and when price and delivery were more important concerns than design differences among vendors. If design differences were significant, Commercial Chemicals engineers always made their own evaluations. Price was not a governing factor if the total cost of a new manufacturing line or new plant fell within the authorization. If it didn't, then usually the whole project was scrutinized and often redesigned. However, if any bid but the lowest was accepted on a particular piece of equipment or a contract, Commercial Chemicals Engineering prepared a routine letter for the files, documenting the reason for making the award as it did. A copy of this letter was sent to Mr. Steele.

Turning to discuss his experience at Amsdeer with reactors Mr. Weston recalled that construction on the Central plant (far and away the largest user of this equipment in Amsdeer) was started originally in 1958 and completed in 1961 and every two years since then there had been a major expansion.

The idea was to make this the most modern resin plant in existence and the reactors had to be designed for rugged duty since they would be cycling daily from ambient temperatures to 500°F. The first reactors had dimpled jackets. We took the lowest bidder, a small ''shade tree'' shop in New Jersey, and we had nothing but problems. Almost from the time they were installed they began leaking and we got in a local welder (ASME[2] approved). He must have come in more than a hundred times in that first year. We had to shut the plant down each time because we were handling highly flammable materials and

2. American Society of Mechanical Engineers

using a welding torch was risky. We lost a lot of reactor time. And we couldn't get good welds. Then we discovered that the fabricator had done a lousy job, even using below-standard materials on the inside where it didn't show. After bringing in a consulting metallurgist, we decided to scrap those units and buy new ones. It actually cost us more to take out those first reactors than they cost in the first place.

After that experience Commercial Chemicals Engineering personnel studied the whole matter of reactor design and procurement. They consulted with two large chemical companies that used similar equipment extensively, and also with three large steel companies which made the stainless steel from which reactors were made. It was concluded, first, that Commercial Chemicals would never again go to small, unproven vendors. Second, it was decided that while the dimpled jacket might possibly be satisfactory for low temperature processes (up to 200°F), it was certainly not suitable for applications involving high temperatures and pressures. As a result of conversations with engineers in the companies Commercial Chemicals engineers visited, five reactor manufacturers were identified as being qualified to meet Amsdeer's standards. One of these five, Thomas, had worked extensively for Ajax and was known to Mr. Weston. Another, Smith, had been a long-time Amsdeer supplier. In fact, some Smith reactors made 25 years ago were still in operation in one Commercial Chemicals plant. Outside sources of information gave Smith the highest recommendations for the quality of its work although noting often that Smith was usually late on delivery.

In late 1969 Commercial Chemicals Engineering solicited bids from the five companies for three reactors for the Central plant; Smith was the low bidder and won the job. Mr. Weston recalled that:

> Smith was late on delivery—but we made allowance for that—and the quality of the work was very, very good. There was one leak in one vessel and they were there right away to fix it.

In 1972, a reactor was purchased for Commercial Chemicals Far West plant. This time Thomas was the low bidder. That unit was installed in 1974 and performed very satisfactorily.

In January 1973, bids were solicited on four units for Western. Baker-Core, the consulting engineer on the project (Baker-Core, itself, had had wide experience in purchasing reactors), suggested that the Flat Iron Company be added to the bid list. Although Flat Iron was low bidder, Smith the second low bidder, was awarded the job.

> Replacing a reactor is a horrendous job. There's so much piping and a lot of auxiliary vessels around the main reactor. A relatively minor difference in original cost is peanuts.

In early 1974, bids (on RFQ #578 and #579) were solicited from five manufacturers for two reactors for Central. Smith was low; Thomas didn't bid and Mr. Weston speculated that it was perhaps because their shops were full.

The reactor ordered in late January 1974 for Western (RFQ #580) was originally designed as a conventional unit and then, according to Mr. Weston, it was changed to a half-pipe coil design.

Smith proposed this design and we chose it because it was technically okay, delivery was faster and there was a cost saving. We didn't think there was much of a risk because this reactor would operate at relatively low temperatures (250°F) and pressures. Also it was a design that had been used in Europe and South America for at least 15 years. Two of our plants in South America have installed half-pipe coil reactors and they're working very well. One has been operating for two years and another for five years. I've seen these in operation and I've also visited plants of other companies in South America which have half-pipe coil units. Smith is the sole licensee to make half-pipe coil reactors in this country.

No, we haven't bought a dimpled jacket reactor since those original Central vessels in the late '50s. We never would buy one again for high temperature work and on low temperature—well—we'd probably take a half-pipe coil design instead.

On all three units that had been ordered in January 1974, work was being delayed because of inability to get delivery on the manway covers. This component had been supplied regularly to Smith by Syracuse Cover. Syracuse Cover, however, had gone bankrupt and had sold its patents to Dorman-Hathaway. The latter had taken over the order for manways on the three Commercial Chemicals reactors and was having difficulty making manways that would operate properly. (Commercial Chemicals and Smith engineers were in constant touch on this problem.) Fabrication had been complicated by the requirement that the manways be hydraulically automated. The idea for automating the manways came out of the Central plant where some mechanically operated manways had been rebuilt to operate hydraulically after being installed. Mr. Weston noted:

The Central plant takes the lead on reactor design because they are Amsdeer's largest user of reactors.

Asked about the RFQs that went out in November for three reactors in two different Commercial Chemicals plants, Mr. Weston commented:

We've had an awful time in getting anybody to bid. We did receive quotes from Smith, Thomas and Brown, a new fabricator that Corporate dug up. Brown is a small shop in University City, started by some professors. They say they're doing business for Ajax.

Brown is low bidder by about 10% but that's not enough to take the risk. Smith is second lowest and Thomas came in very high on price and very long on delivery.

I'm not greatly disturbed by the lack of bidders as long as we think we're getting fair prices. I would be upset if I thought we were locked in and the vendor was getting fat profits. Actually there is a tendency to go back to the same suppliers once you've developed a rapport and you know from experience that his work is good. It's reassuring from an engineering point of view. You don't have to be so exacting with the specifications. Sometimes you can even pick up the telephone and say ''Send me another unit like the one you sent me last time.'' And you can be in constant communication while the equipment is being built.

Index